Contents Table

Appendices

~ Conclusion

Welcome & What You'll Learn

Welcome, fellow Kotlin Android developers, to "Jetpack Compose: A Complete Guide for Kotlin Android Developers"! If you're ready to revolutionize the way you build Android user interfaces (UIs) and embrace a modern, declarative approach, then you're in the right place. This book is your comprehensive roadmap to mastering Jetpack Compose and unleashing its full potential to create stunning, efficient, and user-friendly Android apps.

Why Jetpack Compose?

In the ever-evolving world of Android development, Jetpack Compose emerges as a game-changer. It's more than just a new UI toolkit; it's a paradigm shift that empowers you to design, develop, and iterate on your UIs with unprecedented ease and flexibility. Here's why Jetpack Compose is causing so much excitement:

- **Declarative UI Paradigm:** Jetpack Compose embraces a declarative way of building UIs. Instead of imperatively manipulating views, you describe your UI as functions of its state. This leads to code that is more concise, easier to reason about, and less prone to errors.
- **Modern Kotlin API:** Jetpack Compose is built from the ground up with Kotlin, taking full advantage of the language's expressive power, including coroutines, extension functions, and lambdas. This results in a clean and intuitive API that feels like a natural extension of Kotlin itself.
- **Increased Productivity:** Jetpack Compose streamlines your UI development workflow. The declarative nature allows for rapid iterations and a tighter feedback loop between your code and the UI preview.
- **Built-in Performance Optimizations:** Jetpack Compose is designed with performance in mind. It leverages intelligent recomposition algorithms and efficient rendering mechanisms to ensure smooth and responsive UIs, even in complex layouts.
- **Thriving Community:** Jetpack Compose is rapidly gaining adoption and boasts an active and supportive community of developers. You'll find a wealth of resources, tutorials, and libraries to accelerate your learning and development journey.

What You'll Learn

This book is your one-stop resource for learning Jetpack Compose. Here's a glimpse of the exciting topics we'll cover:

- **Fundamentals:** We'll start with the core concepts of declarative UIs and how Jetpack Compose implements them. You'll gain a solid foundation in composables, layouts, styling, and state management.
- **Building Interactive UIs:** You'll learn how to create engaging and interactive user interfaces with buttons, text fields, images, and other UI elements. We'll dive into state management techniques to keep your UI in sync with your data.
- **Working with Data:** We'll explore how to seamlessly integrate data sources into your Jetpack Compose UIs, including working with lists, Room databases, and network requests using Retrofit.
- **Advanced Layouts:** You'll master advanced layout techniques using ConstraintLayout and even create your own custom layouts to perfectly match your design vision.
- **Architecture and Navigation:** We'll guide you through best practices for structuring your Jetpack Compose apps using architectural patterns like MVVM and modularizing your code for better maintainability. You'll also learn how to seamlessly navigate between screens.
- **Additional Features:** We'll cover a wide range of topics, including animations, testing, integrating with device features like the camera, and even publishing your app to the Google Play Store.

Who This Book Is For

This book is ideal for Kotlin Android developers who are eager to embrace the future of Android UI development. Whether you're a seasoned Android pro or just starting your Kotlin journey, you'll find valuable insights and practical guidance to elevate your skills.

Section A:
Getting Started with Jetpack Compose

Introduction to Declarative UIs and Jetpack Compose

Outline

- What is a Declarative UI?
- Benefits of Declarative UIs
- Introduction to Jetpack Compose
- The Compose Mindset
- Basic Building Blocks: Composables
- Declarative vs. Imperative UI (A Comparison)
- Chapter Summary

What is a Declarative UI?

In the world of UI development, a **declarative UI** is a paradigm shift from the traditional imperative approach. At its core, declarative UI programming revolves around these key principles:

Describing the Desired State:

The essence of declarative UI lies in focusing on **what** the UI should look like at any given moment, rather than getting bogged down in the nitty-gritty details of **how** to make it happen. Instead of writing step-by-step instructions to manipulate views (e.g., "find this button, change its text, then hide this image"), you simply declare the final state you want your UI to be in.

UI as a Function of State:

In the declarative paradigm, your UI is a direct **function of its underlying state**. The state represents the data and variables that influence the appearance and behavior of your UI. Whenever the state changes (for instance, due to user input, data fetching, or internal logic), the UI automatically re-renders itself to accurately reflect the new state.

Automatic UI Updates:

One of the most powerful aspects of declarative UIs is their ability to **automatically update** themselves when the state changes. The underlying framework (in our case, Jetpack Compose) takes care of figuring out the most efficient way to transition the UI from its current state to the new desired state. This eliminates the need for you to manually track and update individual UI elements, significantly reducing the risk of errors and inconsistencies.

Key Advantages:

This approach brings a host of benefits:

- **Increased Readability and Maintainability:** Declarative UI code is often more concise, easier to understand, and less prone to errors.
- **Reduced Boilerplate:** You write less code because you're not focused on low-level UI manipulations.
- **Enhanced UI Consistency:** Since the UI always reflects the current state, it's less likely to fall out of sync.
- **Easier State Management:** The framework handles the complexities of state updates, making it simpler for you to manage your app's data and logic.
- **Improved Performance:** The framework can optimize UI updates, potentially leading to smoother and more responsive user experiences.

Let's illustrate with a simple example (using pseudocode):

Imperative Approach (Traditional):

```
// Find the button
Button myButton = findViewById(R.id.myButton);

// Change the button's text
myButton.setText("New Text");

// Hide an image view
ImageView myImage = findViewById(R.id.myImage);
myImage.setVisibility(View.GONE);
```

Declarative Approach (Jetpack Compose):

```
@Composable
fun MyUI(buttonText: String, showImage: Boolean) {
    Button(onClick = { /* ... */ }) {
        Text(text = buttonText)
    }

    if (showImage) {
        Image(painter = painterResource(id = R.drawable.my_image),
contentDescription = "My Image")
    }
}
```

In the declarative example, the MyUI function describes the desired state of the UI based on the buttonText and showImage variables. If these variables change, Jetpack Compose automatically re-renders the UI to match the new state.

Benefits of Declarative UIs

Declarative UIs, as exemplified by Jetpack Compose, offer a compelling set of advantages over traditional imperative approaches to UI development:

1. Increased Code Readability and Maintainability:

Declarative UI code tends to be more concise and easier to understand. By focusing on describing the desired UI state rather than the procedural steps to achieve it, developers can write code that closely mirrors the visual structure of the UI. This makes it easier for both the original author and other developers to grasp the intent of the code and make modifications with confidence.

2. Reduced Boilerplate Code:

Imperative UI code often involves a significant amount of boilerplate – repetitive code for finding views, setting properties, and handling updates. Declarative UIs abstract away much of this boilerplate, allowing developers to express their UI logic more succinctly. This reduction in code volume can lead to faster development cycles and fewer opportunities for errors to creep in.

3. Enhanced UI Consistency and Predictability:

In a declarative UI, the UI always reflects the current state of the application. This tight coupling between state and UI ensures that the UI remains consistent and predictable, regardless of how the state changes. This can be particularly valuable in complex UIs where managing the synchronization between state and UI elements can be challenging in an imperative approach.

4. Easier State Management:

Declarative UIs typically come with built-in mechanisms for state management. Frameworks like Jetpack Compose provide tools and patterns that help developers manage the state of their UI components efficiently. This simplifies the process of keeping the UI in sync with the underlying data, reducing the cognitive load on developers and leading to more robust applications.

5. Improved Performance Through Optimized UI Updates:

Declarative UI frameworks often employ intelligent algorithms to optimize UI updates. When the state changes, the framework analyzes the differences between the old and new state and updates only the necessary parts of the UI. This can lead to significant performance improvements, especially in complex and dynamic UIs where unnecessary redraws can be costly.

Real-World Impact:

The benefits of declarative UIs translate into tangible advantages in real-world development scenarios. Teams adopting declarative frameworks often experience faster development cycles, reduced bug counts, and improved collaboration due to the inherent clarity and structure of declarative code. Additionally, the performance optimizations offered by these frameworks can lead to smoother and more responsive user experiences.

Introduction to Jetpack Compose

Jetpack Compose is a revolutionary UI toolkit introduced by Google that is poised to reshape the landscape of Android UI development. Designed with modern principles and built upon the solid foundation of Kotlin, Jetpack Compose offers a fresh and efficient approach to crafting native Android user interfaces.

Key Features and Highlights:

- **Declarative UI Paradigm:** Jetpack Compose wholeheartedly embraces the declarative UI paradigm, a fundamental shift from the traditional imperative approach. In this paradigm, developers describe the desired state of the UI rather than explicitly instructing how to achieve it. This declarative nature results in code that is more concise, easier to reason about, and less prone to errors.
- **Built on Kotlin:** Jetpack Compose is seamlessly integrated with Kotlin, Google's modern and expressive programming language for Android development. This integration allows developers to leverage Kotlin's powerful features such as coroutines, extension functions, and lambda expressions to create clean, intuitive, and maintainable UI code.
- **Seamless Integration:** While Jetpack Compose represents a new way of building UIs, it is designed to seamlessly integrate with existing Android codebases. Developers can incrementally

adopt Compose in their projects, gradually replacing traditional UI elements with composable functions. This flexibility enables teams to transition to Compose at their own pace without disrupting ongoing development efforts.

- **Material Design Integration:** Jetpack Compose is deeply integrated with Material Design, Google's comprehensive design system for creating visually appealing and user-friendly interfaces. Compose provides a rich set of pre-built Material Design components and styling options, allowing developers to quickly create beautiful and consistent UIs that adhere to modern design principles.

Why Choose Jetpack Compose?

Jetpack Compose offers a compelling array of benefits that make it a compelling choice for Android UI development:

- **Increased Productivity:** The declarative nature of Compose, coupled with its intuitive Kotlin API, significantly boosts developer productivity. With less boilerplate code and a focus on describing UI states, developers can iterate rapidly and bring their ideas to life more efficiently.
- **Enhanced Maintainability:** Compose code is inherently more maintainable due to its declarative structure and reduced complexity. The separation of UI descriptions from the underlying implementation details makes it easier to understand, modify, and debug UI-related code.
- **Modern UI Development:** Jetpack Compose represents the future of Android UI development. By adopting Compose, developers position themselves at the forefront of Android technology and gain access to the latest tools and best practices for creating cutting-edge user interfaces.

Jetpack Compose is more than just a new UI toolkit; it's a paradigm shift that empowers developers to build Android UIs with unprecedented ease, expressiveness, and efficiency. Whether you're starting a new project or enhancing an existing one, Jetpack Compose opens up a world of possibilities for creating exceptional Android applications.

The Compose Mindset

Transitioning to Jetpack Compose requires adopting a new way of thinking about UI development. This shift involves embracing several key concepts that are fundamental to the declarative UI paradigm:

Thinking in Terms of Composable Functions

In Jetpack Compose, the building blocks of your UI are **composable functions**. These functions, annotated with @Composable, describe the UI's structure and content. Unlike traditional Android views, which are mutable objects manipulated imperatively, composable functions are immutable and purely functional. This means that the UI is a direct output of the function's parameters, making it easier to reason about and predict the UI's behavior.

Embracing Unidirectional Data Flow

Jetpack Compose encourages a **unidirectional data flow** model. In this model, data flows down from the top-level composables to their children, and events flow up from child composables to their parents. This one-way data flow simplifies state management and helps prevent unexpected side effects, leading to more predictable and maintainable UIs.

Understanding Recomposition

Recomposition is the heart of how Jetpack Compose updates the UI. Whenever the state that a composable function depends on changes, Compose re-executes the function to determine the new UI state. This process is intelligent and efficient, as Compose only recomposes the parts of the UI that are affected by the state change. Understanding recomposition is crucial for optimizing your Compose UIs and avoiding unnecessary re-renders.

Emphasizing State Management

State management is a critical aspect of building Jetpack Compose UIs. State represents the data that drives your UI. Properly managing state ensures that your UI remains consistent and reflects the latest data accurately. Jetpack Compose offers various tools and patterns for state management, such as `remember`, `mutableStateOf`, and `ViewModel`, which you'll learn about in later chapters.

Key Takeaways:

- **Composables as Building Blocks:** Think of composable functions as the fundamental units of your UI.
- **Unidirectional Data Flow:** Ensure data flows down and events flow up for predictable UI behavior.
- **Recomposition as the Update Mechanism:** Understand how Compose efficiently updates the UI based on state changes.
- **State Management is Key:** Master state management techniques to keep your UI in sync with your data.

By adopting the Compose mindset, you'll be well-equipped to harness the full power of Jetpack Compose and create beautiful, maintainable, and performant Android UIs. This paradigm shift may require some adjustment, but the benefits in terms of code quality, developer productivity, and user experience are well worth the effort.

Basic Building Blocks: Composables

In Jetpack Compose, **composables** are the fundamental building blocks for constructing your user interface. They are essentially functions annotated with @Composable, which signals to the Compose compiler that this function is responsible for describing a part of your UI.

Core Characteristics of Composables:

- **Functions:** Composables are defined as Kotlin functions, making them a natural fit for the language and allowing you to leverage all of Kotlin's expressive power.
- **Annotated with @Composable:** The @Composable annotation is a special marker that informs the Compose compiler that this function is intended to be used for UI construction.
- **Describe UI Structure and Content:** Composables declare the arrangement of UI elements (such as text, images, buttons, layouts) and their content (e.g., the text displayed within a Text composable).
- **Automatic Recomposition:** One of the most powerful features of composables is their ability to recompose automatically. When the inputs to a composable function change (e.g., when the text content changes or a button is clicked), Compose intelligently re-executes the function to update the UI accordingly.

Example Composables:

Let's look at some basic examples of composables:

Greeting Composable:

```
@Composable
fun Greeting(name: String) {
    Text(text = "Hello, $name!")
}
```

This simple composable function, `Greeting`, takes a name parameter and renders a "Hello, [name]!" message using the Text composable.

Image Composable:

```
@Composable
fun MyImage() {
    Image(
        painter = painterResource(id = R.drawable.my_image),
        contentDescription = "My Image"
    )
}
```

The `MyImage` composable displays an image loaded from your project's resources (`R.drawable.my_image`) using the `Image` composable. The `contentDescription` is an important accessibility feature that provides a textual description of the image for users who rely on screen readers.

Composing Your UI:

Composables are designed to be composable (hence the name!). You can combine them like building blocks to create complex and interactive UIs. Here's how you might use the `Greeting` and `MyImage` composables:

```
@Composable
fun MyScreen() {
    Column {
        Greeting(name = "Alice")
        MyImage()
    }
}
```

In this example, the `MyScreen` composable uses the `Column` composable to arrange the `Greeting` and `MyImage` composables vertically.

Key Points:

- Composables are the core building blocks of Jetpack Compose UIs.
- They are Kotlin functions annotated with @Composable.
- They describe the structure and content of your UI.
- They automatically recompose when their inputs change.

Understanding composables is fundamental to working with Jetpack Compose. Throughout this book, you'll learn how to create custom composables, work with layouts, manage state, and build complex UIs using this powerful declarative approach.

Declarative vs. Imperative UI (A Comparison)

Understanding the differences between declarative and imperative UI paradigms is crucial for appreciating the unique strengths of Jetpack Compose. Let's break down these two approaches side-by-side:

Feature	Imperative UI (Traditional Android)	Declarative UI (Jetpack Compose)
How UI is Described	Focus on **how** to change UI elements step-by-step.	Focus on **what** the final UI state should be.

Code Style	Procedural, often with many lines of code to manipulate views.	Declarative, using functions and expressions to describe the UI.
State Management	Often requires manual tracking and updating of UI element states.	State is managed implicitly by the framework, leading to automatic UI updates.
UI Updates	UI updates are triggered explicitly by the developer's code.	UI updates are triggered automatically when the state changes.
Flexibility	High flexibility to manipulate UI elements directly.	Flexibility is achieved by describing different UI states based on data.
Error Proneness	More prone to errors due to manual UI manipulation.	Less prone to errors due to the declarative nature and framework's control.

Code Examples: Updating a Text View

Imperative (Traditional Android - Java):

```java
TextView myTextView = findViewById(R.id.myTextView);
myTextView.setText("New Text");
if (someCondition) {
    myTextView.setTextColor(Color.RED);
} else {
    myTextView.setTextColor(Color.BLACK);
}
```

Declarative (Jetpack Compose - Kotlin):

```kotlin
@Composable
fun MyTextView(text: String, isHighlighted: Boolean) {
    Text(
        text = text,
        color = if (isHighlighted) Color.Red else Color.Black
    )
}
```

Differences and Advantages

In the imperative example, we explicitly find the `TextView`, set its text, and then conditionally change its color. This involves multiple steps and direct manipulation of the view.

In contrast, the declarative example simply describes what the `TextView` should look like based on the `text` and `isHighlighted` parameters. Jetpack Compose handles the UI updates automatically whenever these parameters change.

Advantages of the Declarative Approach:

- **Conciseness:** The declarative code is significantly shorter and more expressive.
- **Maintainability:** The code is easier to understand and modify due to its focus on describing the UI state.

- **Error Reduction:** The declarative approach eliminates common errors related to manual UI updates, such as forgetting to update a view when the data changes.
- **Predictability:** The UI always reflects the current state, making it more predictable and easier to reason about.

By adopting the declarative approach of Jetpack Compose, you can streamline your UI development process, write more maintainable code, and ultimately create more robust and user-friendly Android applications.

Chapter Summary

In this chapter, we delved into the fundamental concepts that underpin Jetpack Compose and declarative UI development. We started by defining declarative UIs and exploring their key advantages over traditional imperative approaches. You learned how Jetpack Compose embodies these principles, offering a modern and efficient way to build Android user interfaces.

We introduced the core building blocks of Compose – composable functions – and discussed how they describe the structure and content of your UI. You gained insights into the Compose mindset, emphasizing the importance of thinking in terms of composable functions, embracing unidirectional data flow, understanding recomposition, and mastering state management.

Through code examples and comparisons, you saw how declarative UIs, like those built with Jetpack Compose, can be more concise, maintainable, and less error-prone than their imperative counterparts.

In the next chapter, you'll take your first practical steps with Jetpack Compose. We'll guide you through setting up your development environment and creating your first simple UI using this exciting new toolkit.

Setting Up Your Development Environment for Jetpack Compose

Outline

- Prerequisites
- Creating an Android Studio Project
- Adding Jetpack Compose Dependencies
- Enabling Compose in Your Project
- Exploring the Compose Tooling
- Creating Your First Composable Function
- Building and Running Your Compose App
- Chapter Summary

Prerequisites

Before you embark on your Jetpack Compose journey, it's essential to ensure your development environment is properly set up. Here's what you'll need:

Software Requirements:

- **Android Studio:** You'll need the latest stable version of Android Studio. Jetpack Compose is tightly integrated with Android Studio, and the latest version provides the best tooling and support for Compose development. You can download it from the official Android Studio website: https://developer.android.com/studio.
- **Kotlin Plugin:** The Kotlin plugin is essential for working with Jetpack Compose, as Compose is built on Kotlin. Ensure that the Kotlin plugin is enabled in Android Studio (it typically is by default in new installations).
- **Minimum SDK Version:** Jetpack Compose requires a minimum SDK version of 21 (Android 5.0 Lollipop). Make sure your project's minSdkVersion is set to 21 or higher.

Recommended Hardware Configuration:

- **Processor:** A modern multi-core processor (Intel i5 or equivalent or better) is recommended for smooth Android Studio performance and faster build times.
- **RAM:** At least 8GB of RAM is advisable. More RAM allows for smoother multitasking within Android Studio and better performance when working with the Compose preview and emulator.
- **Storage:** A solid-state drive (SSD) is highly recommended for faster project loading and build times.

Optional Tools and Plugins:

While not strictly required, the following tools can enhance your Jetpack Compose development experience:

- **Android Emulator:** The Android Emulator allows you to test your Compose apps on various virtual devices without needing a physical device. You can customize the emulator's configuration to match different Android versions and screen sizes.
- **Jetpack Compose Plugins:** Consider exploring plugins specifically designed for Jetpack Compose. These plugins can provide additional features like live templates, code navigation enhancements, and UI inspection tools.

By ensuring you have the necessary software and hardware, you'll be well-equipped to dive into the exciting world of Jetpack Compose and start building modern, declarative Android UIs.

Creating an Android Studio Project

Let's get started by creating a new project in Android Studio specifically tailored for Jetpack Compose development. Follow these steps:

1. **Launch Android Studio:** Open Android Studio. If you see the welcome screen, click on "Start a new Android Studio project." If you already have a project open, go to "File" -> "New" -> "New Project."
2. **Select a Project Template:** In the "New Project" dialog, you'll see a list of project templates. Choose the "Empty Compose Activity" template. This template provides a basic structure for a Jetpack Compose project, including the necessary dependencies and a simple composable function to get you started.
3. **Configure Project Settings:**
* **Name:** Give your project a meaningful name (e.g., "MyComposeApp").
* **Package name:** Choose a unique package name for your app (e.g., "com.yourcompany.mycomposeapp").
* **Save location:** Select the directory where you want to save your project files.
* **Language:** Ensure that "Kotlin" is selected as the programming language. Jetpack Compose is built on Kotlin, and using Kotlin will allow you to take full advantage of its features and integrations.
* **Minimum SDK:** Set the "Minimum SDK" to API 21: Android 5.0 (Lollipop) or higher. This is the minimum Android version required to use Jetpack Compose.
4. **Click "Finish":** After configuring the project settings, click the "Finish" button. Android Studio will create your new project and set up the basic structure for you.

Why Empty Compose Activity?

The "Empty Compose Activity" template is an excellent starting point for Jetpack Compose projects. It includes:

* **Essential Dependencies:** The template automatically adds the necessary Jetpack Compose dependencies to your project's `build.gradle` file.
* **MainActivity:** A basic `MainActivity` class is provided, which serves as the entry point for your app. It contains the `setContent` block where you'll define your composable functions to build your UI.
* **Default Composable:** A simple "Hello World" composable function is included as an example to get you started.

Key Points:

* **Project Template:** Choosing the "Empty Compose Activity" template streamlines the setup process for Jetpack Compose projects.
* **Kotlin:** Kotlin is the preferred language for Jetpack Compose development due to its seamless integration and expressive syntax.
* **Minimum SDK:** The minimum SDK version of 21 is required for Jetpack Compose compatibility.

With your new project created, you're ready to start exploring the exciting world of Jetpack Compose!

Adding Jetpack Compose Dependencies

To leverage the power of Jetpack Compose in your Android Studio project, you need to include the necessary dependencies. These dependencies provide the core Compose libraries, tooling, and foundational components for building your declarative UIs.

Required Dependencies:

The following dependencies are essential for Jetpack Compose development:

```
// Jetpack Compose UI
implementation("androidx.compose.ui:ui:1.5.4")

// Tooling support (Previews, etc.)
implementation("androidx.compose.ui:ui-tooling-preview:1.5.4")
debugImplementation("androidx.compose.ui:ui-tooling:1.5.4")

// Foundation (Border, Background, Box, Image, Scroll, shapes, animations,
etc.)
implementation("androidx.compose.foundation:foundation:1.5.4")

// Material Design
implementation("androidx.compose.material:material:1.5.4")

// Material design icons
implementation("androidx.compose.material:material-icons-core:1.5.4")
implementation("androidx.compose.material:material-icons-extended:1.5.4")

// Integration with activities
implementation("androidx.activity:activity-compose:1.8.2")

// Integration with ViewModels
implementation("androidx.lifecycle:lifecycle-viewmodel-compose:2.6.2")

// Integration with observables
implementation("androidx.compose.runtime:runtime-livedata:1.5.4")
implementation("androidx.compose.runtime:runtime-rxjava2:1.5.4")
```

Explanation:

- `androidx.compose.ui:ui`: The core Compose library, providing essential composables, layouts, and modifiers.
- `androidx.compose.ui:ui-tooling-preview`: Tooling support for the Compose preview in Android Studio.
- `androidx.compose.ui:ui-tooling`: Tooling support for debugging and inspecting Compose UIs.
- `androidx.compose.foundation:foundation`: Additional composables and building blocks for common UI elements.
- `androidx.compose.material:material`: Implementation of Material Design components and styling in Compose.
- `androidx.compose.material:material-icons-core` and `androidx.compose.material:material-icons-extended`: Material Design icons to use in your Compose UIs.
- `androidx.activity:activity-compose`: Integration between Compose and traditional Android activities.

- `androidx.lifecycle:lifecycle-viewmodel-compose`: Integration between Compose and the `ViewModel` component from Android Architecture Components.
- `androidx.compose.runtime:runtime-livedata` and `androidx.compose.runtime:runtime-rxjava2`: Integration between Compose and the LiveData and RxJava2 observable libraries for data streams.

How to Add Dependencies:

1. **Open `build.gradle (Module :app)`:** In your Android Studio project, navigate to the `build.gradle (Module :app)` file.
2. **Add Dependencies:** In the `dependencies` block of your `build.gradle` file, add the Compose dependencies listed above.
3. **Sync Project:** Click the "Sync Project with Gradle Files" button (the elephant icon) in the toolbar to download and incorporate the dependencies into your project.

Version Compatibility:

It's crucial to pay attention to version compatibility. Ensure that you're using compatible versions of the Compose libraries and other dependencies. The versions listed above (`1.5.4` for Compose UI, etc.) are current as of June 2024, but always check for the latest stable versions on the official Jetpack Compose documentation.

Additional Considerations:

- As you explore more advanced Compose features or integrate with other libraries, you might need to add additional dependencies. Consult the official documentation for guidance on specific use cases.

By carefully adding and managing your Jetpack Compose dependencies, you'll create a solid foundation for building modern and expressive Android UIs.

Enabling Compose in Your Project

After adding the Jetpack Compose dependencies, you need to explicitly enable Compose in your project's Gradle configuration. This step activates the Compose compiler plugin, which is responsible for transforming your composable functions into efficient UI code.

1. **Open `build.gradle (Module :app)`:** Navigate to your project's `build.gradle (Module :app)` file in Android Studio. This is where you'll make the necessary configuration changes.
2. **Enable Compose:** Inside the `android` block of your `build.gradle` file, locate the `buildFeatures` block. If it's not already present, add it. Within this block, set the `compose` option to `true`:

```
android {
    // ... other configurations ...

    buildFeatures {
        compose true
    }

    // ... other configurations ...
}
```

3. **Compose Options (Optional):** While not strictly required, you can add a `composeOptions` block to configure additional settings for the Compose compiler. The most important setting within this block is `kotlinCompilerExtensionVersion`:

```
android {
    // ... other configurations ...

    composeOptions {
        kotlinCompilerExtensionVersion '1.5.4' // Update to the latest
version
    }

    // ... other configurations ...
}
```

- **kotlinCompilerExtensionVersion:** This property specifies the version of the Jetpack Compose compiler plugin to use. It's essential to keep this version aligned with the version of the Compose libraries you're using for compatibility. Always refer to the official Jetpack Compose documentation for the latest recommended version.

Key Points:

- **buildFeatures:** The `buildFeatures` block is used to enable or disable various build features in your Android project. Setting `compose` to `true` activates the Compose compiler plugin.
- **composeOptions:** The `composeOptions` block allows for additional customization of the Compose compiler. The `kotlinCompilerExtensionVersion` is the most critical setting here.
- **Version Compatibility:** Ensure that the `kotlinCompilerExtensionVersion` matches the version of your Compose libraries to avoid compatibility issues.

By enabling Compose and configuring the compiler options correctly, you've taken a crucial step in setting up your development environment for building modern Android UIs with Jetpack Compose.

Exploring the Compose Tooling

Android Studio offers a suite of powerful tools specifically designed to enhance your Jetpack Compose development experience. These tools streamline your workflow, provide real-time feedback, and help you visualize and debug your composable UIs. Let's delve into some of the key features:

Compose Preview: Your Real-Time UI Window

The Compose Preview is an invaluable tool that allows you to visualize your composable functions in real-time, directly within Android Studio. To use the preview:

1. **Annotate Your Composable:** Ensure that the composable function you want to preview is annotated with `@Preview`:

```
@Preview(showBackground = true) // Optional: Show background

@Composable
fun MyComposablePreview() {
    // ... your composable content ...
}
```

2. **Open the Preview Pane:** Locate the "Split" icon in the top-right corner of the code editor and click it. This will open a split view with the preview pane alongside your code.
3. **Interact and Iterate:** The preview updates in real-time as you modify your composable function. You can experiment with different parameters, styles, and layouts to see how they affect the UI's appearance.

Interactive Mode: Test Your UI's Behavior

Interactive Mode takes the preview a step further by allowing you to interact with your composable UI directly in the preview pane. To enable Interactive Mode:

1. **Click the Interactive Button:** In the top-right corner of the preview pane, click the button with the hand icon.
2. **Interact with Your UI:** You can now click buttons, enter text, and trigger other interactions within your composable UI as if it were running on a real device.

Additional Helpful Features:

Android Studio offers several other tools to streamline Compose development:

- **Compose Layout Inspector:** This tool allows you to inspect the layout hierarchy of your composable UIs. You can visualize how composables are nested and arranged, examine their properties, and identify potential layout issues.
- **Compose Recomposition Counts:** Recomposition is the process by which Compose updates the UI when the state changes. Android Studio provides a way to visualize how often your composables are recomposing, which can help you optimize your UI for performance.
- **Live Templates:** Android Studio includes live templates (code snippets) for common composable functions and patterns. These templates can save you time and ensure consistency in your code.
- **Debugging Tools:** You can use standard Android Studio debugging tools, such as breakpoints and log statements, to debug your composable functions.

By leveraging these tools, you can significantly accelerate your Jetpack Compose development, iterate more quickly on your UIs, and create polished and user-friendly Android applications.

Creating Your First Composable Function

Let's dive into the practical side of Jetpack Compose by creating a simple "Hello, World!" composable function. This will serve as a gentle introduction to the structure and syntax of Compose code.

The "Hello, World!" Example

```
@Composable
fun Greeting(name: String) {
    Text(text = "Hello, $name!")
}

@Composable
fun DefaultPreview() {
    Greeting("World")
}
```

In your MainActivity, you'll typically have a setContent block:

```
class MainActivity : ComponentActivity() {
    override fun onCreate(savedInstanceState: Bundle?) {
```

```
        super.onCreate(savedInstanceState)
        setContent {
            Greeting("World")
        }
    }
}
```

Explanation:

- **@Composable Annotation:** This annotation is essential for any function that describes part of your UI. It tells the Compose compiler that this function is a composable and can be used to build the UI.
- **Greeting Function:** This is our composable function. It takes a name parameter (a String) and uses the Text composable to display "Hello, [name]!" on the screen.
- **DefaultPreview Function:** This is another composable function annotated with @Preview. This is special annotation to let you see preview of composable within Android Studio without building and running your application. The Greeting composable is used in the DefaultPreview composable to show the text Hello, World!.
- **setContent Block:** The setContent block within MainActivity is where you define the root composable of your app's UI. In this case, we're calling the Greeting composable and passing "World" as the name parameter.

Structure of a Composable Function:

A typical composable function in Jetpack Compose has the following structure:

1. **@Composable Annotation:** The function starts with this annotation to mark it as a composable.
2. **Function Name:** Choose a descriptive name for your function (e.g., Greeting, MyImage).
3. **Parameters:** If your composable needs input data, you can define parameters (e.g., name: String).
4. **Composable Content:** The body of the function contains other composables (like Text, Image, Button, etc.) or custom composables that you create. These composables are combined to describe the layout and content of your UI.

Key Points:

- **Composables are Functions:** Think of composables as building blocks for your UI.
- **The @Composable Annotation is Essential:** Don't forget this annotation when defining composable functions.
- **setContent is the Starting Point:** Your UI starts within the setContent block of your activity.
- **Composable Structure:** Composables can be nested within each other to create complex layouts.

By understanding this basic structure, you're ready to start building your own composables and creating more complex and interactive user interfaces with Jetpack Compose.

Building and Running Your Compose App

After creating your first composable function, it's time to see it in action! Here's how you can build and run your Jetpack Compose app:

Building the Project:

1. **Click the Build Button (Hammer Icon):** In the toolbar at the top of Android Studio, you'll find a button with a hammer icon. Click this button to initiate the build process.
2. **Wait for the Build to Complete:** Android Studio will compile your code and create an APK (Android Package Kit), which is the installation file for your app. You'll see messages in the "Build" output window at the bottom of Android Studio as the build progresses.

Running the App:

Option 1: Run on an Emulator:

1. **Create or Select an Emulator:** If you haven't already, create or select an Android Virtual Device (AVD) from the AVD Manager in Android Studio.
2. **Click the Run Button (Green Play Icon):** In the toolbar, you'll see a green play button next to the device you've selected. Click this button to run your app on the emulator.
3. **Wait for the Emulator to Launch:** The emulator will start up (which may take some time, especially the first time you run it). Once it's running, your app will automatically install and launch on the emulator.

Option 2: Run on a Physical Device:

1. **Enable USB Debugging:** On your physical Android device, go to "Settings" -> "Developer Options" and enable "USB debugging." If you don't see "Developer Options," you may need to enable it by going to "Settings" -> "About phone" and tapping the "Build number" several times.
2. **Connect Your Device:** Connect your Android device to your computer using a USB cable.
3. **Click the Run Button:** In the toolbar, click the green play button next to your connected device. Your app will be installed and launched on your device.

Verifying Jetpack Compose:

Once your app is running, you should see the "Hello, World!" message displayed on the screen. This confirms that Jetpack Compose is working correctly and rendering your composable function. Additionally, you can inspect your app's layout using the Layout Inspector tool in Android Studio to verify that the composables are arranged as expected.

Troubleshooting:

- **Build Errors:** If you encounter errors during the build process, check the "Build" output window for detailed messages. These messages can often help you pinpoint and resolve the issue.
- **Runtime Errors:** If your app crashes, look for error messages in the "Logcat" window. These messages can provide clues about what went wrong.
- **Emulator/Device Issues:** If you have trouble running your app on an emulator or a physical device, make sure your device is properly connected and that you have the correct drivers installed.

By following these steps and using the available tools, you can successfully build and run your Jetpack Compose apps and start exploring the exciting possibilities of declarative UI development.

Chapter Summary

In this chapter, you took crucial steps towards building Jetpack Compose applications. We covered the prerequisites for starting your Compose journey, guiding you through setting up Android Studio with the necessary dependencies and enabling the Compose compiler.

You also learned how to create a new Android Studio project using the "Empty Compose Activity" template, ensuring a smooth start with the right configuration. We discussed the essential dependencies required for Jetpack Compose development and how to add them to your project's `build.gradle` file.

We then explored the invaluable Compose Tooling in Android Studio, including the powerful Preview feature and Interactive Mode. You now know how to visualize your composable functions in real-time, experiment with different UI elements, and interact with your UI before even running the app.

Finally, we guided you through creating your first simple composable function, a "Hello, World!" example, and explained the key concepts like the @Composable annotation and the setContent block. You also gained knowledge on building and running your Compose app, either on an emulator or a physical device.

Now that you have your development environment set up and a basic understanding of Compose concepts, you're well-prepared to move on to the next chapter, where we'll delve into the core composables that form the foundation of your Jetpack Compose UIs.

Section B:
Building Your First UI with
Jetpack Compose

Core Composables: Text, Images, Buttons, and Layouts

Outline

- Introducing the Basic Composables
- The Text Composable
- The Image Composable
- The Button Composable
- Exploring Basic Layouts
- Combining Composables
- Chapter Summary

Introducing the Basic Composables

In the world of Jetpack Compose, **core composables** are the foundational elements upon which you'll build your Android user interfaces. These composables are pre-built UI components provided by the Compose framework, and they serve as the essential building blocks for creating everything from simple text displays to complex interactive layouts.

Purpose of Core Composables:

- **Simplify UI Development:** Core composables abstract away the complexities of creating and managing UI elements. Instead of writing verbose code to inflate layouts, create views, and set properties, you can simply use a composable function to achieve the same result with much less effort.
- **Ensure Consistency:** Core composables adhere to Material Design principles, ensuring a visually consistent and user-friendly experience across your app. They provide a standardized set of components that follow established design guidelines, saving you the time and effort of creating custom UI elements from scratch.
- **Optimize Performance:** Jetpack Compose is designed with performance in mind. Core composables are optimized for efficient rendering and state management, contributing to smoother and more responsive user interfaces.

Fundamental Building Blocks:

Core composables can be thought of as the basic vocabulary of Jetpack Compose. They include elements for displaying text (Text), images (Image), buttons (Button), and many others. These elements can be combined and arranged within layouts (such as Column, Row, and Box) to create complex UI structures.

Importance in UI Creation:

Without core composables, building Jetpack Compose UIs would be a daunting task. They provide a solid foundation and a convenient starting point for your UI development. By understanding how to use and customize these core building blocks, you can create a wide range of user interfaces with relative ease.

In the following sections, we'll delve deeper into some of the most commonly used core composables: `Text`, `Image`, and `Button`. You'll learn how to use their attributes, customize their appearance, and handle user interactions. As you gain familiarity with these basic composables, you'll be well on your way to mastering the art of building beautiful and functional Android UIs with Jetpack Compose.

The Text Composable

The `Text` composable is your go-to tool for rendering text content in Jetpack Compose. It's incredibly versatile, allowing you to display simple strings, styled text, and even rich text with formatting.

Basic Usage:

At its simplest, the `Text` composable takes a `text` parameter, which is the string you want to display:

```
@Composable
fun SimpleText() {
    Text(text = "Hello, Jetpack Compose!")
}
```

Styling Your Text:

The `Text` composable offers numerous attributes to customize the appearance of your text:

- `fontSize`: Controls the size of the text. You can use `sp` (scale-independent pixels) for font sizes that adapt to the user's screen density:

  ```
  Text(text = "Large Text", fontSize = 24.sp)
  ```

- `fontWeight`: Determines the thickness of the text (e.g., `FontWeight.Normal`, `FontWeight.Bold`).

  ```
  Text(text = "Bold Text", fontWeight = FontWeight.Bold)
  ```

- `color`: Sets the color of the text. You can use standard color values or create custom ones:

  ```
  Text(text = "Blue Text", color = Color.Blue)
  ```

- `style`: Allows you to apply a `TextStyle` to your text. A `TextStyle` encompasses font family, size, weight, color, and other text attributes.

  ```
  val myStyle = TextStyle(
      fontFamily = FontFamily.Serif,
      fontSize = 18.sp,
      fontWeight = FontWeight.SemiBold
  )
  Text(text = "Styled Text", style = myStyle)
  ```

Modifiers for Customization:

Modifiers are a powerful feature in Jetpack Compose that enables you to modify the appearance, behavior, and layout of composables. You can apply modifiers to `Text` composables to achieve various effects:

- `padding`: Adds padding around the text.
- `background`: Sets a background color for the text.
- `border`: Adds a border around the text.
- `clickable`: Makes the text clickable (like a hyperlink).
- …and many more!

```
Text(
    text = "Padded and Clickable Text",
    modifier = Modifier
        .padding(16.dp)
        .clickable { /* Handle click */ }
)
```

Examples:

- **Different Font Sizes:**

```
Text(text = "Small Text", fontSize = 12.sp)
Text(text = "Medium Text", fontSize = 16.sp)
Text(text = "Large Text", fontSize = 20.sp)
```

- **Different Font Weights:**

```
Text(text = "Normal Text", fontWeight = FontWeight.Normal)
Text(text = "Bold Text", fontWeight = FontWeight.Bold)
```

- **Different Colors:**

```
Text(text = "Red Text", color = Color.Red)
Text(text = "Green Text", color = Color.Green)
```

By combining these attributes and modifiers, you have full control over the visual presentation of your text in Jetpack Compose.

The Image Composable

The `Image` composable is your essential tool for displaying images within your Jetpack Compose UIs. Whether it's a simple icon, a photograph, or a complex vector graphic, the `Image` composable provides a flexible and efficient way to integrate visuals into your app.

Loading Images from Various Sources:

The `Image` composable can load images from a variety of sources:

- **Drawable Resources:** Images stored in your project's `res/drawable` folder. You can load them using `painterResource`:

```
Image(

    painter = painterResource(id = R.drawable.my_image),

    contentDescription = "My Image"

)
```

- **Bitmaps:** Images represented as `Bitmap` objects.

```
val bitmap = BitmapFactory.decodeResource(resources, R.drawable.my_image)

Image(bitmap = bitmap.asImageBitmap(), contentDescription = "My Image")
```

- **Vector Drawables:** Scalable vector images stored in your project's `res/drawable` folder. You can load them using `painterResource`:

```
Image(

    painter = painterResource(id = R.drawable.my_vector_image),

    contentDescription = "My Vector Image"

)
```

- **Image URIs:** Images loaded from URLs or other sources represented by `Uri` objects.

```
val imageUri = "https://www.example.com/my_image.jpg"

AsyncImage(

    model = imageUri,

    contentDescription = "My Image",

)
```

- **Other Sources:** Jetpack Compose also supports loading images from other sources like `File` objects and more. Refer to the official documentation for specific details.

Key Attributes:

The `Image` composable has several important attributes:

- **painter:** The most essential attribute. It specifies how to load the image. You can use `painterResource`, `painterFile`, or other `Painter` implementations depending on your image source.
- **contentDescription:** A crucial attribute for accessibility. It provides a textual description of the image for users who are visually impaired or using screen readers. Always provide a meaningful description to enhance the accessibility of your app.
- **contentScale:** Determines how the image is scaled to fit within the available space. Common values include `ContentScale.Fit`, `ContentScale.Crop`, and `ContentScale.FillBounds`.
- **modifier:** As with other composables, you can use modifiers to customize the appearance and behavior of the `Image` composable.

Examples:

Here are examples showcasing how to load and display different types of images:

```
// Drawable Resource
Image(
    painter = painterResource(id = R.drawable.my_image),
    contentDescription = "My Image"
)

// Vector Drawable
Image(
    painter = painterResource(id = R.drawable.my_vector_image),
    contentDescription = "My Vector Image"
)

// Image from URL
AsyncImage(
    model = "https://www.example.com/my_image.jpg",
    contentDescription = "My Image",
)
```

ContentDescription and Accessibility:

The contentDescription attribute is essential for making your app accessible to users with visual impairments. When you provide a contentDescription, screen readers can announce the description of the image, allowing users to understand its content.

Example:

```
Image(
    painter = painterResource(id = R.drawable.profile_picture),
    contentDescription = "Profile picture of the user"
)
```

By thoughtfully utilizing the Image composable and paying attention to accessibility, you can enrich your Jetpack Compose UIs with engaging visuals that cater to all users.

The Button Composable

The Button composable is a fundamental element for creating interactive user interfaces in Jetpack Compose. Buttons are the primary way users trigger actions within your app, making them crucial for navigation, form submission, and other interactive tasks.

Basic Usage:

The simplest way to create a button is to provide the text you want to display within the button's content:

```
@Composable
fun MyButton() {
    Button(onClick = { /* Handle button click */ }) {
        Text("Click Me")
    }
}
```

In this example, the onClick lambda is where you'll define the action that should happen when the button is clicked.

Button Attributes:

The Button composable offers several attributes to customize its appearance and behavior:

- onClick: A lambda function that gets executed when the button is clicked. This is where you'll place the code to handle the button's action.
- modifier: Used to apply modifiers to the button, just like you would with other composables. You can add padding, change the background color, add a border, and more.
- enabled: A boolean value that controls whether the button is enabled or disabled. Disabled buttons appear grayed out and are not clickable.
- colors: Allows you to customize the colors of the button in different states (e.g., normal, pressed, disabled).

Styling and Customization:

You can style your buttons to match your app's design using modifiers and the colors attribute. Here are a few examples:

```
// Simple button with padding and elevated style
Button(
    onClick = { /* ... */ },
    modifier = Modifier.padding(8.dp),
    elevation = ButtonDefaults.elevation(
        defaultElevation = 6.dp,
        pressedElevation = 8.dp,
        disabledElevation = 0.dp
    )
) {
    Text("Elevated Button")
}


// Button with custom colors
val buttonColors = ButtonDefaults.buttonColors(
    backgroundColor = Color.Blue,
    contentColor = Color.White
)
Button(
    onClick = { /* ... */ },
    colors = buttonColors
) {
    Text("Custom Button")
}
```

Handling Button Clicks:

To define the action that happens when a button is clicked, you'll write code within the onClick lambda. Here's an example that shows a message when the button is pressed:

```
Button(onClick = {
    Toast.makeText(context, "Button clicked!", Toast.LENGTH_SHORT).show()
}) {
```

```
    Text("Click Me")
}
```

Important Considerations:

- **Accessibility:** Always provide a `contentDescription` for image buttons or buttons that don't have text labels. This ensures that users with visual impairments can understand the button's purpose.
- **State Management:** In more complex scenarios, you'll likely need to manage the state of your button (e.g., whether it's enabled or disabled) based on the app's data or user interactions. Use state management techniques like `remember` or `ViewModel` to handle these scenarios effectively.

By mastering the `Button` composable and its customization options, you can create engaging and intuitive user experiences in your Jetpack Compose applications.

Exploring Basic Layouts

Layouts are the backbone of your Jetpack Compose UI. They provide the structure for organizing and arranging your composable functions (like `Text`, `Image`, and `Button`) on the screen. In this section, we'll cover the three fundamental layouts that you'll use most often: `Column`, `Row`, and `Box`.

Introduction to Layouts:

Layouts in Jetpack Compose are themselves composables. They act as containers that hold other composables as their children. By nesting composables within layouts and using modifiers to control their positioning and styling, you can create complex and visually appealing UIs.

`Column` Layout:

The `Column` layout arranges its child composables vertically, from top to bottom. Think of it as a stack of UI elements. Here's an example:

```
Column {
    Text("Item 1")
    Text("Item 2")
    Image(painter = painterResource(id = R.drawable.my_image),
contentDescription = null)
}
```

In this example, the two `Text` composables and the `Image` composable will be stacked vertically.

`Row` Layout:

The `Row` layout, on the other hand, arranges its children horizontally, from left to right. It's like placing UI elements side-by-side.

```
Row {
    Image(painter = painterResource(id = R.drawable.my_image),
contentDescription = null)
    Text("Item 1")
    Button(onClick = { /* ... */ }) {
        Text("Click Me")
    }
}
```

In this case, the Image, Text, and Button composables will be arranged horizontally in a row.

Box Layout:

The Box layout is designed for overlapping elements. Its children are stacked on top of each other, with the last child being drawn on top.

```
Box {
    Image(painter = painterResource(id = R.drawable.background), contentDescription
= null)
    Text(
        text = "Hello from behind the image!",
        modifier = Modifier.align(Alignment.Center)
    )
}
```

Here, the Text composable will be displayed on top of the Image composable.

Modifiers for Positioning and Sizing:

Modifiers play a crucial role in customizing how composables are laid out within a layout. Here are a few common modifiers used for positioning and sizing:

- padding: Adds space around a composable.
- size: Sets the width and height of a composable.
- fillMaxWidth, fillMaxHeight: Makes a composable fill the available width or height.
- align: Controls the alignment of a composable within its parent layout (e.g., Alignment.Center, Alignment.TopStart).

```
Column {
    Text(
        text = "Item 1",
        modifier = Modifier
            .padding(8.dp)
            .fillMaxWidth()
    )
    // ... other composables ...
}
```

By combining these basic layouts and modifiers, you can create a wide range of UI structures. Remember, layouts are the foundation for organizing your composables, and mastering them is essential for building complex and visually appealing Android apps with Jetpack Compose.

Combining Composables

The true power of Jetpack Compose shines when you start combining the core composables (Text, Image, Button, etc.) within layouts (Column, Row, Box). This allows you to create more complex and functional UI elements that can be reused throughout your app.

Combining Composables Within Layouts:

Let's consider a few examples of how to combine composables:

Example 1: Product Card

```
@Composable
fun ProductCard(product: Product) {
    Column(
        modifier = Modifier
            .padding(16.dp)
            .fillMaxWidth()
            .border(1.dp, Color.Gray)
    ) {
        Image(
            painter = painterResource(id = product.imageResourceId),
            contentDescription = product.name,
            modifier = Modifier
                .fillMaxWidth()
                .height(180.dp)
        )
        Column(modifier = Modifier.padding(16.dp)) {
            Text(text = product.name, fontWeight = FontWeight.Bold)
            Text(text = product.description)
            Spacer(modifier = Modifier.height(8.dp))
            Button(onClick = { /* Handle purchase */ }) {
                Text("Buy Now")
            }
        }
    }
}
```

In this example, we create a `ProductCard` composable that displays a product's image, name, description, and a "Buy Now" button. We use a `Column` to arrange the elements vertically and a nested `Column` for the text content and button.

Example 2: User Profile Header

```
@Composable
fun UserProfileHeader(user: User) {
    Row(
        modifier = Modifier
            .padding(16.dp)
            .fillMaxWidth()
    ) {
        Image(
            painter = painterResource(id = user.profileImageResourceId),
            contentDescription = "Profile picture of ${user.name}",
            modifier = Modifier
                .size(64.dp)
                .clip(CircleShape)
        )
        Spacer(modifier = Modifier.width(16.dp))
        Column {
            Text(text = user.name, fontWeight = FontWeight.Bold)
            Text(text = "@${user.username}")
        }
    }
}
```

This composable displays a user's profile picture, name, and username in a horizontal row. We use Row to arrange the elements and a nested `Column` for the text content.

Best Practices for Organizing Composables:

- **Break Down into Smaller Composables:** Divide your UI into smaller, reusable composable functions. This makes your code more modular, easier to test, and promotes reusability.
- **Name Composables Meaningfully:** Choose descriptive names for your composables that reflect their purpose. This enhances code readability and makes it easier to understand the structure of your UI.
- **Use a Consistent Style:** Follow a consistent style guide for your Compose code. This includes naming conventions, indentation, and code formatting.
- **Separate Concerns:** Try to keep the UI logic (presentation) separate from the business logic (data fetching, calculations). This separation of concerns improves code maintainability and testability.

Real-World Scenarios:

- **List Items:** You can create reusable composables for list items in a `LazyColumn` or `LazyRow`.
- **App Bars:** Design custom app bars with icons, titles, and actions.
- **Dialog Boxes:** Build dialog boxes with custom content and buttons.
- **Forms:** Create forms with input fields, labels, and validation messages.
- **Complex Screens:** Break down complex screens into smaller composable components.

By mastering the art of combining composables, you'll be equipped to build sophisticated and user-friendly Android interfaces with Jetpack Compose. Remember, these are just a few examples, and the possibilities are endless. Get creative and experiment with different combinations to craft unique and engaging UIs!

Chapter Summary

This chapter introduced you to the core building blocks of Jetpack Compose UIs: composable functions. You learned how to work with fundamental composables like `Text` for displaying text, `Image` for rendering images, and `Button` for creating interactive buttons. We explored how to customize these composables using attributes and modifiers, enabling you to tailor their appearance and behavior to your specific needs.

You also gained a foundational understanding of layouts (`Column`, `Row`, and `Box`) and how to arrange composables within them to create structured UIs. We discussed the importance of modifiers for positioning and sizing elements, giving you the tools to build more complex and visually appealing layouts.

Finally, we explored the art of combining composables, demonstrating how to create reusable UI components like product cards and user profile headers. You learned best practices for organizing your composables and maintaining a clean and maintainable codebase.

Equipped with this knowledge of core composables and layouts, you're now ready to dive deeper into the world of Jetpack Compose. In the next chapter, we'll explore how to manage state and handle user input, two essential concepts for building interactive and dynamic Android applications.

State Management and User Input in Jetpack Compose

Outline

- Understanding State in Jetpack Compose
- The Importance of State
- The Problem with Mutable State
- Managing State with `remember`
- Mutable State Holders
- Handling User Input
- Chapter Summary

Understanding State in Jetpack Compose

In the world of Jetpack Compose, **state** is the heart and soul of your dynamic and interactive user interfaces. It represents the data or values that influence how your UI looks and behaves at any given moment. State can include things like:

- **User input:** Text entered in a text field, checkboxes toggled, sliders adjusted.
- **Data from network requests:** Information fetched from APIs or databases.
- **Internal application data:** Variables or objects that control UI elements.
- **UI configuration:** Settings that affect the appearance of your UI.

Composables as Functions of State:

In Jetpack Compose, your UI is built using composable functions. These functions are not just code that describes how the UI looks; they are *functions of their state*. This means that the output of a composable function (the UI it renders) is determined by the current values of the state variables it depends on.

Whenever the state changes, Jetpack Compose re-executes the relevant composable functions to reflect those changes in the UI. This process is called **recomposition**. Recomposition is the mechanism that allows your UI to dynamically update in response to state changes, making it interactive and responsive to user actions.

Unidirectional Data Flow:

Jetpack Compose promotes a **unidirectional data flow** model for state management. This means that state typically flows in a single direction:

1. **Downward Flow:** State flows down from parent composables to their child composables. Parents pass state values as parameters to their children.
2. **Upward Flow:** Events (like button clicks or text input) flow up from child composables to their parents. Children emit events, and parents handle them by modifying the state, which then triggers recomposition.

This unidirectional flow helps maintain a clear separation of concerns, making your code easier to reason about and debug. It also ensures that your UI remains consistent with the latest state, preventing unexpected side effects or inconsistencies.

Example:

Consider a simple composable function to display a counter:

```
@Composable
fun Counter(count: Int, onIncrement: () -> Unit) {
    Column {
        Text("Count: $count")
        Button(onClick = onIncrement) {
            Text("Increment")
        }
    }
}
```

In this example:

- `count` is the state that determines the displayed value.
- `onIncrement` is an event handler that flows up to the parent when the button is clicked.
- The parent composable would be responsible for holding and updating the `count` state and passing it down to the `Counter` composable.

By understanding the role of state and the concept of unidirectional data flow, you'll be well-equipped to build robust and interactive UIs in Jetpack Compose. State management is a fundamental pillar of Compose development, and we'll delve deeper into various techniques and tools for managing state effectively in the upcoming sections.

The Importance of State

State is the lifeblood of interactive user interfaces. It's what empowers your Jetpack Compose UIs to respond dynamically to user actions, fetch and display data, and adapt to changing conditions. Let's explore how state plays a crucial role in crafting engaging and user-friendly experiences.

Dynamic and Responsive UIs:

Without state, your UI would be a static picture, unable to react to the user or reflect changes in your app's data. State allows you to build UIs that:

- **Respond to User Input:** State variables can store values from text fields, checkboxes, radio buttons, and other input elements. When the user interacts with these elements, the state changes, triggering recomposition and updating the UI to reflect the new input.
- **Display Data:** State can hold data fetched from network requests, local databases, or other sources. This data is then displayed in the UI, and any updates to the data automatically refresh the corresponding UI elements.
- **Adapt to Conditions:** State can be used to represent the internal state of your app or its components. For instance, a boolean state variable can track whether a loading indicator should be visible, or an enum can represent the current screen in a navigation flow.

State Hoisting: Sharing State Between Composables:

In complex UIs, multiple composables might need access to the same state. Instead of duplicating state variables in each composable, you can use **state hoisting**. This involves lifting the state to a higher level in the composable hierarchy, typically to a parent composable or a shared ViewModel. This parent composable then passes the state down to its children as parameters.

State hoisting has several benefits:

- **Single Source of Truth:** It ensures that there's only one copy of the state, avoiding inconsistencies.
- **Improved Communication:** Child composables can communicate with each other by triggering events that modify the shared state.
- **Simplified Testing:** By centralizing the state, you can more easily test your composables in isolation.

Examples of State-Driven Interactions:

Let's see how you can use state to create interactive features:

Toggling Visibility:

```
@Composable
fun MyComposable() {
    var showImage by remember { mutableStateOf(false) }
    Column {
        Button(onClick = { showImage = !showImage }) {
            Text(if (showImage) "Hide Image" else "Show Image")
        }
        if (showImage) {
            Image(painterResource(id = R.drawable.my_image), contentDescription =
"My Image")
        }
    }
}
```

In this example, the showImage state variable controls whether the Image composable is visible. Clicking the button toggles this state, triggering recomposition and updating the UI.

Updating Text Content:

```
@Composable
fun MyComposable() {
    var text by remember { mutableStateOf("Hello") }
    Column {
        TextField(value = text, onValueChange = { text = it }) // Update
'text' on change
        Text("You entered: $text")
    }
}
```

The text state variable stores the input from the TextField. The UI updates to display the entered text in real-time.

Changing Colors:

```
@Composable
fun MyComposable() {
    var isRed by remember { mutableStateOf(false) }
    val buttonColor = if (isRed) Color.Red else Color.Blue
    Button(
        onClick = { isRed = !isRed },
        colors = ButtonDefaults.buttonColors(backgroundColor = buttonColor)
    ) {
        Text("Change Color")
    }
}
```

The `isRed` state variable determines the color of the button. Clicking the button toggles the state and updates the button color.

These examples demonstrate how state, combined with Jetpack Compose's declarative nature and recomposition mechanism, empowers you to build dynamic and engaging user interfaces that respond seamlessly to user actions and data changes.

The Problem with Mutable State

While mutable state is essential for creating dynamic UIs, it presents a challenge when working with Jetpack Compose due to its immutable nature. Let's delve into the issues that arise when attempting to directly modify mutable state in Compose.

Compose's Immutability Principle:

Jetpack Compose is built on the foundation of immutability. Composables are essentially pure functions of their state, meaning their output solely depends on their input parameters. Modifying the state directly within a composable violates this principle and can lead to unexpected consequences.

Unexpected Behavior and UI Inconsistencies:

Directly modifying mutable state can cause:

- **Missed UI Updates:** Compose relies on recomposition to update the UI when state changes. If you modify a mutable state variable without notifying Compose, it won't trigger recomposition, and your UI won't reflect the updated state. This results in a stale UI that doesn't match the underlying data.
- **Incorrect Recompositions:** In some cases, directly modifying mutable state can lead to unnecessary or incorrect recompositions. This can impact performance and cause unexpected UI glitches.
- **State Management Difficulties:** Managing mutable state in a complex UI becomes increasingly difficult as your app grows. Tracking which composables depend on which state variables and ensuring proper updates can become error-prone.

Need for a Controlled Mechanism:

To overcome these challenges, Jetpack Compose provides mechanisms to manage state changes in a controlled and predictable way. These mechanisms:

- **Ensure Proper Recomposition:** They notify Compose whenever a state variable is modified, triggering the necessary recompositions to keep the UI up-to-date.
- **Enforce Unidirectional Data Flow:** They encourage a unidirectional flow of data, where state changes are initiated by events or actions, leading to more predictable UI behavior.
- **Simplify State Management:** They offer tools and patterns to centralize and manage state effectively, making it easier to reason about and maintain your UI logic.

In the following sections, we'll explore the key mechanisms that Jetpack Compose offers for managing state, including the `remember` function, `mutableStateOf`, and `MutableState`.

Managing State with `remember`

Jetpack Compose's `remember` function is a key tool for effectively managing state in a declarative and immutable environment. Let's break down how it works and how you can use it to your advantage.

How `remember` Solves the Mutable State Problem:

- **Caching Across Recompositions:** The core idea behind `remember` is caching. When you use `remember` to store a value, Compose calculates that value once during the initial composition. On subsequent recompositions (triggered by state changes), Compose retrieves the cached value instead of recalculating it.
- **Stable Reference to Mutable State:** This caching mechanism allows you to store mutable state objects (like `MutableList`, `MutableMap`, or custom data classes) within `remember`. The reference to the mutable state object remains stable across recompositions, while you can safely modify the object's internal state.
- **Recomposition Trigger:** Whenever you modify the state within a `remember` block, Jetpack Compose is notified of the change and triggers a recomposition. This ensures that the UI is updated to reflect the new state.

Using `remember` to Store and Update State:

Here's how you can use `remember` to manage different types of state variables:

Counters:

```
@Composable
fun Counter() {
    var count by remember { mutableStateOf(0) }

    Button(onClick = { count++ }) {
        Text("Count: $count")
    }
}
```

In this example, `remember` is used to store the count variable. The `mutableStateOf` function creates a `MutableState` object that holds the integer value, and the by keyword delegates the getter and setter properties to the `MutableState` object. When you click the button, `count` is incremented, and Compose automatically recomposes the `Counter` function to display the updated count.

Text Inputs:

```
@Composable
fun MyTextField() {
    var text by remember { mutableStateOf("") }

    TextField(
        value = text,
        onValueChange = { text = it },
        label = { Text("Enter text") }
    )
}
```

Here, `remember` stores the `text` variable, representing the content of the `TextField`. As the user types, `onValueChange` updates the `text` variable, and Compose recomposes the `TextField` to display the new input.

Boolean Flags:

```
@Composable
fun MyToggle() {
    var isChecked by remember { mutableStateOf(false) }
```

```
    Switch(
        checked = isChecked,
        onCheckedChange = { isChecked = it }
    )
}
```

In this case, remember holds a boolean isChecked state. When the Switch is toggled, onCheckedChange updates the isChecked value, and Compose recomposes the Switch to reflect the new state.

Key Points:

- remember provides a solution to the problem of mutable state in Jetpack Compose by caching values and ensuring stable references.
- It allows you to safely modify the internal state of objects while triggering recomposition for UI updates.
- remember is a versatile tool for storing and updating various types of state variables in your composable functions.

By understanding and utilizing remember, you can confidently manage state in your Jetpack Compose applications, leading to dynamic, interactive, and reliable user interfaces.

Mutable State Holders

Jetpack Compose offers a variety of mechanisms to help you manage state effectively. In this section, we'll focus on the key mutable state holders: remember, mutableStateOf, and MutableState, and explore how they work together to maintain a predictable and reactive UI.

remember

- **Role:** The remember function is your primary tool for storing state values in Jetpack Compose. It caches the value across recompositions, providing a stable reference to the state even if the composable function is re-executed. This ensures that the state isn't lost or recalculated unnecessarily, leading to predictable UI behavior.
- **When to Use:** Use remember whenever you want to store a value that should persist across recompositions and potentially be modified. This includes counters, user input values, flags, and even complex objects like lists or custom data classes.

mutableStateOf

- **Role:** The mutableStateOf function is a convenience function that creates a MutableState object. MutableState is a special type of object in Compose that allows you to store a mutable value and automatically triggers recomposition when that value changes.
- **When to Use:** Use mutableStateOf when you need to store a simple value (like an Int, String, Boolean, etc.) that can be directly modified. The by keyword is often used in conjunction with mutableStateOf to delegate the getter and setter properties to the MutableState object, making it easier to read and write.

MutableState

- **Role:** `MutableState` is the underlying interface for mutable state objects in Jetpack Compose. It provides functions like `value` (for getting the current value) and `setValue` (for updating the value).
- **When to Use:** You can work directly with `MutableState` if you need more fine-grained control over how state changes are handled. However, in most cases, `mutableStateOf` provides a more convenient way to create and use `MutableState` objects.

Combining State Holders with State Hoisting

For efficient and maintainable state management in larger applications, you'll often combine these state holders with **state hoisting**. State hoisting involves lifting the state to a common ancestor composable or a `ViewModel`. This allows you to share the state between multiple child composables and avoid unnecessary recompositions.

Example:

```
@Composable
fun ParentComposable() {
    val sharedState = remember { mutableStateOf(0) } // Hoisted state
    Column {
        ChildComposable1(sharedState)
        ChildComposable2(sharedState)
    }
}


@Composable
fun ChildComposable1(sharedState: MutableState<Int>) {
    Button(onClick = { sharedState.value++ }) { // Modify shared state
        Text("Increment from Child 1")
    }
}


@Composable
fun ChildComposable2(sharedState: MutableState<Int>) {
    Text("Count: ${sharedState.value}") // Read shared state
}
```

In this example, the `sharedState` is hoisted to the `ParentComposable` and passed down to both `ChildComposable1` and `ChildComposable2`.

By skillfully combining these state holders with state hoisting, you can create a well-structured and maintainable approach to managing state in your Jetpack Compose applications. Remember to choose the right state holder for the job and consider hoisting state when it needs to be shared among multiple composables.

Handling User Input

Interactive UIs are built on the foundation of handling user input. Jetpack Compose provides a straightforward and elegant way to capture user actions and respond to them, creating a seamless and engaging experience for your app's users.

Handling Button Clicks:

The most basic form of user interaction is the button click. You've already seen the `Button` composable in action:

```
Button(onClick = { /* Handle button click */ }) {
    Text("Click Me")
}
```

The onClick parameter is a lambda function that gets executed when the button is clicked. Inside this lambda, you'll write the code to handle the click event, such as updating state, navigating to a new screen, or performing some other action.

Text Input with `TextField`:

The `TextField` composable is used to capture text input from the user:

```
@Composable
fun MyTextField() {
    var text by remember { mutableStateOf("") }

    TextField(
        value = text,
        onValueChange = { newText ->
            text = newText
        },
        label = { Text("Enter text") }
    )
}
```

In this example:

- `text` is a state variable that stores the current input value.
- `onValueChange` is a lambda function that gets called whenever the text changes. It receives the new text value and updates the `text` state, triggering recomposition and updating the UI.

Event Handlers and Lambda Functions:

Jetpack Compose uses **event handlers** to respond to user actions. Event handlers are functions or lambda expressions that you pass as parameters to composables. These handlers are invoked when the corresponding event occurs, such as a button click or text input change.

Lambda functions are a concise way to define event handlers in Kotlin. They allow you to write a block of code that will be executed when the event happens. For example, the `onClick` lambda in the `Button` composable is an event handler for button click events.

Capturing and Updating State:

When a user interacts with your UI, you often need to capture their input and update the app's state accordingly. This can involve:

1. **Capturing Input:** Use composables like `TextField` or custom composables to capture user input.
2. **Updating State:** Modify your state variables based on the captured input. Use `mutableStateOf` or other statemanagement techniques.
3. **Triggering Recomposition:** The state change automatically triggers recomposition, updating the UI to reflect the new state.

Example: Counter App:

```
@Composable
fun Counter() {
    var count by remember { mutableStateOf(0) }

    Column {
        Text(text = "Count: $count")
        Button(onClick = { count++ }) {
            Text("Increment")
        }
    }
}
```

In this counter app, clicking the button increments the count state variable, which triggers recomposition and updates the Text composable to display the new count.

Gesture Handling:

Jetpack Compose also provides modifiers for handling gestures like tap, double-tap, long press, and drag. You'll learn more about gestures and their modifiers in later chapters.

By mastering user input handling and state management, you can create truly interactive and engaging Android apps with Jetpack Compose. Remember, user input is the primary way users interact with your app, so crafting a smooth and responsive input experience is crucial for a successful application.

Chapter Summary

This chapter delved into the core principles of state management and user input in Jetpack Compose. You learned how state serves as the driving force behind dynamic and interactive user interfaces, enabling your app to respond to user actions and data changes. We explored the concept of state hoisting, a technique for sharing state efficiently between composables, and discussed the challenges of working with mutable state in Compose's immutable environment.

The remember function was introduced as a powerful tool for managing state, providing a mechanism for caching values across recompositions and ensuring stable references to mutable state objects. You saw how to use remember with mutableStateOf and MutableState to store and update various types of state, such as counters, text inputs, and boolean flags.

Finally, we explored how to handle user input in Jetpack Compose, focusing on button clicks and text input. You learned about event handlers, lambda functions, and the importance of updating state to trigger UI updates in response to user interactions.

With a solid understanding of state management and user input handling, you're well-equipped to create dynamic and interactive Android apps with Jetpack Compose. In the next chapter, we'll delve into advanced layout techniques and explore how to customize the appearance of your UIs with styling and theming.

Section C:
Mastering Layouts and Customization

Advanced Layout Techniques: ConstraintLayout and Custom Layouts

Outline

- Revisiting Layouts in Jetpack Compose
- The Power of ConstraintLayout in Compose
- Creating Custom Layouts
- Exploring Layout Modifiers
- Chapter Summary

Revisiting Layouts in Jetpack Compose

In the previous chapter, we explored the foundational layouts in Jetpack Compose: Column, Row, and Box. These layouts provide the basic building blocks for arranging composables vertically, horizontally, or in an overlapping manner. However, as your UI designs become more intricate and your app's functionality grows, you'll inevitably encounter scenarios where these basic layouts alone might not suffice.

The Need for Advanced Layouts:

Consider these situations where advanced layout techniques become essential:

- **Complex Positioning:** You might need to position elements precisely relative to each other or the screen edges, creating layouts that don't fit the simple linear or overlapping patterns of Column, Row, and Box.
- **Responsive Design:** Different screen sizes and orientations require layouts that can adapt gracefully to varying dimensions. Basic layouts often fall short in handling these variations effectively.
- **Custom UI Elements:** When you need to create unique UI elements that don't fit into standard molds, you'll need the flexibility to define custom layout behaviors.
- **Performance Optimization:** In complex layouts with numerous elements, optimizing the layout process becomes crucial for maintaining smooth performance. Advanced layout techniques can help you achieve this.

The Importance of Flexibility and Customization:

The ability to create flexible and customizable layouts is paramount in Jetpack Compose. Here's why:

- **Visual Appeal:** Advanced layouts allow you to craft visually engaging UIs that go beyond the limitations of simple arrangements.
- **User Experience:** Responsive layouts ensure a seamless user experience across different devices and screen sizes.

- **Uniqueness:** Custom layouts enable you to create distinctive UI elements that set your app apart.
- **Efficiency:** Optimized layouts contribute to a smoother and more responsive app experience.

In the following sections, we'll dive into two powerful layout techniques in Jetpack Compose: ConstraintLayout and custom layouts. ConstraintLayout offers a declarative way to define complex relationships between elements, while custom layouts give you the ultimate flexibility to create unique UI structures tailored to your specific needs. By mastering these techniques, you'll be equipped to tackle even the most challenging UI design requirements with confidence.

The Power of ConstraintLayout in Compose

ConstraintLayout, a powerful layout tool familiar to Android developers from the traditional View system, has made its way into the world of Jetpack Compose. It brings with it the same flexibility and declarative power, allowing you to create complex layouts with ease.

What is ConstraintLayout in Compose?

In essence, ConstraintLayout in Compose is a composable function (ConstraintLayout) that enables you to define relationships (constraints) between composables within a layout. These constraints dictate how composables are positioned and sized relative to each other and their parent container.

Translating ConstraintLayout to Compose:

The core concepts of ConstraintLayout remain the same in Compose. You define constraints using references to composables and anchors (top, bottom, start, end, etc.). These constraints are declarative, meaning you specify the desired relationships, and Compose takes care of calculating the actual positions and sizes based on those constraints.

Advantages of ConstraintLayout:

ConstraintLayout offers several significant advantages:

1. **Flexibility:** You can easily create complex layouts with precise positioning and alignment of elements.
2. **Responsiveness:** ConstraintLayout makes it easier to design layouts that adapt to different screen sizes and orientations.
3. **Performance:** ConstraintLayout is optimized for performance, especially in complex layouts.
4. **Familiarity:** If you're already familiar with ConstraintLayout in the View system, the transition to Compose is smooth.

Creating a Layout with ConstraintLayout (Step-by-Step):

1. **Import the dependency:**

```
implementation("androidx.constraintlayout:constraintlayout-compose:1.1.0-alpha13")
```

2. **Define the ConstraintLayout:**

```
@Composable

fun MyConstraintLayout() {
```

```
ConstraintLayout {

    val (button, text) = createRefs() // Create references


    Button(
        onClick = { /* TODO */ },
        modifier = Modifier.constrainAs(button) {
            top.linkTo(parent.top, margin = 16.dp)
            start.linkTo(parent.start, margin = 16.dp)
        }
    ) {
        Text("Button")
    }


    Text("Text", Modifier.constrainAs(text) {
        top.linkTo(button.bottom, margin = 16.dp)
        start.linkTo(parent.start, margin = 16.dp)
    })
    }
}
```

Defining Constraints:

- **createRefs():** This function creates references (button and text in the example) that you can use to identify your composables within the ConstraintLayout.
- **constrainAs(ref):** This modifier is applied to a composable to define its constraints. The ref parameter is the reference you created for that composable.
- **Constraint Functions:** Within the constrainAs block, you use constraint functions to establish relationships between composables and their anchors. For example:
  - top.linkTo(parent.top, margin = 16.dp): Position the top of the button 16 dp below the top of its parent.
  - start.linkTo(parent.start, margin = 16.dp): Position the start of the button 16 dp to the right of the start of its parent.
  - top.linkTo(button.bottom, margin = 16.dp): Position the top of the text 16 dp below the bottom of the button.

ConstraintLayout in Compose provides you with a powerful tool to create flexible, responsive, and visually appealing layouts for your Android applications.

Creating Custom Layouts

While Jetpack Compose provides a rich set of built-in layouts, there will be times when you need to create your own custom layouts to achieve unique UI designs or specific layout behaviors. In this section, we'll delve into the world of custom layouts and show you how to craft them using the Layout composable.

Why Create Custom Layouts?

Here are some scenarios where custom layouts become invaluable:

- **Unique Layouts:** When you need to create a layout that doesn't fit the mold of existing layouts (e.g., a circular arrangement, a staggered grid, or a custom calendar view).
- **Specific Behaviors:** You might want to control the precise placement of elements, implement custom scrolling behavior, or handle touch events in a unique way.
- **Performance Optimization:** For complex layouts, crafting a custom layout optimized for your specific use case can improve performance compared to using a more general-purpose layout.

The Layout Composable:

The Layout composable is the foundation for creating custom layouts in Jetpack Compose. It provides a powerful and flexible way to measure and position your composable children.

Here's a simplified overview of how Layout works:

1. **Measure:** The measure function is responsible for determining the size requirements of each child composable. It takes the constraints provided by the parent layout and calculates the minimum and maximum size that each child needs to be properly displayed.
2. **Layout:** The layout function is responsible for placing and sizing the child composables within the available space. It uses the measurements obtained in the measure step to determine the final position and size of each child.

Implementing a Custom Layout:

To create a custom layout, you need to follow these steps:

1. **Create a Composable Function:** Define a composable function that takes a content parameter of type @Composable () -> Unit. This content lambda is where you'll place the child composables of your layout.
2. **Override measure and layout:** Inside your composable function, call the Layout function and override its measure and layout parameters. Implement the logic to measure and position your child composables within these functions.

Practical Example: Circular Arrangement

Let's create a custom layout that arranges its children in a circle:

```
@Composable
fun CircularLayout(
    modifier: Modifier = Modifier,
    content: @Composable () -> Unit
) {
    Layout(
        modifier = modifier,
        content = content
```

```
    ) { measurables, constraints ->
        // 1. Measure children
        val placeables = measurables.map { measurable ->
            measurable.measure(constraints)
        }

        // 2. Determine layout dimensions
        val radius = max(constraints.maxWidth, constraints.maxHeight) / 2

        // 3. Place children in a circle
        layout(radius * 2, radius * 2) {
            val angleIncrement = 360f / placeables.size
            var currentAngle = 0f
            placeables.forEach { placeable ->
                val x = radius + radius *
cos(Math.toRadians(currentAngle.toDouble())).toFloat() - placeable.width / 2
                val y = radius + radius *
sin(Math.toRadians(currentAngle.toDouble())).toFloat() - placeable.height / 2
                placeable.placeRelative(x.toInt(), y.toInt())
                currentAngle += angleIncrement
            }
        }
    }
}
```

(Remember to replace the comment with the actual code, and please note the use of trigonometry is needed to calculate the x and y coordinates on a circle)

In this example:

1. We measure each child composable to determine their size.
2. We calculate the radius of the circle based on the layout's constraints.
3. We iterate through the children and place them equidistantly around the circle using trigonometric calculations.

Now you can use this layout in your code:

```
CircularLayout {
    Image(painter = painterResource(id = R.drawable.image1), contentDescription =
"Image 1")
    Image(painter = painterResource(id = R.drawable.image2), contentDescription =
"Image 2")
    // Add more composables here
}
```

By creating custom layouts like this, you unlock a vast array of possibilities for designing unique and engaging user interfaces in Jetpack Compose.

Exploring Layout Modifiers

Layout modifiers are essential tools in Jetpack Compose for customizing the appearance and behavior of layouts and their child composables. They provide a declarative way to modify properties such as size, positioning, alignment, and more. By chaining modifiers together, you can achieve precise control over how your UI elements are displayed.

What are Layout Modifiers?

Layout modifiers are functions that you apply to composables using the `.modifier` property. They intercept the layout process and allow you to adjust how composables are measured, laid out, and drawn. Modifiers can be applied to both layouts (like `Column` or `Row`) and individual composables (like `Text` or `Image`).

Commonly Used Layout Modifiers:

- **offset:** Shifts a composable by a specified amount in the x and y directions.

```
Text(
    "Offset Text",
    modifier = Modifier.offset(x = 10.dp, y = 20.dp)
)
```

- **size:** Sets the width and height of a composable to fixed values.

```
Image(
    painter = painterResource(id = R.drawable.my_image),
    contentDescription = "My Image",
    modifier = Modifier.size(width = 100.dp, height = 150.dp)
)
```

- **fillMaxWidth, fillMaxHeight:** Makes a composable fill the available width or height of its parent layout.

```
Button(
    onClick = { /* ... */ },
    modifier = Modifier.fillMaxWidth()
)
```

- **weight:** Distributes available space proportionally among composable elements within a Row or Column.

```
Row {
    Text(
        "Item 1",
        modifier = Modifier.weight(1f)
    )
    Text(
        "Item 2",
        modifier = Modifier.weight(2f) // Twice the width of Item 1
    )
}
```

- **padding:** Adds space (padding) around a composable.

```
Text(
    "Padded Text",
    modifier = Modifier.padding(16.dp)
)
```

Creating Custom Modifiers:

You can create your own custom modifiers to encapsulate specific layout behaviors. Here's a simple example:

```
fun Modifier.borderWithPadding(width: Dp, color: Color, padding: Dp) = this
    .border(width, color)
    .padding(padding)
```

(The actual implementation of a custom modifier will typically be more complex than in the above example. It will likely override certain layout functions to provide more control over placement and sizing.)

You can then use this modifier like this:

```
Text(
    "Custom Border and Padding",
    modifier = Modifier.borderWithPadding(2.dp, Color.Red, 8.dp)
)
```

`Modifier.layout` for Advanced Customization:

For more complex layout logic, you can use the `Modifier.layout` function. This function allows you to intercept the layout process and manually control the positioning and sizing of a composable.

```
Text(
    "Custom Layout",
    modifier = Modifier.layout { measurable, constraints ->
        // ... custom layout logic ...
    }
)
```

Within the `layout` lambda, you receive the measurable object of the composable and the constraints imposed by the parent layout. You can then measure the composable, determine its desired size, and place it at the desired coordinates within the parent's layout.

Key Takeaways:

- Layout modifiers provide a flexible and declarative way to customize the appearance and behavior of your composables.
- Commonly used modifiers include `offset`, `size`, `fillMaxWidth`, `weight`, and `padding`.
- You can create custom modifiers to encapsulate specific layout behaviors.
- `Modifier.layout` allows for more advanced and fine-grained control over layout customization.

By mastering layout modifiers, you gain a powerful toolset for creating complex and visually appealing layouts in Jetpack Compose. Experiment with different modifiers and combinations to achieve your desired UI designs.

Chapter Summary

This chapter delved into advanced layout techniques in Jetpack Compose, equipping you with the skills to create complex and customized UIs. You learned how `ConstraintLayout`, a powerful tool from the traditional Android View system, seamlessly integrates into Compose, offering flexibility and responsiveness for intricate layouts. We explored the process of creating custom layouts using the `Layout` composable, giving you the ability to craft unique UI elements tailored to your specific design needs.

You also gained a deeper understanding of layout modifiers, learning how they modify the behavior and appearance of composables within layouts. We covered commonly used modifiers like `offset`, `size`, `fillMaxSize`, `weight`, and `padding`, demonstrating their usage through practical examples.

Additionally, you discovered how to create your own custom modifiers and even manipulate layouts directly using the `Modifier.layout` function for ultimate customization.

With these advanced layout techniques under your belt, you're well-prepared to tackle a wide range of UI challenges in your Jetpack Compose projects. In the next chapter, we'll focus on styling and theming, exploring how to make your Compose UIs visually appealing and consistent with Material Design principles.

Styling and Theming: Material Design and Custom Styles

Outline

- Styling in Jetpack Compose
- Material Design Principles in Compose
- Theming in Jetpack Compose
- Creating Custom Themes
- Chapter Summary

Styling in Jetpack Compose

In Jetpack Compose, **styling** plays a pivotal role in shaping the visual appearance and presentation of your user interface. It encompasses everything from basic modifications like adding padding and colors to creating complex themes that define the overall look and feel of your app. Let's delve into how styling works in Compose and how it differs from the traditional Android approach.

Styling vs. Traditional Android Styling:

Jetpack Compose takes a fresh approach to styling compared to the XML-based styling in traditional Android views. Here's a comparison:

Feature	Traditional Android Styling (XML)	Jetpack Compose Styling (Kotlin)
Declaration	Styles are defined in separate XML files (e.g., `styles.xml`).	Styles are defined directly in Kotlin code using modifiers or composable functions.
Application	Styles are applied to views using attributes (e.g., `style="@style/MyStyle"`).	Styles are applied using modifiers or by passing style objects as parameters to composables.
Flexibility	Limited to pre-defined attributes and styles.	Highly flexible, allowing custom styles and dynamic styling based on state.
Type Safety	No type safety for style attributes.	Type-safe styling due to the use of Kotlin.
Readability	Styling code can be scattered across XML files, making it harder to track.	Styling code is often co-located with the composable function, improving readability.

Modifiers for Basic Styling:

Modifiers are your primary tool for basic styling in Jetpack Compose. You can use modifiers to:

- **Add Padding:**

```
Text("Hello", modifier = Modifier.padding(16.dp))
```

- **Set Background Color:**

```
Box(modifier = Modifier.background(Color.LightGray))
```

- **Add a Border:**

```
Text("Bordered Text", modifier = Modifier.border(2.dp, Color.Black))
```

- **Apply Shapes:**

```
Image(
    painter = painterResource(id = R.drawable.my_image),
    contentDescription = null,
    modifier = Modifier.clip(RoundedCornerShape(8.dp))
)
```

Composable Functions for Reusable Styles:

To create reusable styles, you can define composable functions that encapsulate specific styles. This promotes consistency and makes your code more maintainable:

```
@Composable
fun MyTextStyle(content: @Composable () -> Unit) {
    Text(
        content(),
        style = TextStyle(fontWeight = FontWeight.Bold, color = Color.Blue)
    )
}


// Usage
MyTextStyle {
    Text("This text is bold and blue")
}
```

Applying Styles to Composables:

You can apply styles to individual composables or groups of composables. For instance, you can wrap a group of composables in a `Column` and apply a modifier to the `Column` to style all its children:

```
Column(modifier = Modifier.background(Color.Yellow)) {
    Text("Text 1")
    Text("Text 2")
    // ...
}
```

In the following sections, we'll delve deeper into Material Design principles and explore how to create custom themes in Jetpack Compose to further enhance the visual aesthetics of your applications.

Material Design Principles in Compose

Material Design is Google's comprehensive design system that aims to create visually appealing, user-friendly, and consistent experiences across platforms and devices. Jetpack Compose seamlessly embraces Material Design principles, offering a rich set of pre-built components and styling options that adhere to these guidelines.

Embracing Material Design in Compose:

Jetpack Compose is designed to be Material Design-first. The framework provides composables that directly map to Material Design components, such as buttons, cards, text fields, and more. Additionally, Compose offers flexible styling options that allow you to customize the appearance of these components while maintaining the core principles of Material Design.

Core Concepts of Material Design:

Material Design is based on a few fundamental concepts:

- **Material is the Metaphor:** Material Design draws inspiration from the physical world, using surfaces, shadows, and motion to create a tangible and intuitive feel.
- **Bold, Graphic, Intentional:** Material Design emphasizes clear typography, vibrant colors, and deliberate use of white space to create visually striking interfaces.
- **Meaningful Motion:** Motion is used to guide the user's attention, provide feedback, and create a sense of continuity between actions.

Let's delve into some of the key principles you'll encounter in Material Design:

- **Material Surfaces:** UI elements are treated as sheets of digital "material" with varying elevation levels. Shadows and depth cues create a sense of hierarchy and realism.
- **Elevation:** Elevation (z-axis) is used to indicate the relative importance and interactivity of elements. Higher elevation implies greater prominence.
- **Color System:** Material Design offers a well-defined color system with primary, secondary, and accent colors. You can use predefined palettes or create custom color schemes.
- **Typography:** A clear and legible typography system is essential. Material Design emphasizes the use of Roboto and Noto fonts.
- **Motion:** Meaningful motion enhances the user experience by providing visual feedback and transitions between states.

Using Material Design Components in Compose:

Jetpack Compose provides a wide array of Material Design composables, including:

- **Button:** Creates interactive buttons with various styles (e.g., `filled`, `outlined`, `text`).
- **Card:** A versatile container for displaying content in a visually distinct manner.
- **AppBar:** A top-level bar that provides structure to your screen, typically including a title and actions.
- **Scaffold:** A basic structure for your app's UI, including an app bar, a navigation drawer (optional), and a content area.
- **Many More:** Explore the full range of Material Design composables in the official documentation.

Customization:

While Material Design components provide a solid foundation, you can customize them to align with your app's branding and style. You can modify colors, typography, shapes, and even create custom composables while still adhering to the overall Material Design principles.

Example: Customizing a Button:

```
Button(
    onClick = { /* ... */ },
```

```
    colors = ButtonDefaults.buttonColors(
        backgroundColor = Color.Green, // Custom background color
        contentColor = Color.White      // Custom text color
    ),
    shape = RoundedCornerShape(8.dp)    // Custom shape
) {
    Text("Custom Button")
}
```

In this example, we customize the button's background color, text color, and shape.

By embracing Material Design principles and leveraging the rich set of composables and styling options in Jetpack Compose, you can create visually stunning and user-friendly Android applications that adhere to Google's design guidelines and deliver a consistent and enjoyable experience for your users.

Theming in Jetpack Compose

Theming in Jetpack Compose is a powerful mechanism for applying a consistent visual style to your entire application. It allows you to define a set of colors, typography, shapes, and other design elements that are used throughout your UI. This ensures a cohesive and polished look for your app while making it easier to maintain and update your styles.

`MaterialTheme`: Your Default Style Foundation

Jetpack Compose comes with a built-in `MaterialTheme` composable. This composable provides a default Material Design theme, which is a great starting point for your app. The default theme includes:

- **Color Palette:** A set of colors for primary, secondary, background, surface, error, and other elements.
- **Typography:** Predefined styles for different text elements (e.g., headlines, body text, captions).
- **Shapes:** Default shapes for components like buttons, cards, and dialogs.

You can use `MaterialTheme` like this:

```
@Composable
fun MyApp() {
    MaterialTheme {
        // Your composable content here
    }
}
```

All composables within the `MaterialTheme` block will inherit the default styles provided by the theme.

Creating Custom Themes:

While the default `MaterialTheme` is a good starting point, you'll often want to create custom themes to match your app's branding and design. Custom themes allow you to:

- **Define Your Color Palette:** Choose colors that align with your app's identity.
- **Customize Typography:** Select fonts and text styles that suit your content.
- **Create Unique Shapes:** Design shapes that complement your overall design aesthetic.

To create a custom theme, you can use the `MaterialTheme` composable and provide your own values for colors, typography, and shapes:

```
@Composable
fun MyApp() {
    val myColors = lightColors(
        primary = Color.Red,
        secondary = Color.Yellow,
        // ... other colors ...
    )

    val myTypography = Typography(
        h1 = TextStyle(fontSize = 24.sp, fontWeight = FontWeight.Bold),
        // ... other text styles ...
    )

    val myShapes = Shapes(
        small = RoundedCornerShape(4.dp),
        medium = RoundedCornerShape(8.dp),
        // ... other shapes ...
    )

    MaterialTheme(colors = myColors, typography = myTypography, shapes =
myShapes) {
        // Your composable content here
    }
}
```

Applying Themes and Dynamic Switching:

To apply your custom theme, simply wrap your composable content within the `MaterialTheme` block, as shown in the examples above.

You can also switch between themes dynamically (e.g., for light/dark mode) by making the theme parameters (`colors`, `typography`, `shapes`) state variables and updating them based on user preferences or system settings.

Light and Dark Themes:

Creating light and dark themes is a common practice to accommodate different user preferences and lighting conditions. Here's a simplified example:

```
val isDarkTheme = isSystemInDarkTheme() // Detect system theme

val lightColors = lightColors(
    // ... light theme colors ...
)

val darkColors = darkColors(
    // ... dark theme colors ...
)

MaterialTheme(colors = if (isDarkTheme) darkColors else lightColors) {
    // ... your composable content ...
}
```

By mastering theming in Jetpack Compose, you'll be able to create visually cohesive and engaging apps that offer a delightful user experience. Remember, a well-designed theme is an essential part of any modern Android application.

Creating Custom Themes

While Jetpack Compose provides a default Material Theme, creating custom themes allows you to truly tailor the look and feel of your app. Let's explore how to define your own color palettes, typography, shapes, and more.

Step-by-Step Guide to Creating a Custom Theme:

1. **Define Color Palettes:**
   - Create a data class to hold your color scheme:

   ```
   data class AppColors(
       val primary: Color,
       val secondary: Color,
       val background: Color,
       val surface: Color,
       val onPrimary: Color,
       val onSecondary: Color,
       val onBackground: Color,
       val onSurface: Color,
       // ...add other colors you'll use
   )
   ```

   - Create instances of light and dark color palettes:

   ```
   val LightColorPalette = AppColors(
       // ... light colors ...
   )

   val DarkColorPalette = AppColors(
       // ... dark colors ...
   )
   ```

2. **Customize Typography:**
   - Create a Typography object to define text styles for different elements (e.g., h1, h2, body1, button):

   ```
   val MyTypography = Typography(
       h1 = TextStyle(
           fontFamily = FontFamily.SansSerif,
           fontWeight = FontWeight.Bold,
           fontSize = 24.sp
       ),
       // ... other text styles ...
   )
   ```

3. **Define Custom Shapes:**
   - Create a Shapes object to define the shapes of your UI elements:

   ```
   val MyShapes = Shapes(
       small = RoundedCornerShape(4.dp),
   ```

```
    medium = RoundedCornerShape(8.dp),
    large = RoundedCornerShape(16.dp)
)
```

4. **Create Your Theme:**
   ○ Create a composable function that encapsulates your theme:

```
@Composable
fun MyTheme(
    darkTheme: Boolean = isSystemInDarkTheme(),
    content: @Composable () -> Unit
) {
    val colors = if (darkTheme) DarkColorPalette else
LightColorPalette

    MaterialTheme(colors = colors, typography = MyTypography, shapes
= MyShapes) {
        CompositionLocalProvider(LocalAppColors provides colors) {
            content()
        }
    }
}
```

(Notice we've added a `CompositionLocalProvider` that provides the colors for easy access within child composables.)

5. **Use Your Theme:**

```
MyTheme { // Wrap your app's content
    // ... your composable functions ...
}
```

`CompositionLocalProvider`:

`CompositionLocalProvider` lets you inject values (like your color palette) into the composition tree. Child composables can then access these values without needing them passed explicitly as parameters.

```
@Composable
fun MyComposable() {
    val colors = LocalAppColors.current
    Text("Text with primary color", color = colors.primary)
}
```

Best Practices:

- **Organize Your Theme Files:** Create separate files for colors, typography, shapes, and your theme composables for better organization.
- **Name Clearly:** Use descriptive names for your color, typography, and shape variables.
- **Keep it Maintainable:** Design your theme to be easily adaptable to future changes.

Example: Branding Your App:

```
data class AppColors(
    val primary: Color = Color(0xFF6200EE),  // Brand primary
    val secondary: Color = Color(0xFF03DAC5), // Brand secondary
    // ...other colors
```

```
)

// In your MyTheme composable:
MaterialTheme(colors = AppColors()) { ... }
```

By investing time in creating a well-crafted custom theme, you'll elevate the visual appeal and consistency of your Jetpack Compose applications, leaving a lasting impression on your users.

Chapter Summary

This chapter has illuminated the power of styling and theming in Jetpack Compose, crucial tools for creating visually appealing and consistent Android apps. You've learned how to leverage modifiers for basic styling, adding visual enhancements like padding, colors, borders, and shapes to your composable functions.

We then explored the principles of Material Design and how Jetpack Compose embraces this design language. You discovered a plethora of Material Design components readily available in Compose, allowing you to quickly build interfaces that adhere to modern design principles.

The concept of theming in Compose was unveiled, showcasing how to define and apply consistent styles across your entire application. You learned how to create custom themes from scratch, defining color palettes, typography, and shapes to align with your app's unique branding and personality. The use of `CompositionLocalProvider` for convenient access to theme values within composables was also explained.

By the end of this chapter, you are equipped with the knowledge to transform your Jetpack Compose UIs into visually stunning and user-friendly experiences.

Section D:
Working with Data and Lists

Displaying Lists with LazyColumn and LazyRow

Outline

- Efficiently Displaying Lists in Compose
- LazyColumn
- LazyRow
- Advanced List Customization
- LazyGrids: Compose 1.4.0+
- Chapter Summary

Efficiently Displaying Lists in Compose

Lists are a fundamental UI element for displaying collections of data, and Jetpack Compose provides powerful tools to make working with lists a breeze. However, when dealing with large datasets, using traditional layouts like Column or Row to display lists can quickly become problematic.

Challenges with Traditional Layouts:

- **Performance Bottleneck:** If you have a list with hundreds or thousands of items, attempting to render them all simultaneously using Column or Row can overwhelm your app's performance. This can result in slow scrolling, janky animations, and an overall sluggish user experience.
- **Memory Overhead:** Rendering all items at once consumes a significant amount of memory, especially if each item contains complex layouts or large images. This can lead to memory pressure and even app crashes on devices with limited resources.

The Concept of Lazy Lists:

Jetpack Compose addresses these challenges with **lazy lists**. Lazy lists, implemented as LazyColumn (for vertical lists) and LazyRow (for horizontal lists), are designed to optimize performance by only rendering the items that are currently visible on the screen. As the user scrolls, items that move off-screen are removed from the composition, and new items that become visible are composed and displayed.

This approach offers several key benefits:

- **Improved Performance:** By rendering only a subset of items at a time, lazy lists significantly reduce the computational and memory overhead associated with large lists. This results in smoother scrolling and a more responsive UI.
- **Reduced Memory Consumption:** Lazy lists efficiently manage memory by recycling composables that are no longer visible. This means that even with very large lists, your app's memory footprint remains manageable.
- **Simplified Development:** The API for LazyColumn and LazyRow is designed to be intuitive and easy to use. You provide your list data and a composable function to define how each item should be displayed, and Compose handles the rest.

Benefits for Large Datasets:

The advantages of lazy lists become particularly evident when working with large datasets:

- **Smooth Scrolling:** Lazy lists ensure smooth scrolling even when dealing with thousands of items.
- **Responsive UI:** The UI remains responsive to user interactions, as only a small portion of the list is being updated at any given time.
- **Memory Efficiency:** Memory usage is kept in check, preventing memory-related issues and crashes.
- **Faster Loading Times:** Your app will start up faster because it doesn't need to load and render all list items upfront.

By leveraging lazy lists in Jetpack Compose, you can confidently handle large datasets and deliver a seamless and enjoyable user experience. In the following sections, we'll dive deeper into the specifics of LazyColumn and LazyRow, exploring their features and customization options.

LazyColumn

The LazyColumn composable is your workhorse for displaying vertical lists of items in Jetpack Compose. It's designed for efficiency, rendering only the items that are visible on the screen and recycling them as the user scrolls. This makes it ideal for handling large lists without compromising performance.

How LazyColumn Works:

Under the hood, LazyColumn creates a vertically scrollable container and manages the composition of list items dynamically. As the user scrolls, LazyColumn intelligently decides which items to compose and which to discard. It reuses composables from items that have scrolled off-screen, reducing the need to create new composables constantly.

The items Parameter:

The items parameter is the heart of the LazyColumn. It's where you provide the data that you want to display in the list. You can pass a List, an Array, or even an integer range to specify the number of items.

```
val items = listOf("Apple", "Banana", "Cherry", "Date")
LazyColumn {
    items(items) { item ->
        Text(text = item)
    }
}
```

In this example, items is a list of strings, and the lambda function item -> Text(text = item) defines how each item (a string) should be displayed in the list.

The key Parameter:

When working with dynamic lists where items can be added, removed, or rearranged, it's crucial to provide a unique key for each item. The key helps LazyColumn identify individual items during recomposition, ensuring smooth animations and correct behavior.

```
@Composable
fun MyLazyColumn() {
    val items = listOf(
```

```
        ListItem("Apple", R.drawable.apple),
        ListItem("Banana", R.drawable.banana),
        ListItem("Cherry", R.drawable.cherry),
        ListItem("Date", R.drawable.date)
    )
    LazyColumn {
        items(items, key = { item -> item.name }) { item ->
            ListItemRow(item)
        }
    }
}

@Composable
fun ListItemRow(item: ListItem) {
    Row(modifier = Modifier.padding(8.dp)) {
        Image(
            painter = painterResource(id = item.imageRes),
            contentDescription = item.name,
            modifier = Modifier.size(48.dp)
        )
        Spacer(modifier = Modifier.width(8.dp))
        Text(text = item.name)
    }
}

data class ListItem(val name: String, val imageRes: Int)
```

Examples of LazyColumn with Different Item Types:

- **Text List:**

```
LazyColumn {
    items(100) { index -> // Display 100 items
        Text(text = "Item $index")
    }
}
```

- **Image List:**

```
val images = listOf(R.drawable.image1, R.drawable.image2, ...)

LazyColumn {
    items(images) { imageRes ->
        Image(painter = painterResource(id = imageRes),
contentDescription = null)
    }
}
```

- **Custom Item List:**

```
data class Item(val title: String, val description: String)

val items = listOf(
    Item("Title 1", "Description 1"),
    Item("Title 2", "Description 2"),
    // ...
```

```
    )

    LazyColumn {
        items(items) { item ->
            ItemCard(item) // Assuming you have an ItemCard composable
        }
    }
```

By understanding the workings of LazyColumn and its key parameters, you can efficiently display lists of any size in your Jetpack Compose applications. Remember to use the key parameter for smooth updates and explore the various customization options to tailor the appearance and behavior of your lists.

LazyRow

The LazyRow composable is the horizontal counterpart of LazyColumn. It shares the same efficiency principles, rendering only the items visible within the viewport and recycling them as the user scrolls horizontally. This makes LazyRow perfect for displaying image carousels, galleries, or any content that naturally flows horizontally.

How LazyRow Works:

Like LazyColumn, LazyRow is designed to handle large datasets efficiently. It only composes and displays the items that are currently within the horizontal viewport. When the user scrolls, items that move out of view are removed from the composition, and new items are composed as they become visible. This dynamic rendering minimizes resource usage and ensures smooth scrolling performance.

Similarity to LazyColumn:

The usage of LazyRow mirrors that of LazyColumn. You provide a list of data using the items parameter and a lambda function to define the content of each item.

```
val items = listOf("Item 1", "Item 2", "Item 3", "Item 4") // Example data

LazyRow {
    items(items) { item ->
        Text(text = item, modifier = Modifier.padding(8.dp))
    }
}
```

(The code provides a horizontal list of Text composables)

Code Examples for LazyRow:

- **Horizontal Image Gallery:**

```
val images = listOf(R.drawable.image1, R.drawable.image2, ...)

LazyRow {
    items(images) { imageRes ->
        Image(
            painter = painterResource(id = imageRes),
            contentDescription = null,
            modifier = Modifier
                .size(128.dp)
```

```
                    .padding(8.dp)
        )
    }
}
```

(This creates a horizontal list of images loaded from drawable resources. The images are displayed at 128x128 DP and padded with 8 DP.)

- **Custom Item Row:**

```
@Composable
fun MyLazyRow() {
    val items = listOf(
        ListItem("Apple", R.drawable.apple),
        ListItem("Banana", R.drawable.banana),
        ListItem("Cherry", R.drawable.cherry),
        ListItem("Date", R.drawable.date)
    )
    LazyRow {
        items(items, key = { item -> item.name }) { item ->
            ListItemRow(item)
        }
    }
}
```

```
// (ListItem and ListItemRow composables are same as were defined in the
code of LazyColumn in the previous response.)
```

(This is a horizontal list of images and texts.)

Customization Options:

Like LazyColumn, LazyRow offers various customization options:

- **Item Spacing:** Use horizontalArrangement and verticalAlignment to control the spacing and alignment of items.
- **Item Padding:** Add padding around each item using modifiers.
- **Scrolling Behavior:** Customize the scrolling behavior with modifiers like scrollable and flingBehavior.
- **Item Animations:** Apply animations to items as they enter or exit the viewport.
- **Content Padding:** Add padding around the entire list using the contentPadding modifier.

Example: Customizing Item Spacing and Alignment:

```
LazyRow(
    modifier = Modifier.fillMaxWidth(),
    horizontalArrangement = Arrangement.spacedBy(16.dp),
    verticalAlignment = Alignment.CenterVertically
) {
    // ... your items ...
}
```

By harnessing the power of LazyRow and its customization options, you can effortlessly create horizontal lists that are both visually appealing and performant, even when dealing with large amounts of data.

Advanced List Customization

Both `LazyColumn` and `LazyRow` offer a rich set of customization options beyond the basic functionality. These advanced features allow you to create visually engaging and interactive lists that cater to your specific design and usability requirements.

Item Spacing and Padding:

Controlling the spacing between list items and adding padding around them are common customization tasks. You can achieve this using modifiers and layout parameters:

```
LazyColumn(
    contentPadding = PaddingValues(horizontal = 16.dp), // Padding around the
list
    verticalArrangement = Arrangement.spacedBy(8.dp)    // Spacing between
items
) {
    items(items) { item ->
        // ... your item content ...
    }
}
```

In this example, we add 16 dp of horizontal padding around the entire list and 8 dp of spacing between each item.

Headers and Footers:

Headers and footers are special items that appear at the beginning and end of your list, respectively. You can create them using the `item` parameter:

```
LazyColumn {
    item {
        Text("Header", style = MaterialTheme.typography.h6)
    }
    items(items) { item ->
        // ... your item content ...
    }
    item {
        Text("Footer")
    }
}
```

Sticky Headers:

Sticky headers remain fixed at the top of the list as the user scrolls, providing a helpful way to group and label list items. You can achieve sticky headers using the `stickyHeader` parameter:

```
LazyColumn {
    stickyHeader { // This item will act as a sticky header
        Text("Section Title", style = MaterialTheme.typography.h6)
    }
    items(items) { item ->
        // ... your item content ...
    }
}
```

Item Animations:

Adding animations to list items can make your lists more engaging. Jetpack Compose provides various animation modifiers you can apply to items:

```
LazyColumn {
    items(items) { item ->
        AnimatedVisibility(visible = true) { // Animate item appearance
            ListItemContent(item)
        }
    }
}
```

(The code is a LazyColumn with animated visibility for each list item.)

Custom Scroll Behavior:

You can customize the scrolling behavior of lazy lists using the `flingBehavior` and `userScrollEnabled` modifiers. For example:

```
LazyColumn(
    modifier = Modifier.scrollable(
        state = rememberScrollState(),
        orientation = Orientation.Vertical
    ),
    flingBehavior = rememberSnapFlingBehavior(lazyListState =
rememberLazyListState())
) {
    // ... your items ...
}
```

(This LazyColumn has customized scrolling and fling behavior.)

Remember:

This chapter has just scratched the surface of the many customization options available for `LazyColumn` and `LazyRow`. Be sure to explore the official documentation for even more ways to tailor your lists to perfection!

LazyGrids: Compose 1.4.0+

If your Jetpack Compose project targets version 1.4.0 or higher, you gain access to two additional powerful composables for displaying lists in a grid format: `LazyVerticalGrid` and `LazyHorizontalGrid`. These composables bring the same efficiency and performance benefits of lazy lists to grid layouts, making them ideal for scenarios like image galleries, product catalogs, or dashboards.

Introducing `LazyVerticalGrid` **and** `LazyHorizontalGrid`:

- **LazyVerticalGrid:** Renders items in a vertical grid, where items flow from top to bottom, filling columns.
- **LazyHorizontalGrid:** Renders items in a horizontal grid, where items flow from left to right, filling rows.

Both of these composables share similar concepts and functionalities with LazyColumn and LazyRow, making the transition to grid layouts quite seamless.

Using LazyGrids:

To create a lazy grid, follow these steps:

1. **Import the dependency:** Ensure that the Jetpack Compose Grids dependency is included in your build.gradle file:

```
implementation("androidx.compose.foundation:foundation:1.4.0") // or higher
```

2. **Choose the Grid Type:** Decide whether you want a LazyVerticalGrid (columns) or LazyHorizontalGrid (rows).
3. **Define Columns or Rows:** Specify the number of columns (GridCells.Fixed(count)) or rows (GridCells.Fixed(count)) for your grid layout.
4. **Provide Items:** Use the items parameter to supply your list of data.
5. **Define Item Content:** Create a composable function to define the content of each grid item.

Code Examples:

LazyVerticalGrid (3 Columns):

```
val items = (1..20).toList() // Example data (numbers 1 to 20)

LazyVerticalGrid(
    columns = GridCells.Fixed(3),
    contentPadding = PaddingValues(8.dp),
    verticalArrangement = Arrangement.spacedBy(8.dp),
    horizontalArrangement = Arrangement.spacedBy(8.dp),
    modifier = Modifier.fillMaxWidth()
) {
    items(items) { item ->
        Text(
            text = "Item $item",
            modifier = Modifier
                .padding(8.dp)
                .fillMaxWidth()
        )
    }
}
```

(LazyVerticalGrid arranged in 3 columns.)

LazyHorizontalGrid (2 Rows):

```
LazyHorizontalGrid(
    rows = GridCells.Fixed(2),
    contentPadding = PaddingValues(8.dp),
    horizontalArrangement = Arrangement.spacedBy(8.dp),
    verticalArrangement = Arrangement.spacedBy(8.dp),
    modifier = Modifier.fillMaxHeight()
) {
    items(items) { item ->
        Image(
```

```
        painter = painterResource(id = item.imageResource),
        contentDescription = null,
        modifier = Modifier.size(128.dp)
    )
  }
}
```

(LazyHorizontalGrid arranged in 2 rows with images.)

Customization:

Lazy grids offer similar customization options to LazyColumn and LazyRow:

- **Item Spacing:** Use horizontalArrangement and verticalArrangement to control spacing.
- **Content Padding:** Apply padding around the entire grid using contentPadding.
- **Item Content:** Design each grid item using composables.
- **Spanning Items:** Make items occupy multiple cells using span in the items function.

By incorporating LazyVerticalGrid and LazyHorizontalGrid into your Jetpack Compose toolbox, you can effortlessly create stunning grid layouts that are optimized for performance and user experience, even when dealing with extensive datasets.

Chapter Summary

This chapter has equipped you with the knowledge and tools to efficiently display lists of data in your Jetpack Compose applications. You learned about the limitations of traditional layouts like Column and Row when dealing with large datasets, and how lazy lists like LazyColumn and LazyRow address these challenges by rendering only visible items and recycling composables.

We explored the core concepts of LazyColumn and LazyRow, focusing on the items parameter for providing data and the key parameter for maintaining item identity during updates. Through practical examples, you saw how to create vertical and horizontal lists with various item types, including text, images, and custom composables.

Furthermore, we delved into advanced list customization techniques, such as adjusting item spacing, adding headers and footers, creating sticky headers, and applying animations to list items. We also touched upon how to customize the scrolling behavior of lazy lists to create a more tailored user experience.

For those targeting Compose 1.4.0 or higher, we introduced LazyVerticalGrid and LazyHorizontalGrid, which offer a convenient way to display lists in a grid format. You learned how to configure these grids with different numbers of columns or rows and customize their appearance.

With the knowledge gained in this chapter, you're now prepared to build efficient, flexible, and visually appealing lists in your Jetpack Compose applications. As you continue your Compose journey, remember that lists are a powerful tool for presenting data to your users, and mastering their nuances will greatly enhance your ability to create engaging and informative app experiences.

Integrating with Data Sources: Room Persistence Library

Outline

- Persistence in Android
- Introduction to Room
- Setting Up Room in Your Project
- Defining Entities
- Data Access Objects (DAOs)
- The Room Database
- Integrating Room with Jetpack Compose
- Advanced Room Usage (Optional)
- Chapter Summary

Persistence in Android

In the dynamic world of mobile apps, data is king. Whether it's user preferences, cached information, or critical business data, the ability to store and retrieve data persistently is essential for providing a seamless and personalized user experience. This is where **data persistence** comes into play.

What is Data Persistence?

Data persistence refers to the mechanism by which your Android app can store data and retrieve it even after the app has been closed or the device has been restarted. It's like giving your app a memory that outlives its current session.

Why is Persistence Needed?

Persistence is essential for several reasons:

- **Preserving User Data:** Imagine a user customizing their app settings or entering data into a form. Without persistence, this information would be lost the moment they close the app, leading to frustration and a poor user experience.
- **Offline Availability:** Many apps need to function offline, even when the device doesn't have an internet connection. Persistence allows you to store data locally, making it accessible offline.
- **Caching Data:** Caching data locally can significantly improve app performance by reducing the need to fetch the same data repeatedly from remote sources.
- **Data Synchronization:** Persistence is a crucial component of data synchronization strategies, allowing you to reconcile changes between the local and remote versions of your data.

Types of Data Persistence in Android:

Android offers several options for storing data persistently:

- **SharedPreferences:** This mechanism is best suited for storing simple key-value pairs, such as user preferences, settings, or small amounts of structured data. It's easy to use but not ideal for complex data structures or large datasets.
- **Files:** You can store data in files on the device's internal storage or external storage (SD card). Files are versatile and can store various types of data, from text and images to structured data formats like JSON or XML.

- **Databases (SQLite):** SQLite is a lightweight relational database engine that's embedded in Android. It's ideal for storing structured data that requires querying, filtering, and relationships between entities. However, working directly with SQLite can involve a significant amount of boilerplate code.

Room: A Powerful Persistence Library

To simplify working with SQLite databases in Android, Google introduced the **Room Persistence Library**. Room acts as an abstraction layer over SQLite, providing a clean, object-oriented API for defining your database schema, accessing data, and performing queries.

Room offers several key benefits:

- **Reduced Boilerplate:** Room eliminates much of the repetitive code associated with raw SQLite operations.
- **Compile-Time Verification:** Room checks your SQL queries at compile time, catching errors early in the development process.
- **Easier Database Migrations:** Room simplifies the process of updating your database schema when your app evolves.

By leveraging the Room Persistence Library, you can streamline your data storage and retrieval tasks, focusing on your app's logic rather than the intricacies of SQLite. In the following sections, we'll dive deeper into Room, exploring its core components and how to integrate it seamlessly with your Jetpack Compose UIs.

Introduction to Room

Room is a powerful persistence library from Google that makes working with SQLite databases in Android a breeze. It acts as an abstraction layer over the raw SQLite API, providing a more convenient, object-oriented, and type-safe way to interact with your data.

Room as an Abstraction Layer:

Think of Room as a bridge between your Kotlin code and the underlying SQLite database. It allows you to model your data as Kotlin objects (entities), define how to access those objects (DAOs), and manage the database itself (database class). This abstraction simplifies database operations and eliminates the need to write raw SQL queries manually.

Benefits of Using Room:

Room offers numerous benefits for Android developers:

- **Reduced Boilerplate:** Room significantly reduces the amount of boilerplate code you need to write compared to using SQLite directly. It handles tasks like creating tables, mapping data to objects, and executing queries, saving you time and effort.
- **Compile-Time Verification:** One of Room's standout features is its ability to verify your SQL queries at compile time. This means that if you make a mistake in a query, Room will flag it as an error during compilation, preventing runtime crashes and bugs.
- **Easier Database Migrations:** As your app evolves, your database schema might need to change. Room simplifies the process of migrating your database to a new version, ensuring data integrity and a smooth transition for your users.
- **Improved Testability:** Room's architecture makes it easier to write unit tests for your database interactions, ensuring the reliability and correctness of your data access logic.
- **Kotlin Integration:** Room seamlessly integrates with Kotlin, leveraging its features like data classes and extension functions to provide a more intuitive and expressive API.

Core Components of Room:

Room's architecture revolves around three main components:

1. **Entities:** Entities are data classes annotated with @Entity. They represent tables in your SQLite database, and their properties correspond to the columns in those tables.
2. **Data Access Objects (DAOs):** DAOs are interfaces annotated with @Dao. They define the methods for accessing and manipulating the data in your database. These methods can be simple queries or more complex operations involving multiple tables.
3. **Database Class:** The database class is an abstract class annotated with @Database. It ties together your entities and DAOs, providing a single access point for your entire Room database. You define your database class by specifying the list of entities and the database version.

Room Architecture Overview:

Here's how these components interact:

1. Your app interacts with the database class to get instances of DAOs.
2. DAOs provide methods for querying and modifying the database.
3. Entities represent the data stored in the database tables.
4. Room handles the mapping between entities and database rows, as well as the execution of SQL queries.

In the following sections, we'll dive deeper into each of these components and explore how to use Room to create, read, update, and delete data in your Android app.

Setting Up Room in Your Project

To start using Room in your Jetpack Compose project, you need to include the Room library and enable the necessary compiler plugin. Follow these steps:

1. **Add Room Dependencies:**

   Open your project's build.gradle (Module: app) file and add the following dependencies to the dependencies block:

   ```
   // Room dependencies
   implementation("androidx.room:room-runtime:2.6.0") // Room runtime library
   annotationProcessor("androidx.room:room-compiler:2.6.0") // Room annotation
   processor
   kapt("androidx.room:room-compiler:2.6.0") // If using Kotlin Annotation
   Processing Tool
   implementation("androidx.room:room-ktx:2.6.0") // Kotlin Extensions and
   Coroutines support for Room
   ```

   - **room-runtime:** The core Room library providing the runtime implementation.
   - **room-compiler:** The Room annotation processor, responsible for generating code to simplify database access.
   - **room-ktx:** Provides Kotlin extensions and Coroutines support for Room, making it easier to work with the library in Kotlin.
   - **kapt:** This is required for Kotlin projects to enable annotation processing.

2. **Enable the Room Compiler Plugin:**

   Inside the build.gradle (Module: app) file, under the android block, locate or create the buildFeatures block and enable the buildConfig flag:

```
android {
    // ... other configurations ...
    buildFeatures {
        buildConfig = true
    }
    // ... other configurations ...
}
```

After that, under the android block, locate or create the defaultConfig block and enable the javaCompileOptions flag:

```
android {
    // ... other configurations ...
    defaultConfig {
        // ... other configurations ...

        javaCompileOptions {
            annotationProcessorOptions {
                arguments += ["room.schemaLocation":
                        "$projectDir/schemas".toString()]
            }
        }
    }
    // ... other configurations ...
}
```

3. **Sync Gradle:** Click the "Sync Project with Gradle Files" button (the elephant icon) in the toolbar to download and incorporate the dependencies into your project.

Room Library Versions:

The version numbers (2.6.0 in the example above) are subject to change as new versions of Room are released. Always refer to the official Room documentation for the latest stable versions and any compatibility considerations.

Compatibility with Compose:

Room is fully compatible with Jetpack Compose. You can seamlessly integrate Room with your composable functions to read and write data to your database, creating dynamic and data-driven UIs.

Additional Tips:

- **Kotlin Symbol Processing (KSP):** If you're using Kotlin Symbol Processing (KSP) in your project, you might need to replace the kapt configuration with the appropriate KSP configuration. Consult the Room documentation for instructions.

By following these steps, you've successfully added the Room persistence library to your project. You're now ready to start defining your database schema, creating data access objects, and building a robust data layer for your Jetpack Compose application.

Defining Entities

In the world of Room, **entities** are the heart of your data model. They represent tables in your SQLite database, and each property of an entity corresponds to a column in that table. By defining entities, you're essentially creating a blueprint for how your data will be structured and stored within the database.

Creating Entity Classes:

To create an entity, you define a Kotlin data class and annotate it with @Entity. Here's a basic example:

```
@Entity
data class User(
    @PrimaryKey(autoGenerate = true) val id: Int = 0,
    @ColumnInfo(name = "first_name") val firstName: String,
    @ColumnInfo(name = "last_name") val lastName: String,
    val age: Int
)
```

Let's break down the annotations:

- **@Entity:** This annotation marks the class as an entity, indicating that it should be represented as a table in the database.
- **@PrimaryKey:** Every entity must have a primary key, a unique identifier for each row in the table. In this case, the id property is the primary key, and it's set to auto-generate, meaning Room will automatically assign unique IDs to each user.
- **@ColumnInfo:** You can use this annotation to customize the name of a column in the database table. For example, firstName in Kotlin becomes first_name in the database.

Supported Data Types:

Room supports a wide range of data types for entity properties:

- **Primitive Types:** Int, Long, String, Double, Float, etc.
- **Boxed Types:** Integer, Long, etc. (use these for nullable columns).
- **Date and Time:** Date, Calendar, Long (for timestamps).
- **Byte Arrays:** ByteArray (for storing BLOB data like images).

Entity Examples:

Let's look at some examples of entity classes for common data models:

User:

```
@Entity
data class User(
    // ... as shown above ...
)
```

Product:

```
@Entity
data class Product(
    @PrimaryKey(autoGenerate = true) val id: Int = 0,
    val name: String,
    val price: Double,
    val category: String
)
```

Message:

```
@Entity
data class Message(
```

```
@PrimaryKey(autoGenerate = true) val id: Int = 0,
val senderId: Int,
val recipientId: Int,
val text: String,
val timestamp: Long // Store as a timestamp (milliseconds since epoch)
)
```

Additional Considerations:

- **Relationships:** You can define relationships between entities using foreign keys. Room provides convenient annotations like @Embedded and @Relation to manage relationships efficiently.
- **Indices:** For better query performance, consider adding indices to your entity columns.

By carefully designing your entity classes, you create the foundation for your Room database. Entities represent the structure of your data, and in the following sections, we'll explore how to interact with that data using DAOs (Data Access Objects).

Data Access Objects (DAOs)

Data Access Objects (DAOs) are the bridge between your Kotlin code and the underlying Room database. They are interfaces that define the methods you'll use to interact with your data. Room takes care of implementing these methods, generating efficient SQL queries behind the scenes.

Creating DAO Interfaces:

DAOs are defined as Kotlin interfaces annotated with @Dao. Within the interface, you define functions for different database operations. Each function is annotated with a specific Room annotation that indicates the type of operation to perform.

Here's a basic example of a DAO for the User entity:

```
@Dao
interface UserDao {

    @Query("SELECT * FROM user")
    fun getAllUsers(): List<User>

    @Query("SELECT * FROM user WHERE id = :id")
    fun getUserById(id: Int): User

    @Insert
    fun insertUser(user: User)

    @Update
    fun updateUser(user: User)

    @Delete
    fun deleteUser(user: User)
}
```

Let's break down the annotations:

- **@Dao:** Marks the interface as a DAO.

- **@Query:** Used to write SELECT queries. The query string is standard SQL, and you can use placeholders (: followed by a name) for parameters.
- **@Insert:** Used for inserting new entities into the database.
- **@Update:** Used for updating existing entities in the database.
- **@Delete:** Used for deleting entities from the database.

Types of Queries in Room:

Room supports a variety of SQL query types:

- **SELECT:** Used to retrieve data from the database. You can write complex queries with filters, sorting, and joins.
- **INSERT:** Used to add new rows to a table.
- **UPDATE:** Used to modify existing rows in a table.
- **DELETE:** Used to remove rows from a table.

DAO Examples for CRUD Operations:

Here are examples of DAO functions for common CRUD operations:

```
// CREATE (Insert)
@Insert
fun insertUsers(vararg users: User) // Insert multiple users

// READ (Select)
@Query("SELECT * FROM user ORDER BY age DESC")
fun getUsersByAgeDescending(): Flow<List<User>> // Return a Flow

// UPDATE
@Update
fun updateUserName(userId: Int, newName: String)

// DELETE
@Delete
fun deleteUser(user: User)

@Query("DELETE FROM user") // Delete all users
fun deleteAllUsers()
```

(The code includes a query to return data in a Flow. Flow is used to represent asynchronous data streams.)

By defining DAO interfaces, you establish a clear contract for how your app will interact with the database. Room takes care of generating the SQL queries and providing efficient implementations for these methods.

The Room Database

The Room database class is the central hub for accessing and managing your Room database. It acts as the main entry point for obtaining Data Access Objects (DAOs) and provides configuration options for your database.

Creating the Database Class:

1. **Abstract Class:** Define an abstract class that extends RoomDatabase. This class will be annotated with @Database and serve as your database's representation in code.
2. **@Database Annotation:** Annotate the class with @Database, providing the following parameters:
   - **entities:** An array listing all the entity classes that are part of your database schema.
   - **version:** An integer representing the current version of your database schema. You'll need to increment this version whenever you make changes to the schema (e.g., adding a new table or column).
   - **exportSchema:** (Optional) A boolean indicating whether to export the schema to a file. This is useful for debugging and version control purposes.
3. **Abstract DAO Properties:** Include abstract properties for each of your DAO interfaces. Room will automatically generate implementations for these properties.

```
@Database(
    entities = [User::class, Product::class], // List your entities here
    version = 1,
    exportSchema = false
)
abstract class AppDatabase : RoomDatabase() {
    abstract val userDao: UserDao
    abstract val productDao: ProductDao
}
```

Obtaining a Database Instance:

To interact with your Room database, you need to obtain an instance of your database class. Room provides the Room.databaseBuilder method for this purpose.

```
val db = Room.databaseBuilder(
    applicationContext,
    AppDatabase::class.java,
    "app_database"
).build()

val userDao = db.userDao()
val productDao = db.productDao()
```

(The code initializes the AppDatabase and gets references for userDao and productDao.)

Here's a breakdown of the databaseBuilder parameters:

- **context:** The application context.
- **klass:** The Java class of your database (e.g., AppDatabase::class.java).
- **name:** The name of your database file (e.g., "app_database").

The build() method creates and opens the database if it doesn't exist. You can then use the generated properties (e.g., userDao, productDao) to obtain instances of your DAOs and perform database operations.

Singleton Pattern (Recommended):

It's generally recommended to use the Singleton pattern to ensure that you have only one instance of the database class in your application. This helps avoid conflicts and resource wastage. Here's an example:

```
object DatabaseProvider {
```

```
    val db: AppDatabase by lazy {
        Room.databaseBuilder(
            // ... same as above ...
        ).build()
    }
}
```

(The code provides a singleton object called `DatabaseProvider` to hold the database instance. It lazily creates the database instance the first time it's accessed.)

By understanding the role of the Room database class and how to create and access it, you establish a solid foundation for interacting with your database in a structured and efficient manner. The next section will cover the integration of Room into your Jetpack Compose project, enabling you to create dynamic, data-driven user interfaces.

Integrating Room with Jetpack Compose

Integrating Room with Jetpack Compose enables you to build dynamic UIs that seamlessly react to changes in your database. The key to this integration lies in using Kotlin Flows, which provide a reactive way to observe database updates and trigger UI refreshes in your composable functions.

Flows for Observing Database Changes:

Room's query methods can return `Flow` objects, which are asynchronous streams of data. When the data in the database changes, the `Flow` emits new values, allowing your composable functions to react to these changes and update the UI accordingly.

Example: Observing a List of Users:

In your DAO interface:

```
@Query("SELECT * FROM user")
fun getAllUsers(): Flow<List<User>> // Return a Flow
```

(This DAO function returns a Flow that emits a list of users.)

In your composable function:

```
@Composable
fun UserListScreen(userDao: UserDao) {
    val users by userDao.getAllUsers().collectAsState(initial = emptyList())
// Use collectAsState

    LazyColumn {
        items(users) { user ->
            UserItem(user)
        }
    }
}
```

(The composable function `UserListScreen` displays the list of users in a `LazyColumn`.)

`collectAsState`: Bringing Flows to Composables:

The collectAsState function is your bridge between Flows and Jetpack Compose. It collects values from a Flow and represents them as a State object, which Compose can observe to trigger recomposition when the data changes.

In the example above:

1. userDao.getAllUsers() returns a Flow<List<User>>.
2. collectAsState(initial = emptyList()) collects values from the Flow, starting with an initial empty list.
3. The users variable is a State object that holds the latest list of users from the database.
4. Whenever the database is updated, the Flow emits a new list, collectAsState updates the users state, and Compose recomposes the UserListScreen composable to display the updated list.

Complete Example: Fetching and Displaying Users:

```
@Composable
fun UserListScreen(db: AppDatabase) { // Assuming you have a reference to your
database
    val userDao = db.userDao()
    val users by userDao.getAllUsers().collectAsState(initial = emptyList())

    LazyColumn {
        items(users) { user ->
            UserItem(user) // A composable to display a single user item
        }
    }
}


@Composable
fun UserItem(user: User) {
    Row(modifier = Modifier.padding(8.dp)) {
        Text(text = user.firstName)
        Spacer(modifier = Modifier.width(8.dp))
        Text(text = user.lastName)
    }
}
```

(The function UserListScreen takes the database, AppDatabase, as a parameter, retrieves the DAO, and collects the Flow of all users from the database into the users state variable. It then displays the list of users in a LazyColumn. The UserItem composable is called for each user to display their details in the list.)

By leveraging Flows and collectAsState, you can easily build reactive Jetpack Compose UIs that stay in sync with your Room database, providing a smooth and engaging user experience.

Advanced Room Usage

Beyond the basics, Room offers a wealth of advanced features to handle complex database scenarios and optimize performance. In this optional section, we'll touch on some of these features and provide tips for integrating Room effectively with your Jetpack Compose projects.

Database Migrations:

As your app evolves, your database schema might need to change. Room simplifies this process with migrations. You can create migration classes that define how to transform the database from one version to another, ensuring data integrity during the upgrade process.

```
val MIGRATION_1_2 = object : Migration(1, 2) {
    override fun migrate(database: SupportSQLiteDatabase) {
        database.execSQL("ALTER TABLE user ADD COLUMN email TEXT")
    }
}


// In your Room.databaseBuilder:
.addMigrations(MIGRATION_1_2) // Add migrations
.build()
```

Complex Queries:

Room supports complex SQL queries, including JOINs and subqueries. You can write these queries directly in your DAO functions using the @Query annotation.

```
@Query("SELECT * FROM user JOIN orders ON user.id = orders.user_id")
fun getUsersWithOrders(): Flow<List<UserWithOrders>> // Use @Relation to
create a custom object
```

@Transaction:

The @Transaction annotation ensures that a block of database operations is executed atomically. This is crucial when you need to perform multiple operations that should either all succeed or all fail together.

```
@Transaction
fun updateUserAndOrders(user: User, orders: List<Order>) {
    userDao.updateUser(user)
    orderDao.updateOrders(orders)
}
```

Tips and Best Practices:

- **Use the Right Data Type:** Choose appropriate data types for your entity properties. For example, use INTEGER for IDs, TEXT for strings, and REAL for floating-point numbers.
- **Indexes:** Add indexes to columns frequently used in queries to improve performance.
- **Background Threads:** Perform database operations on background threads to avoid blocking the UI. Room provides suspend functions and coroutine support for this purpose.
- **Data Validation:** Validate input data before inserting or updating it in the database to prevent data corruption.
- **Testing:** Write unit tests for your DAO functions to ensure the correctness of your database logic.
- **Observing Data Changes:** Utilize Flows and collectAsState to seamlessly integrate Room with Jetpack Compose UIs.
- **Dependency Injection:** Consider using dependency injection (e.g., Hilt) to manage database instances and DAOs in your Compose project.

By mastering these advanced Room techniques, you can unlock its full potential and build robust and efficient data layers for your Android applications.

Important Note: Remember, these are advanced concepts and might not be necessary for simpler use cases. Focus on mastering the fundamentals first and gradually incorporate these advanced features as needed.

Chapter Summary

This chapter delved into integrating the Room Persistence Library with your Jetpack Compose projects. We started by highlighting the importance of data persistence in Android apps and discussing various storage options, with a particular focus on Room as a powerful and efficient way to work with SQLite databases.

You learned how Room simplifies database interactions by acting as an abstraction layer over SQLite, reducing boilerplate code and providing compile-time query verification. We explored the core components of Room: entities, DAOs, and the database class, understanding their roles in the overall architecture.

The chapter provided a step-by-step guide on setting up Room in your project, including adding the necessary dependencies and enabling the Room compiler plugin. We then delved into defining entities to represent your data models and creating DAOs to interact with the database. You learned how to write various types of SQL queries using Room annotations and how to obtain a database instance to access your DAOs.

Furthermore, we explored the seamless integration of Room with Jetpack Compose by utilizing Kotlin Flows and the `collectAsState` function. You learned how to observe changes in the database and automatically update your composable UIs, ensuring your app remains in sync with the underlying data.

For those seeking to expand their Room expertise, we touched on advanced topics like database migrations, complex queries, and the use of `@Transaction` for atomic operations. We also shared some valuable tips and best practices for effectively working with Room in Jetpack Compose projects.

Armed with this knowledge, you are now ready to build robust, data-driven Android applications that can store and retrieve data efficiently using Room. In the next chapter, we will shift our focus to architectural patterns and explore how to structure your Jetpack Compose projects for maintainability and scalability.

Section E:
Architectural Patterns with Jetpack Compose

MVVM (Model-View-ViewModel) Architecture with Jetpack Compose

Outline

- Understanding Software Architecture
- Introduction to MVVM (Model-View-ViewModel)
- The Model
- The View
- The ViewModel
- Implementing MVVM with Jetpack Compose
- Best Practices and Considerations
- Chapter Summary

Understanding Software Architecture

Software architecture is the fundamental structure of a software system, defining its components, their relationships, and how they interact with each other. It's like the blueprint of a building, providing a roadmap for how the different parts fit together to create a cohesive whole.

Importance of Software Architecture:

In the context of app development, a well-designed architecture is crucial for several reasons:

- **Maintainability:** A well-structured architecture makes your codebase easier to understand, modify, and maintain over time. This is particularly important for large and complex applications that involve multiple developers.
- **Scalability:** A good architecture allows your app to grow and evolve gracefully. You can add new features, change existing ones, or scale your app to handle more users without major refactoring.
- **Testability:** An architecture with clear separation of concerns makes it easier to write unit and integration tests for your app, ensuring its quality and reliability.
- **Code Reusability:** A well-organized architecture promotes code reuse, saving you time and effort in the long run.
- **Collaboration:** A clearly defined architecture facilitates communication and collaboration among team members, making it easier to work together on a project.

Separation of Concerns:

One of the core principles of software architecture is **separation of concerns (SoC)**. This principle suggests that a software system should be divided into distinct sections, each addressing a separate concern. In the context of app development, common concerns include:

- **Presentation Logic:** How the UI is displayed and how user interactions are handled.
- **Business Logic:** The core rules and operations of your app, independent of the UI.
- **Data Access:** How the app interacts with data sources, such as databases or network APIs.

By separating these concerns into different layers or modules, you make your codebase more modular, easier to understand, and less prone to errors. Changes to one concern are less likely to affect others, making development and maintenance more predictable.

Common Android Architectural Patterns:

Android development has seen the evolution of several architectural patterns, each with its own strengths and weaknesses:

- **MVC (Model-View-Controller):** MVC is a classic pattern where the Model represents data, the View displays the UI, and the Controller handles user input and updates the Model and View.
- **MVP (Model-View-Presenter):** MVP is similar to MVC, but the Presenter has a more active role in mediating between the View and the Model.
- **MVVM (Model-View-ViewModel):** MVVM introduces the ViewModel, which holds UI state and exposes data and actions to the View. The View observes the ViewModel for changes and updates the UI accordingly.

Jetpack Compose, with its declarative UI paradigm, is well-suited for the MVVM architecture. In this book, we'll focus primarily on MVVM as our recommended architectural pattern for building Jetpack Compose applications.

By understanding the importance of software architecture and embracing principles like separation of concerns, you can lay a solid foundation for your Jetpack Compose projects. A well-designed architecture will make your codebase more maintainable, scalable, and enjoyable to work with.

Introduction to MVVM (Model-View-ViewModel)

Model-View-ViewModel (MVVM) is a popular architectural pattern that has gained widespread adoption in Android development, especially with the rise of Jetpack Compose. MVVM provides a structured approach to organizing your code, promoting separation of concerns, and making your app more maintainable, testable, and scalable.

Core Components of MVVM:

MVVM consists of three key components:

1. **Model:** The Model represents the data and business logic of your application. It's responsible for fetching data from various sources (e.g., network, database, local storage), encapsulating data objects, and performing business operations. The Model is typically unaware of the UI and interacts with the ViewModel to provide data and receive updates.
2. **View:** The View is the visual representation of your app's UI. In Jetpack Compose, the View is built using composable functions. The View's primary responsibility is to display data provided by the ViewModel and handle user interactions (e.g., button clicks, text input). The View doesn't contain complex logic; it primarily focuses on rendering UI elements and delegating events to the ViewModel.
3. **ViewModel:** The ViewModel acts as the intermediary between the View and the Model. It holds the UI state, prepares data for presentation, and exposes this data to the View using observable data structures (e.g., `LiveData` or `StateFlow`). The ViewModel also handles user interactions by executing actions requested by the View, such as fetching data from the Model or triggering updates.

Benefits of Using MVVM:

MVVM offers several compelling advantages:

- **Improved Testability:** MVVM's clear separation of concerns makes it easier to write unit tests for each component independently. You can test your ViewModel's logic without involving the UI, and vice-versa.
- **Code Reusability:** ViewModels can be reused by multiple Views, reducing code duplication. For example, you can have different screens in your app that display the same data, each using the same ViewModel.
- **Separation of Concerns:** MVVM enforces a clean separation between UI logic (in the View) and business logic (in the Model). This makes your codebase more organized, maintainable, and easier to reason about.
- **Lifecycle Awareness:** ViewModels are lifecycle-aware, meaning they can survive configuration changes (e.g., screen rotation) and automatically handle data persistence.
- **Data Binding (Optional):** While not strictly part of MVVM, data binding libraries (like the View Binding library in Android) can be used in conjunction with MVVM to further streamline the process of binding data from the ViewModel to the View.

MVVM in Jetpack Compose:

Jetpack Compose's declarative nature aligns well with the MVVM architecture. Composables naturally represent the View, and the use of observable data structures like `LiveData` or `StateFlow` allows for seamless communication between the ViewModel and the View.

By adopting MVVM in your Jetpack Compose projects, you can create a solid architectural foundation that promotes code quality, testability, and maintainability, leading to more robust and scalable Android applications.

The Model

In the MVVM architecture, the **Model** layer is the backbone of your application's data and business logic. It's responsible for handling data operations, encapsulating the core functionality of your app, and interacting with external data sources.

What the Model Encompasses:

- **Data Representation:** The Model defines data structures (classes, data classes) that represent the entities or objects within your app's domain. For instance, you might have a `User` class to represent user data or a `Product` class to model products in an e-commerce app.
- **Business Logic:** The Model encapsulates the business rules and operations of your app. This could include calculations, data validation, transformations, or any other logic that determines how your app functions.
- **Data Access:** The Model is responsible for interacting with data sources to fetch, store, or modify data. This could involve communicating with a Room database, making network requests to a REST API using Retrofit, or accessing local files.

Model's Interaction with Data Sources:

The Model acts as the gateway between your app's logic and the outside world. It handles the following interactions:

- **Fetching Data:** The Model fetches data from external sources, such as a database or a network API. It parses the raw data and converts it into the appropriate data structures defined in your Model.
- **Storing Data:** The Model saves data to persistent storage, such as a database or local files. It ensures that the data is stored correctly and can be retrieved later.
- **Updating Data:** The Model modifies existing data in the data sources based on user actions or internal logic.
- **Deleting Data:** The Model removes data from the data sources when it's no longer needed.

Example Model Classes:

Let's illustrate with a few examples of Model classes:

```kotlin
// User Data Class
data class User(
    val id: Int,
    val name: String,
    val email: String
)


// Repository (Interacts with data sources)
class UserRepository(private val userDao: UserDao, private val apiService:
ApiService) {
    suspend fun getUserById(id: Int): User {
        // Fetch from database first
        val user = userDao.getUserById(id)
        if (user != null) {
            return user
        }

        // If not in the database, fetch from network
        val response = apiService.getUserById(id)
        if (response.isSuccessful) {
            val networkUser = response.body()
            userDao.insertUser(networkUser)  // Save to database
            return networkUser
        } else {
            throw Exception("Failed to fetch user")
        }
    }
}
```

(The code includes data class User to represent user data and class UserRepository to encapsulate data access logic for users. UserRepository class interacts with the data source to fetch a user either from the database first and then network, if not found in database.)

Key Points:

- The Model is the foundation of your app's data and logic.
- It defines data structures, encapsulates business logic, and handles interactions with data sources.
- By separating the Model from the View, you achieve better code organization, maintainability, and testability.

In the next sections, we'll see how the ViewModel utilizes the Model to fetch and process data before presenting it to the View, completing the MVVM architecture's elegant separation of concerns.

The View

In the MVVM architecture, the **View** layer is the visual face of your Jetpack Compose application. It's responsible for displaying the user interface, rendering data obtained from the ViewModel, and handling user interactions.

What the View Does:

- **Renders UI Elements:** The View layer is where you define the visual structure and layout of your screens. You use composable functions to build UI elements such as text, images, buttons, lists, and more.
- **Displays Data:** The View receives data from the ViewModel and displays it to the user. This data might be the current state of the UI, information fetched from the Model, or feedback messages.
- **Handles User Interactions:** The View captures user actions, such as button clicks, text input, or gestures. It then communicates these interactions to the ViewModel for further processing.

Observing ViewModel Changes:

Jetpack Compose's declarative nature makes it ideal for observing changes in the ViewModel and updating the UI accordingly. You can use state variables in your composables to hold data from the ViewModel. When the ViewModel's data changes, the state variables are updated, triggering recomposition and refreshing the UI.

In the context of MVVM, the View observes the ViewModel for changes to its state. When the state changes, the View is automatically updated to reflect those changes. This ensures that the UI always stays in sync with the underlying data and logic, creating a seamless and responsive user experience.

Composables in Jetpack Compose:

In Jetpack Compose, the View layer is constructed entirely using composable functions. These functions are annotated with @Composable, and they define the structure, layout, and content of your UI. Composables are the building blocks of your View, allowing you to create complex and interactive UIs by combining and nesting them.

Example: View Implementation

```
@Composable
fun UserListScreen(viewModel: UserListViewModel = viewModel()) { // Assuming
viewModel is used here
    val uiState by viewModel.uiState.collectAsState()

    LazyColumn {
        items(uiState.users) { user ->
            UserItem(user)
        }
    }
}


@Composable
fun UserItem(user: User) {
    // ... composable to display a user item ...
}
```

(The UserListScreen composable observes the uiState in UserListViewModel, and updates the UI whenever it changes.)

In this example, the `UserListScreen` composable observes the `uiState` property of the `UserListViewModel`. The `uiState` likely contains a list of users. When the `uiState` changes (e.g., when the ViewModel fetches new user data), the `LazyColumn` recomposes to display the updated list.

Key Points:

- The View in MVVM is responsible for displaying the UI and handling user interactions.
- The View observes changes in the ViewModel and updates the UI accordingly.
- Jetpack Compose uses composable functions to build the View layer, making it a natural fit for the MVVM architecture.

By understanding the role of the View and how it interacts with the ViewModel, you can effectively design and implement the visual aspect of your Jetpack Compose applications.

The ViewModel

The ViewModel is a crucial component in the MVVM architecture, serving as the communication and coordination center between the View and the Model. It encapsulates the UI logic, manages the UI state, and interacts with the Model to fetch or update data.

ViewModel's Role:

- **UI State Management:** The ViewModel holds the data that drives the UI's appearance and behavior. This data is often represented as state variables within the ViewModel. For instance, the ViewModel might hold a list of items to display in a list, the text entered in a search bar, or a boolean flag indicating whether a loading spinner should be visible.
- **Exposing Data to the View:** The ViewModel makes the UI state observable to the View. In Jetpack Compose, this is typically done using `LiveData` or `StateFlow`. The View can then observe these observable data structures and react to changes, triggering recomposition and UI updates as needed.
- **Handling UI Logic:** The ViewModel contains the logic that drives UI interactions. When the View triggers an event (like a button click), it delegates the handling of that event to the ViewModel. The ViewModel might perform calculations, update the UI state, or interact with the Model to fetch or modify data.
- **Interacting with the Model:** The ViewModel communicates with the Model layer to request data or trigger actions. It might fetch data from a database, make network requests, or perform other operations that involve the Model's business logic.

LiveData and StateFlow: Observable Data Structures:

- **LiveData:** `LiveData` is a lifecycle-aware observable data holder class. It respects the lifecycle of Android components, ensuring that UI updates are only delivered when the View is in an active state. LiveData is well-suited for scenarios where you need to observe data changes from lifecycle-aware components like Activities or Fragments.
- **StateFlow:** `StateFlow` is a type of flow in Kotlin coroutines that represents a read-only state with a single updatable data value. It's suitable for scenarios where you need to observe data changes from any context, including composables.

Example: ViewModel Implementation:

```
class UserListViewModel(private val userRepository: UserRepository) :
ViewModel() {
```

```
    private val _uiState = MutableStateFlow(UserListUiState(isLoading = true))
// Private mutable state flow
    val uiState: StateFlow<UserListUiState> = _uiState.asStateFlow() // Public
read-only state flow

    init {
        viewModelScope.launch { // Launch a coroutine in the ViewModel's scope
            try {
                val users = userRepository.getAllUsers()
                _uiState.value = UserListUiState(isLoading = false, users =
users)
            } catch (e: Exception) {
                _uiState.value = UserListUiState(isLoading = false, error =
e.message)
            }
        }
    }
}

// UI state class
data class UserListUiState(
    val isLoading: Boolean = false,
    val users: List<User> = emptyList(),
    val error: String? = null
)
```

(The code includes the `UserListViewModel` class, which encapsulates the UI state for a user list screen. It also fetches the user data from a repository and exposes the UI state using a `StateFlow`.)

Key Points:

- The ViewModel bridges the View and Model, managing the UI state and logic.
- LiveData or StateFlow are used to make the UI state observable to the View.
- The ViewModel handles UI interactions and communicates with the Model to fetch or update data.

By incorporating the ViewModel into your Jetpack Compose projects, you can achieve a cleaner separation of concerns, making your code more maintainable, testable, and robust.

Implementing MVVM with Jetpack Compose

Let's walk through a practical implementation of the MVVM architecture in a Jetpack Compose project, showcasing how the different components work together to create a well-structured application.

Step 1: Create a ViewModel Class

```
class MainViewModel : ViewModel() {
    private val _counter = MutableStateFlow(0)
    val counter: StateFlow<Int> = _counter.asStateFlow()

    fun incrementCounter() {
        _counter.value++
    }
}
```

(The code initializes the `MainViewModel` class, which encapsulates the logic for managing the counter state. It also defines the function to increment the count.)

This basic ViewModel has a private `MutableStateFlow` variable to hold the counter value. A public, read-only `StateFlow` exposes this value to the UI. The `incrementCounter` function is used to update the counter.

Step 2: Use `viewModel()` in a Composable

```
@Composable
fun MainScreen() {
    val viewModel: MainViewModel = viewModel()
    val count by viewModel.counter.collectAsState()

    Column {
        Text(text = "Count: $count")
        Button(onClick = { viewModel.incrementCounter() }) {
            Text("Increment")
        }
    }
}
```

(The code initializes the `MainScreen` composable and gets a `MainViewModel` instance using `viewModel()`. It also observes the `counter` state flow in the `viewModel` using `collectAsState()`. It then displays the current `count` and provides a button to increment it.)

The `viewModel()` function, imported from `androidx.lifecycle:lifecycle-viewmodel-compose`, retrieves a ViewModel instance. The `collectAsState()` function is used to collect the `counter` StateFlow and convert it into a `State` object that Compose can observe.

Step 3: Expose Data with StateFlow or LiveData

In the ViewModel, expose data using `StateFlow` (for coroutines) or `LiveData` (for compatibility with older components):

```
private val _myData = MutableStateFlow(initialData) // Private mutable
StateFlow
val myData: StateFlow<MyData> = _myData.asStateFlow() // Public immutable
StateFlow
```

Step 4: Use LaunchedEffect to Trigger Actions

Use the LaunchedEffect composable to perform actions in the ViewModel when certain events occur in the UI (e.g., when the screen is first composed):

```
@Composable
fun MainScreen(viewModel: MainViewModel = viewModel()) {
    // ...

    LaunchedEffect(Unit) { // Trigger when the composable enters the
composition
        viewModel.loadData() // Call a function in the ViewModel
    }
```

```
    // ...
}
```

Complete Example (with Repository):

```
// View Model
class MainViewModel(private val repository: MyRepository) : ViewModel() {
    // ... (same as above)
}

// Repository (interacts with your data source)
class MyRepository {
    suspend fun fetchData(): MyData {
        // ... logic to fetch data ...
    }
}

// View
@Composable
fun MainScreen(viewModel: MainViewModel = viewModel(factory =
MyViewModelFactory(MyRepository()))) {
    // ... (same as above)
}
```

(This is a complete example of MVVM with a repository class to interact with the data source.)

In this example, MyRepository (the Model) fetches the data. The ViewModel uses LaunchedEffect to call fetchData() when the screen is composed.

Key Points:

- **ViewModel:** Creates a bridge between your UI and data.
- **viewModel():** Retrieves or creates the ViewModel instance.
- **StateFlow/LiveData:** Makes data observable to the UI.
- **collectAsState():** Collects the data from StateFlow in a composable.
- **LaunchedEffect:** Performs actions in the ViewModel based on UI events.

With these steps, you can effectively implement the MVVM architecture in your Jetpack Compose projects, promoting a clean separation of concerns and making your code more maintainable and testable.

Best Practices and Considerations

Implementing MVVM effectively in Jetpack Compose requires adherence to best practices and careful consideration of various factors. This section aims to provide guidance and insights to ensure a successful and maintainable MVVM architecture in your Compose projects.

Best Practices:

1. **Single Source of Truth:** Maintain a single source of truth for your UI state within the ViewModel. Avoid duplicating state variables or logic in different parts of your code. This ensures consistency and simplifies debugging.
2. **Unidirectional Data Flow:** Strictly adhere to the unidirectional data flow principle. Data should flow down from the ViewModel to the View, and events should flow up from the View to the ViewModel. Avoid bidirectional data binding or direct manipulation of the ViewModel's state from the View.

3. **Immutability:** Embrace immutability whenever possible. Design your state objects as immutable data classes to prevent unintended side effects and simplify state management.
4. **Scoped State:** Use the `remember` function to create state variables within the appropriate scope. Avoid creating state variables at the top level of your composable functions if they are only needed within a specific part of the UI.
5. **ViewModel Communication:** For communication between ViewModels, consider using shared `StateFlow` or `SharedFlow` objects or leverage the `SavedStateHandle` to persist state across configuration changes.
6. **Dependency Injection:** Utilize dependency injection (e.g., Hilt) to manage dependencies like repositories or data sources within your ViewModels. This promotes testability and maintainability.

Handling Complex UI Interactions:

- **Decompose UIs:** Break down complex screens into smaller, reusable composables. This makes your code more manageable and improves testability.
- **State Hoisting:** Lift state to a higher level in the composable hierarchy when it needs to be shared among multiple composables.
- **Event-Driven Architecture:** Use events to communicate actions and data changes between composables.
- **Custom Composables:** Create custom composables for complex UI elements to encapsulate their logic and state.

Navigation and State Management:

- **Navigation Component:** Utilize the Jetpack Compose Navigation component for managing navigation between screens.
- **SavedStateHandle:** Use `SavedStateHandle` within your ViewModels to persist UI state across configuration changes (e.g., screen rotation).

Testing Your ViewModel:

- **Unit Tests:** Write comprehensive unit tests for your ViewModel logic. Use mocking frameworks (like Mockito) to simulate interactions with the Model layer.
- **State Verification:** Verify that the ViewModel's state changes as expected in response to events and interactions.
- **Error Handling:** Test how your ViewModel handles errors that might occur during data fetching or other operations.

Additional Tips:

- **Kotlin Coroutines:** Leverage Kotlin coroutines for asynchronous operations within your ViewModels.
- **State Restoration:** If needed, implement state restoration to preserve the UI state even after the app process is killed by the system.
- **Performance Optimization:** Be mindful of recomposition and avoid unnecessary re-renders by using the appropriate state management techniques and optimizing your composable functions.

By adhering to these best practices and carefully considering the nuances of MVVM architecture in Jetpack Compose, you'll be well on your way to building robust, scalable, and maintainable Android applications.

Chapter Summary

This chapter has illuminated the Model-View-ViewModel (MVVM) architecture as a powerful approach for structuring your Jetpack Compose applications. You learned about the roles of the Model, View, and ViewModel components and how they interact to create a clear separation of concerns. This separation improves code maintainability, testability, and scalability.

We explored the concept of state management within the ViewModel, highlighting the use of `LiveData` and `StateFlow` as observable data holders to communicate state changes to the View. You also learned how to leverage `LaunchedEffect` to trigger actions in the ViewModel from the View.

Through a step-by-step guide, you were shown how to create a ViewModel class, obtain an instance of it within a composable, and expose data using observable data structures. The integration of ViewModel with a repository, representing the Model layer, was also demonstrated, showcasing the complete MVVM flow.

Finally, we discussed best practices for designing and implementing MVVM in Jetpack Compose projects. We covered considerations for handling complex UI interactions, navigation, state management, and testing ViewModels. By following these guidelines, you'll be well-equipped to build robust and maintainable Compose applications.

The next chapter will introduce you to another crucial aspect of modern Android development: dependency injection. You'll discover how to use Hilt, a popular dependency injection library, to streamline dependency management in your Jetpack Compose projects.

Dependency Injection with Hilt in Jetpack Compose

Outline

- Understanding Dependency Injection
- Why Use Dependency Injection?
- Introduction to Hilt
- Setting Up Hilt in Your Project
- Injecting Dependencies into ViewModels
- Injecting Dependencies into Composables
- Testing with Hilt
- Best Practices and Considerations
- Chapter Summary

Understanding Dependency Injection

Dependency Injection (DI) is a software design pattern that promotes loose coupling between classes and their dependencies. Instead of a class creating its own dependencies internally, those dependencies are "injected" into the class from the outside. This approach offers significant benefits in terms of code organization, testability, and flexibility.

What is Dependency Injection?

In essence, dependency injection is the process of providing a class with its required dependencies rather than having the class create them itself. For example, if a class needs to access a database, instead of creating a database connection directly, it would receive the connection as a parameter or through a property.

Types of Dependency Injection:

There are three common types of dependency injection:

1. **Constructor Injection:** Dependencies are passed to a class through its constructor. This is the most common and recommended type of DI, as it ensures that the class has all its required dependencies before it can be used.
2. **Field Injection (Property Injection):** Dependencies are assigned to fields (properties) of a class after the class has been instantiated. This can be useful in some scenarios, but it can make testing more difficult.
3. **Method Injection (Setter Injection):** Dependencies are provided to a class through setter methods. This is less common than constructor injection and can be less desirable due to potential issues with object state.

Benefits of Using Dependency Injection:

- **Improved Testability:** DI makes it easier to write unit tests because you can replace real dependencies with mock objects during testing.
- **Increased Flexibility:** By decoupling classes from their dependencies, DI allows you to easily switch between different implementations of those dependencies without changing the dependent class. This is useful for swapping out components, like using a fake database for testing or supporting different data sources.

- **Better Maintainability:** DI makes your code more modular and easier to understand. Each class is responsible for its own functionality, and dependencies are explicitly defined, leading to clearer code structure.

Dependency Inversion Principle and DI:

Dependency injection is closely related to the Dependency Inversion Principle (DIP), a core principle of SOLID object-oriented design. DIP states that high-level modules should not depend on low-level modules; both should depend on abstractions. DI helps implement DIP by ensuring that classes depend on abstractions (interfaces or abstract classes) rather than concrete implementations of their dependencies.

Example:

```
interface Repository {
    fun getData(): Data
}

class UserRepository : Repository {
    override fun getData(): Data {
        // ... (fetch data from a database)
    }
}

class MyViewModel(private val repository: Repository) : ViewModel() {
    // ... (use the repository to fetch data)
}
```

(The code is a demonstration of Dependency Injection where MyViewModel class takes the Repository dependency as a parameter instead of creating the dependency inside the class.)

In this example, the MyViewModel class depends on the Repository interface, not the concrete UserRepository class. This allows you to easily replace the UserRepository with a different implementation (e.g., a mock repository for testing) without modifying the MyViewModel.

By embracing dependency injection, you empower your code with increased flexibility, testability, and maintainability, paving the way for a more robust and adaptable Jetpack Compose application.

Why Use Dependency Injection?

Dependency injection (DI) may seem like an extra layer of complexity at first, but its benefits far outweigh the initial learning curve. Let's explore some common issues that arise in code without DI and how DI can help you create more robust, maintainable, and testable applications.

Common Problems Without DI:

1. **Tight Coupling:** When classes create their dependencies directly, they become tightly coupled. This means that changes to one class can ripple through the codebase, making modifications and refactoring difficult. Imagine a scenario where a UserInterface class directly creates an instance of a Database class. If you decide to change the type of database you're using, you'll need to modify the UserInterface class, which could lead to unforeseen errors in other parts of your code that depend on it.

2. **Hidden Dependencies:** Dependencies created within a class are often hidden from view. This can make it challenging to understand the full set of dependencies a class relies on, hindering debugging and testing efforts.
3. **Hard to Test:** Tight coupling makes it difficult to isolate classes for testing. You might need to create a complex test environment to simulate all the dependencies a class requires. This can slow down your testing process and make it more prone to errors.

How DI Solves These Problems:

- **Loose Coupling:** With DI, classes receive their dependencies from external sources. This breaks the tight coupling between classes, making them more independent and easier to change.
- **Explicit Dependencies:** Dependencies are declared explicitly in constructors, fields, or methods, making it clear what each class requires to function. This transparency improves code readability and understanding.
- **Easier Testing:** DI allows you to inject mock objects during testing, replacing real dependencies with controlled substitutes. This isolates the class being tested, making it easier to focus on its specific behavior without worrying about the complexities of its dependencies.

Advantages of Using a DI Framework (Hilt):

While you can implement DI manually, using a DI framework like Hilt brings several additional advantages:

- **Simplified Setup:** Hilt automates many of the tedious tasks associated with DI, such as creating components, managing scopes, and generating boilerplate code. This saves you time and reduces the risk of errors.
- **Integration with Jetpack Libraries:** Hilt is designed to seamlessly integrate with other Jetpack libraries like ViewModel, Navigation, and WorkManager, making it easier to adopt DI throughout your app.
- **Compile-Time Safety:** Hilt performs dependency checks at compile time, catching potential issues early and preventing runtime crashes.
- **Reduced Boilerplate:** Hilt's annotations and code generation capabilities eliminate the need to write a lot of repetitive boilerplate code, making your code cleaner and more focused on your app's core logic.

Example: Comparing Manual DI vs. Hilt

Manual DI:

```
class MyViewModel(val repository: MyRepository) { /* ... */ }

// In an Activity or Compose function
val repository = MyRepository() // Create the dependency
val viewModel = MyViewModel(repository)
```

Hilt DI:

```
@HiltViewModel
class MyViewModel @Inject constructor(val repository: MyRepository) { /* ... */ }

// In a Compose function
val viewModel: MyViewModel = viewModel() // Hilt automatically injects the
dependency
```

(Notice Hilt's annotations, e.g. @HiltViewModel and @Inject for constructor injection)

As you can see, Hilt significantly reduces the code required to obtain a ViewModel instance, making it cleaner and easier to work with.

By adopting dependency injection, and particularly leveraging the power of Hilt, you can create a more modular, testable, and flexible architecture for your Jetpack Compose applications. DI is an essential tool in the modern Android developer's arsenal, and it's well worth the investment to learn and apply it in your projects.

Introduction to Hilt

Hilt is Google's recommended dependency injection (DI) library for Android development, specifically designed to simplify and streamline the DI process in your projects. Built on top of the powerful Dagger library, Hilt brings many of Dagger's advantages while eliminating much of its complexity and boilerplate.

Hilt: A Simplified Dagger Experience:

Dagger is a widely used DI framework known for its performance and flexibility. However, setting up and using Dagger can be quite challenging, especially for larger projects. Hilt addresses this by providing a simplified and opinionated way to use Dagger, making it more accessible and easier to integrate into your Android applications.

Benefits of Using Hilt:

- **Simplified Setup:** Hilt significantly reduces the amount of boilerplate code and configuration required compared to manual DI or Dagger. It provides annotations and code generation capabilities that streamline the DI process, allowing you to focus on your app's core logic.
- **Integration with Jetpack Libraries:** Hilt seamlessly integrates with other Jetpack libraries like ViewModel, Navigation, WorkManager, and Compose. This means you can easily inject dependencies into these components, promoting consistency and maintainability across your entire project.
- **Compile-Time Correctness:** Hilt performs dependency checks at compile time. This ensures that if there are any issues with your dependency graph or injection points, you'll get immediate feedback, preventing runtime errors and crashes.
- **Standard Structure:** Hilt enforces a standard structure for your DI setup, making it easier for you and your team to understand and maintain the codebase. This standardized structure also promotes consistency across different parts of your application.

Key Concepts in Hilt:

While Hilt abstracts away many of the complexities of Dagger, it's still helpful to understand some key concepts:

- **Modules:** Modules are classes annotated with `@Module`. They define how to provide dependencies. In a module, you declare functions annotated with `@Provides` that return instances of your dependencies.
- **Components:** Components are responsible for creating and providing instances of your dependencies. Hilt defines several standard components (e.g., `ApplicationComponent`, `ActivityComponent`) and allows you to create custom ones if needed.
- **Scopes:** Scopes define the lifetime of your dependencies. Hilt provides standard scopes like `@Singleton` (application-wide) and `@ActivityScoped` (activity-specific), ensuring that dependencies are created and shared correctly.

Hilt in the Jetpack Compose Architecture:

Hilt fits seamlessly into the MVVM architecture commonly used in Jetpack Compose applications. You can inject dependencies directly into your ViewModels and composables, making it easy to provide them with the necessary data sources, repositories, or other services. Hilt's ability to manage complex dependency graphs ensures that your Compose components receive the correct dependencies effortlessly.

In the following sections, we'll dive into the practical aspects of setting up Hilt in your Jetpack Compose project, injecting dependencies into ViewModels and composables, and testing your Hilt-enabled code.

Setting Up Hilt in Your Project

Getting Hilt up and running in your Jetpack Compose project involves a few simple steps. Let's walk through them together.

1. Add Hilt Dependencies:

Open your project's `build.gradle (Module: app)` file and add the following dependencies to the dependencies block:

```
// Hilt Dependencies
implementation("com.google.dagger:hilt-android:2.48")
kapt("com.google.dagger:hilt-android-compiler:2.48")
implementation("androidx.hilt:hilt-navigation-compose:1.1.0")
```

- **hilt-android:** The core Hilt library for Android.
- **hilt-android-compiler:** The Hilt annotation processor, responsible for generating code related to dependency injection.
- **hilt-navigation-compose:** This dependency helps to integrate Hilt with Compose navigation.

2. Apply the Hilt Gradle Plugin:

In your project's top-level `build.gradle` file, add the Hilt Gradle plugin within the `plugins` block:

```
plugins {
    // ... other plugins ...
    id 'com.google.dagger.hilt.android' version '2.48' apply false
}
```

Then, apply the plugin to your module-level `build.gradle (:app)` file:

```
// In build.gradle (Module: app)
plugins {
    // ... other plugins ...
    id 'com.google.dagger.hilt.android'
}
```

3. Create an Application Class:

Create a new Kotlin class that extends `Application` and annotate it with `@HiltAndroidApp`:

```
@HiltAndroidApp class MyApplication : Application()
```

(The code is of an application class `MyApplication` which will be used by the Hilt library to generate components and modules for your app.)

Add this class to your `AndroidManifest.xml`:

```
<application android:name=".MyApplication" ...> </application>
```

4. Configure Hilt Modules (Optional):

Hilt modules are typically not required in simple Compose projects. Hilt automatically provides default modules for common components like `Application` and `Activity`. However, you'll need to create modules when you want to provide dependencies that Hilt doesn't know how to create by default. We'll cover this in more detail in later sections.

Key Points:

- **Dependencies:** Ensure you have the correct Hilt dependencies in your `build.gradle` file.
- **Plugin:** Apply the Hilt Gradle plugin to your project.
- **Application Class:** Create and annotate your `Application` class with `@HiltAndroidApp`.

By completing these steps, you've successfully set up Hilt in your Jetpack Compose project. This lays the groundwork for injecting dependencies into your ViewModels and composables, making your code cleaner, more modular, and easier to test.

Injecting Dependencies into ViewModels

Hilt makes it incredibly easy to inject dependencies into your ViewModels, ensuring they have access to the resources they need (repositories, data sources, etc.) without manual instantiation. Let's see how this works in practice.

Using `@HiltViewModel` and Constructor Injection:

1. **Annotate Your ViewModel:** Annotate your ViewModel class with `@HiltViewModel`:

   ```
   @HiltViewModel
   class MyViewModel @Inject constructor(
       private val repository: MyRepository
   ) : ViewModel() {
       // ... your ViewModel logic ...
   }
   ```

   (The code initializes the `MyViewModel` class and annotates it with `@HiltViewModel`. `MyRepository` is injected into the ViewModel through the constructor.)

   - `@HiltViewModel`: This annotation tells Hilt that this class is a ViewModel and that it should be created and managed by Hilt.
   - `@Inject constructor(...)`: This annotation tells Hilt how to provide the dependencies for the ViewModel's constructor. In this case, Hilt will automatically create an instance of `MyRepository` and pass it to the `MyViewModel` constructor.

2. **Create a Hilt Module (If Needed):**

   If the dependency you're injecting (`MyRepository` in this case) has its own dependencies, you'll need to create a Hilt module to instruct Hilt on how to provide those dependencies.

   ```
   @Module
   @InstallIn(ViewModelComponent::class)
   object AppModule {
   ```

```
    @Provides
    @ViewModelScoped
    fun provideMyRepository(apiService: ApiService, database: AppDatabase):
MyRepository {
        return MyRepositoryImpl(apiService, database)
    }
}
```

(This module provides an implementation of `MyRepository`.)

- `@Module`: This annotation marks the class as a Hilt module.
- `@InstallIn(ViewModelComponent::class)`: This annotation tells Hilt to install the module into the `ViewModelComponent`, ensuring that its provided dependencies are available within the scope of ViewModels.
- `@Provides`: This annotation is used to mark functions that provide dependencies.
- `@ViewModelScoped`: This annotation indicates that the provided dependency should be scoped to the lifetime of the ViewModel.

3. **Get the ViewModel in Your Composable:**

   You can now get an instance of your ViewModel using the `viewModel()` function, which is provided by the `androidx.hilt:hilt-navigation-compose` library:

```
@Composable
fun MyScreen() {
    val viewModel: MyViewModel = viewModel()
    // Use the viewModel
}
```

   (The code gets an instance of `MyViewModel` in the `MyScreen` composable and then uses it.)

Examples of Injecting Dependencies:

- **Repository:** Injecting a repository gives your ViewModel access to data operations.
- **Data Source:** Inject a data source (e.g., Room DAO, Retrofit API) to abstract the data layer.
- **Shared Preferences:** Inject `SharedPreferences` to handle user preferences.
- **Other Services:** Inject any service or dependency your ViewModel requires, such as analytics trackers, network connectivity checkers, etc.

By leveraging Hilt's dependency injection capabilities, you can simplify your ViewModel creation process, promote loose coupling, and make your code more testable and maintainable.

Injecting Dependencies into Composables

Hilt not only simplifies dependency injection in ViewModels but also extends this convenience to your composable functions. This means you can directly access the dependencies your composables need without the need for manual passing or cumbersome initialization.

Using `@Composable` and `injectedViewModel()`:

To inject a ViewModel or any other dependency directly into a composable function, you can use the `injectedViewModel()` function, which is provided by the `androidx.hilt:hilt-navigation-compose` library:

```
@Composable
fun MyComposable() {
    val viewModel: MyViewModel = viewModel()
    // Now you can use the viewModel instance directly
}
```

In this example:

1. The `viewModel()` function, when called inside a composable function annotated with `@Composable`, will use Hilt to locate or create the `MyViewModel` instance.
2. Hilt then injects any required dependencies (defined in your Hilt modules) into the `MyViewModel` constructor.
3. The `viewModel()` function returns the fully initialized `MyViewModel` instance, ready for you to use within your composable.

Preserving ViewModel Across Recompositions with `remember`:

To ensure that the same ViewModel instance is retained across recompositions (which are triggered by state changes), you can wrap the `viewModel()` call inside a `remember` block:

```
@Composable
fun MyComposable() {
    val viewModel: MyViewModel = remember { viewModel() } // Remember the
ViewModel
    // ... rest of your composable code
}
```

Example: Injecting a ViewModel and a Repository:

```
@HiltViewModel // Annotate your ViewModel with @HiltViewModel
class MyViewModel @Inject constructor(
    private val repository: MyRepository
) : ViewModel() {
    // ... ViewModel logic
}

@Composable
fun MyScreen() {
    val viewModel: MyViewModel = viewModel()
    val data by viewModel.data.collectAsState()

    Column {
        // Use viewModel.data to display UI elements
        Text(text = data)
    }
}
```

(The code initializes the `MyScreen` composable and gets a `MyViewModel` instance using `viewModel()`. It then displays the data from the `viewModel` in a `Column`.)

In this example, Hilt automatically provides an instance of `MyRepository` when creating `MyViewModel`. The `MyScreen` composable can then access `MyViewModel`'s `data` directly without needing to create or manage any dependencies manually.

Key Points:

- **@Composable:** Ensure your composable function is annotated with @Composable.
- **injectedViewModel():** Use this function to obtain your ViewModel instance within a composable.
- **remember:** Wrap the `viewModel()` call in `remember` to preserve the ViewModel across recompositions.
- **Hilt Modules:** If your ViewModel or other dependencies have their own dependencies, define them in Hilt modules.

By leveraging Hilt's capabilities for injecting dependencies directly into composables, you streamline your code, reduce boilerplate, and enhance the maintainability and testability of your Jetpack Compose applications.

Testing with Hilt

Testing is a crucial part of software development, and when you're using dependency injection with Hilt, it's essential to test your ViewModels and composables to ensure they interact correctly with their injected dependencies. Hilt provides a set of testing APIs that make this process smoother and more efficient.

Importance of Testing with DI:

- **Verify Correct Behavior:** Testing classes that rely on dependency injection ensures that they function as expected when they receive different implementations of their dependencies. This helps catch errors early in the development cycle.
- **Isolate Components:** By using mock objects or fake implementations of dependencies, you can isolate the class under test and focus on its specific logic. This makes your tests more reliable and easier to maintain.
- **Prevent Regressions:** Tests act as a safety net, helping you catch unintended side effects when you modify your code. This prevents regressions and ensures that your app remains stable as it evolves.

Using Hilt's Testing APIs:

Hilt provides specific tools and annotations to facilitate testing:

- **HiltAndroidTest:** This annotation tells Hilt to generate a test-specific Hilt component for your test class. It also provides access to the Hilt test rule, which manages the test component's lifecycle.
- **@UninstallModules:** This annotation allows you to replace or disable specific modules during testing. This is useful when you want to provide mock implementations of dependencies.
- **@BindValue:** This annotation lets you inject test-specific values into your Hilt component. You can use this to provide mock data or configuration options for testing.

Example: Testing a ViewModel:

```
@HiltAndroidTest
class MyViewModelTest {
```

```
@get:Rule
var hiltRule = HiltAndroidRule(this)

@Inject lateinit var repository: MyRepository

@Before
fun setup() {
    hiltRule.inject()
}

@Test
fun testFetchData() = runTest {
    // ... (set up mock repository to return test data) ...

    val viewModel = MyViewModel(repository)

    viewModel.fetchData() // Trigger the data fetching logic

    // ... (verify that the UI state is updated correctly) ...
    }
}
```

(The code is a test for MyViewModel class. It sets up the Hilt test rule and injects the repository dependency into the test. It also triggers the fetchData() function and verifies that the UI state is updated as expected.)

In this example:

1. We use the @HiltAndroidTest annotation and the HiltAndroidRule to set up the Hilt test environment.
2. We inject a mock instance of MyRepository (or another dependency).
3. We create the MyViewModel instance and trigger the fetchData() function.
4. We verify that the ViewModel's UI state is updated correctly based on the mock data.

Example: Testing a Composable:

```
@HiltAndroidTest
@RunWith(AndroidJUnit4::class)
class MyComposableTest {

    @get:Rule
    val composeTestRule = createAndroidComposeRule<ComponentActivity>() //
Replace ComponentActivity with the appropriate Activity

    @Test
    fun testComposable() {
        composeTestRule.setContent {
            val viewModel = MyViewModel(repository = mockRepository)

            MyComposable(viewModel) // Pass the mock ViewModel to the
composable

            // ... (interact with the composable and assert UI elements) ...
        }
```

```
        }
}
```

(The code is a test for `MyComposable`. It uses the `createAndroidComposeRule` to set up a test environment for the Composable. It then sets the content of the Composable with a mock ViewModel and interacts with the Composable to verify the correctness of the UI elements.)

Key Points:

- Testing DI components is crucial to ensure they work correctly with their dependencies.
- Hilt provides specialized annotations and APIs to simplify testing with dependency injection.
- Use mock objects or fake implementations to isolate the component under test.
- Write comprehensive unit tests to cover different scenarios and edge cases.

By incorporating Hilt's testing capabilities into your development workflow, you can build robust and reliable Jetpack Compose applications that are easier to maintain and less prone to errors.

Best Practices and Considerations

Using Hilt effectively in larger projects and complex architectures requires following best practices and understanding potential pitfalls. This section will guide you through some essential considerations.

Organizing and Managing Hilt Modules:

- **Modularity:** Organize your modules based on functionality or features. Create separate modules for different layers of your app (e.g., data, domain, presentation) or for distinct features. This promotes a clear separation of concerns and makes your codebase more maintainable.
- **Scoped Modules:** Use scopes (`@Singleton`, `@ActivityScoped`, `@ViewModelScoped`, etc.) to control the lifetime of your dependencies. Inject dependencies with the appropriate scope to ensure they're shared and destroyed correctly.
- **Naming Conventions:** Follow a consistent naming convention for your modules (e.g., `AppModule`, `NetworkModule`, `DataModule`) to improve readability and maintainability.

Hilt in Multi-Module Projects:

- **Shared Modules:** Create shared modules for dependencies that need to be accessed across multiple modules. For example, a `NetworkModule` can provide network-related dependencies (e.g., Retrofit, OkHttp) to other modules.
- **Component Dependencies:** Use component dependencies (`@ComponentDependencies`) to establish relationships between components in different modules. This allows modules to access dependencies provided by other modules.

Handling Dependency Cycles:

Dependency cycles (circular dependencies) can occur when two or more classes depend on each other. This can lead to compilation errors or runtime issues. To avoid dependency cycles:

- **Refactor:** Rethink your design to eliminate the circular dependency. Consider introducing interfaces or abstract classes to break the cycle.
- **Qualified Injection:** Use `@Named` or `@Qualifier` annotations to differentiate between multiple instances of the same type if you encounter conflicts.

Common Pitfalls and How to Avoid Them:

- **Overuse of @Singleton:** Be cautious about using @Singleton for every dependency. Overusing it can lead to memory leaks or make it difficult to replace dependencies for testing.
- **Forgetting to Annotate:** Make sure to annotate all classes that you want Hilt to manage with the appropriate Hilt annotations (e.g., @AndroidEntryPoint, @HiltViewModel, @Inject).
- **Injecting into Private Constructors:** Hilt needs access to the constructor of a class to inject dependencies. Avoid making constructors private if you intend to use Hilt for injection.

Integrating Hilt with Other Jetpack Libraries:

- **ViewModel:** Hilt seamlessly integrates with the ViewModel library. You can use @HiltViewModel to annotate your ViewModels and inject dependencies into them.
- **Navigation:** Hilt supports injecting dependencies into your navigation graphs and destinations. This allows you to easily pass dependencies between different screens in your app.
- **Other Libraries:** Hilt can be integrated with other Jetpack libraries like WorkManager and DataStore to simplify dependency injection in those components as well.

By following these best practices and being mindful of potential issues, you can harness the full power of Hilt to create well-structured, maintainable, and testable Jetpack Compose applications. Remember, dependency injection is a powerful tool, and using Hilt effectively can greatly enhance your development workflow.

Chapter Summary

This chapter has illuminated the world of dependency injection (DI) and how Hilt, a powerful DI library built on Dagger, can streamline your Jetpack Compose development. We started by exploring the concept of DI, discussing its benefits, and highlighting how it addresses common problems like tight coupling and hidden dependencies.

You learned how Hilt simplifies the DI process by providing a clear structure, annotations, and code generation tools. Hilt's seamless integration with other Jetpack libraries, compile-time correctness guarantees, and reduced boilerplate make it a compelling choice for managing dependencies in your Android projects.

We then walked through the steps of setting up Hilt in your Jetpack Compose project, adding the necessary dependencies, applying the Hilt Gradle plugin, and creating an application class. You also learned how to inject dependencies into your ViewModels and composable functions using Hilt annotations and functions, making your code cleaner and more modular.

The chapter also touched on the importance of testing your Hilt-enabled code and provided examples of how to write unit tests for ViewModels and composables. Finally, we discussed best practices for organizing Hilt modules, handling dependency cycles, and integrating Hilt with other Jetpack libraries like ViewModel and Navigation.

Armed with this knowledge of dependency injection and Hilt, you're now equipped to create more maintainable, testable, and scalable Jetpack Compose applications. As you continue your Compose journey, remember that dependency injection is a fundamental technique in modern Android development and mastering it will elevate your skills as a developer.

Section F:
Asynchronous Programming and Networking

Coroutines for Asynchronous Operations in Jetpack Compose

Outline

- The Need for Asynchronicity in Android
- Introducing Kotlin Coroutines
- Basic Coroutine Concepts
- Coroutines in Jetpack Compose
- Structured Concurrency with `coroutineScope` and `LaunchedEffect`
- Error Handling and Cancellation
- Practical Use Cases
- Best Practices and Considerations
- Chapter Summary

The Need for Asynchronicity in Android

Asynchronous programming is a fundamental concept in Android development, playing a crucial role in maintaining the responsiveness and performance of your applications. Let's delve into why asynchronicity is so important and explore the challenges it presents.

What is Asynchronous Programming?

In the context of Android, asynchronous programming refers to the ability to execute tasks in the background without blocking the main thread. The **main thread**, also known as the UI thread, is responsible for rendering the user interface and handling user interactions. If you perform time-consuming operations on the main thread (e.g., network requests, database queries), it can freeze the UI, leading to a frustrating user experience.

Asynchronous operations allow you to offload such tasks to background threads, freeing up the main thread to keep the UI smooth and responsive.

Why Asynchronicity is Essential:

Asynchronicity is crucial for a variety of tasks in Android:

- **Network Requests:** Fetching data from remote servers can take an unpredictable amount of time due to network latency and server response times. Blocking the main thread during a network request would render your app unusable.
- **Database Operations:** Reading or writing data to a database can be time-consuming, especially for larger datasets. Performing these operations asynchronously prevents the UI from freezing while the database is being accessed.

- **Background Processing:** Many apps need to perform background tasks like image processing, data analysis, or complex calculations. Asynchronicity enables you to execute these tasks without hindering the user's interaction with the UI.

Challenges of Traditional Asynchronous Approaches:

Traditional approaches to asynchronous programming in Android, such as callbacks and `AsyncTask`, can lead to several challenges:

- **Callback Hell:** Asynchronous operations often involve chains of callbacks, resulting in deeply nested and difficult-to-read code. This "callback hell" makes it challenging to reason about the flow of execution and can lead to subtle errors.
- **Error Handling:** Managing errors in a callback-based approach can be cumbersome and error-prone. You need to handle errors at each step in the callback chain, leading to repetitive and potentially buggy code.
- **Lifecycle Management:** Callbacks often require manual handling of lifecycle events to prevent memory leaks and crashes. This adds complexity to your code and increases the risk of bugs.

To overcome these challenges, Kotlin introduced coroutines, a powerful and modern way to write asynchronous code. In the next section, we'll explore how coroutines revolutionize asynchronous programming in Android, making it more concise, readable, and maintainable.

Introducing Kotlin Coroutines

Kotlin coroutines provide a fresh and elegant way to handle asynchronous operations in Android development. They revolutionize how you write asynchronous code by enabling you to express asynchronous tasks in a sequential, easy-to-read style. This paradigm shift eliminates many of the complexities associated with traditional approaches like callbacks and `AsyncTask`.

What are Kotlin Coroutines?

At their core, coroutines are lightweight threads that allow you to execute code concurrently without the overhead of traditional threads. They are a language-level feature in Kotlin, providing a more structured and efficient way to handle asynchronous operations.

Simplifying Asynchronous Programming:

Coroutines simplify asynchronous code by allowing you to write it in a sequential manner, using familiar language constructs like loops and conditional statements. This is a significant departure from callback-based approaches, where asynchronous operations often lead to nested callbacks and complex code structures.

Here's a simplified example:

```
fun fetchData() = viewModelScope.launch { // Launch a coroutine
    val data = repository.getData() // Suspend function - waits for result
    updateUI(data)
}
```

In this example, the `fetchData()` function launches a coroutine that calls the `repository.getData()` function. The `getData()` function is a `suspend` function, meaning it can pause the coroutine's execution until the data is fetched. Once the data is available, the coroutine resumes, and the `updateUI()` function is called to update the UI.

Benefits of Kotlin Coroutines:

- **Improved Code Readability:** Coroutines allow you to write asynchronous code that reads like synchronous code, making it easier to understand the flow of your program.
- **Better Error Handling:** Coroutines provide structured concurrency, which simplifies error handling and ensures that exceptions are propagated correctly.
- **Structured Concurrency:** Coroutines introduce the concept of coroutine scopes, which define the lifetime of coroutines and help prevent leaks.
- **Lightweight:** Coroutines are lightweight compared to traditional threads, making them more efficient for managing concurrent tasks.
- **Cancellation Support:** Coroutines can be easily canceled, allowing you to gracefully stop ongoing operations when they're no longer needed.
- **Main-Safety:** Compose functions are *main-safe*, which means you can call suspend functions directly within composables without worrying about blocking the UI thread.

By leveraging Kotlin coroutines in your Jetpack Compose projects, you can write cleaner, more concise, and more maintainable asynchronous code. Coroutines are a powerful tool for simplifying your app's logic and improving its responsiveness and performance.

Basic Coroutine Concepts

To effectively wield the power of coroutines, it's essential to grasp some foundational concepts. Let's delve into the building blocks that form the basis of coroutine-based asynchronous programming.

Coroutine Builders (`launch` and `async`):

Coroutine builders are special functions that create coroutines. The two most common builders are:

1. **launch:** Starts a new coroutine that executes independently and doesn't return a result. Use launch for fire-and-forget tasks where you don't need a specific result from the coroutine.
2. **async:** Starts a new coroutine and returns a Deferred object, which represents a promise of a future result. You can use await() on the Deferred object to get the result once the coroutine completes. Use async when you need to get a result from the coroutine's computation.

suspend **Functions:**

suspend functions are the core of coroutine programming. A suspend function can pause the execution of a coroutine without blocking the underlying thread. This allows other coroutines to run while the suspended coroutine is waiting for a result or performing a long-running operation.

You can only call a suspend function from within another suspend function or a coroutine. This restriction ensures that the calling code is prepared to handle the potential pause in execution.

Coroutine Scopes:

A coroutine scope defines the lifetime and context of a coroutine. It's a way to group coroutines together and manage their cancellation behavior. When you launch a coroutine, you always do it within a coroutine scope.

Here are the main types of coroutine scopes in Jetpack Compose:

- **viewModelScope:** A scope tied to the lifecycle of a ViewModel. Coroutines launched in this scope are automatically canceled when the ViewModel is cleared.
- **rememberCoroutineScope:** A scope tied to a composable function. Coroutines launched in this scope are canceled when the composable leaves the composition.

Using coroutine scopes is crucial for preventing coroutine leaks and ensuring that coroutines are canceled when they're no longer needed.

Coroutine Context:

The coroutine context defines the environment in which a coroutine executes. It includes information like the dispatcher (which thread the coroutine runs on) and any additional elements (like exception handlers or job objects).

Examples:

Delaying Execution:

```
viewModelScope.launch {
    delay(1000) // Wait for 1 second
    println("Hello from the coroutine!")
}
```

(The code is to print a message "Hello from the coroutine!" after one second of delay.)

Running a Background Task:

```
viewModelScope.launch {
    withContext(Dispatchers.IO) { // Switch to IO dispatcher for network request
        val data = fetchDataFromNetwork()
        withContext(Dispatchers.Main) { // Switch back to Main dispatcher for UI
update
            updateUI(data)
        }
    }
}
```

(The code fetches data from the network in a background thread and then updates the UI in the main thread.)

By understanding these fundamental coroutine concepts, you'll be equipped to write efficient and reliable asynchronous code in your Jetpack Compose applications. Remember, coroutines offer a powerful way to simplify asynchronous programming and enhance the responsiveness of your UIs.

Coroutines in Jetpack Compose

Jetpack Compose and Kotlin coroutines are a match made in heaven. Compose is designed to work seamlessly with coroutines, providing convenient tools and APIs that make it easy to write asynchronous code within your composable functions.

Seamless Integration:

Jetpack Compose's declarative nature aligns perfectly with the sequential style of coroutines. You can launch coroutines directly within your composables, allowing you to perform asynchronous tasks like fetching data or running animations without interrupting the UI thread.

`rememberCoroutineScope`:

The `rememberCoroutineScope` function is a crucial tool for using coroutines in Compose. It provides you with a `CoroutineScope` that is tied to the lifecycle of the composable. This means that any coroutines you launch within this scope will be automatically canceled when the composable is removed from the composition.

```
@Composable
fun MyComposable() {
    val scope = rememberCoroutineScope()

    Button(onClick = {
        scope.launch {
            // This coroutine will be canceled if MyComposable is removed
            // ... perform some asynchronous task ...
        }
    }) {
        Text("Start Task")
    }
}
```

(The code is to create a coroutine scope tied to the composable's lifecycle and launch a coroutine to perform an asynchronous task when the button is clicked.)

`LaunchedEffect`:

The `LaunchedEffect` composable is designed to launch coroutines when a composable is first composed or when its dependencies change. It provides a convenient way to trigger side effects or asynchronous actions based on the state of your composable.

```
@Composable
fun MyComposable(viewModel: MyViewModel) {
    val data by viewModel.data.collectAsState()

    LaunchedEffect(key1 = data) { // Launch when data changes
        // ... react to data changes (e.g., update UI, trigger animation)
    }

    // ... rest of your composable code ...
}
```

(The code is to launch a coroutine whenever the `data` state in the `viewModel` changes.)

In this example, the `LaunchedEffect` composable launches a coroutine whenever the `data` value from the `viewModel` changes. This allows you to react to data updates and perform actions like updating the UI or triggering animations.

Examples of Coroutines in Compose:

- **Fetching Data from ViewModel:**

```
@Composable
fun MyScreen(viewModel: MyViewModel) {
    val scope = rememberCoroutineScope()
    var data by remember { mutableStateOf<MyData?>(null) }

    LaunchedEffect(Unit) { // Launch when the composable is first
composed
        data = viewModel.fetchData()
```

```
        }

        // Use data in the UI
    }
```

- **Performing Animations:**

```
@Composable
fun MyAnimatedComposable() {
    var offsetX by remember { mutableStateOf(0f) }
    val scope = rememberCoroutineScope()

    Box(modifier = Modifier.offset(x = offsetX)) {
        // ... your composable content ...
    }

    LaunchedEffect(Unit) {
        while (true) {
            offsetX += 10f // Animate the composable
            delay(100)
        }
    }
}
```

By harnessing the power of Kotlin coroutines and using the provided tools in Jetpack Compose, you can effortlessly handle asynchronous operations within your UI code. This allows you to build responsive, dynamic, and efficient applications that deliver a seamless user experience.

Structured Concurrency with `coroutineScope` and `LaunchedEffect`

Structured concurrency is a powerful concept in Kotlin coroutines that revolutionizes the way we handle multiple asynchronous operations. It's a paradigm shift that addresses common challenges like coroutine leaks, complex error handling, and code readability. Jetpack Compose provides built-in support for structured concurrency through the `coroutineScope` and `LaunchedEffect` composables.

Understanding Structured Concurrency:

Think of structured concurrency as a way to organize and manage your coroutines within a well-defined "block" of code. This block acts as a parent for all the coroutines launched within it, ensuring that:

- **Coroutine Lifecycle Alignment:** Child coroutines cannot outlive their parent. If the parent scope is canceled or completes, all its child coroutines are automatically canceled as well. This prevents coroutine leaks, where a forgotten coroutine keeps running in the background even after it's no longer needed.
- **Simplified Error Handling:** Exceptions thrown within a child coroutine are propagated to the parent scope, allowing you to handle errors gracefully in a centralized location. This eliminates the need for complex error handling mechanisms scattered throughout your code.

`coroutineScope` and `LaunchedEffect`: The Power Duo

In Jetpack Compose, you can achieve structured concurrency using the `coroutineScope` and `LaunchedEffect` composables.

- **coroutineScope:** This composable function creates a coroutine scope within your composable. Any coroutines launched within this scope become children of the `coroutineScope`. This ensures that these coroutines won't outlive the composable itself.
- **LaunchedEffect:** This composable function launches a coroutine and automatically cancels it when the composable leaves the composition. It's particularly useful for launching coroutines that are tied to the lifecycle of the composable, such as fetching data, performing animations, or reacting to state changes.

Example: Using `coroutineScope` to Launch Multiple Coroutines:

```
@Composable
fun MyComposable() {
    val scope = rememberCoroutineScope() // Remember the scope

    Column {
        Button(onClick = {
            scope.launch {
                task1() // Launch coroutine 1
            }
            scope.launch {
                task2() // Launch coroutine 2
            }
        }) {
            Text("Start Tasks")
        }

        // ... other composables
    }
}

suspend fun task1() { /* ... */ }
suspend fun task2() { /* ... */ }
```

(The code creates a coroutine scope using `rememberCoroutineScope` and then launches two coroutines (`task1` and `task2`) inside the scope.)

In this example:

1. `rememberCoroutineScope` creates a `CoroutineScope` that's tied to the lifecycle of `MyComposable`.
2. Clicking the "Start Tasks" button launches two coroutines (`task1` and `task2`) within that scope.
3. If `MyComposable` is removed from the composition, the scope is cancelled, automatically canceling both `task1` and `task2`.
4. If either `task1` or `task2` throws an exception, it will be propagated to the `coroutineScope`, allowing you to handle the error gracefully.

By using `coroutineScope` and `LaunchedEffect`, you can write concise, readable, and maintainable code that gracefully handles multiple asynchronous operations in your Jetpack Compose UIs.

Error Handling and Cancellation

When working with coroutines in Jetpack Compose, it's crucial to have strategies in place for handling errors and gracefully canceling coroutines that are no longer needed. Let's explore these aspects and see how you can implement them effectively in your applications.

Error Handling Strategies:

Coroutines can fail due to various reasons, such as network errors, invalid data, or exceptions thrown within your code. Here are common approaches to handle errors:

1. **try-catch Blocks:** The simplest way to handle errors is using `try-catch` blocks within your coroutine code:

```
coroutineScope.launch {
    try {
        val result = performRiskyOperation()
        // Handle success
    } catch (e: Exception) {
        // Handle error
        // Log the error, show an error message, etc.
    }
}
```

2. **CoroutineExceptionHandler:** For more fine-grained error handling, you can use a CoroutineExceptionHandler. It allows you to define a central handler for exceptions thrown in your coroutines.

```
val handler = CoroutineExceptionHandler { _, exception ->
    // Handle exception globally
    // Log the error, show a generic error message, etc.
}
coroutineScope.launch(handler) {
    // ... your coroutine code ...
}
```

Coroutine Cancellation:

Canceling coroutines is essential when they're no longer needed. This prevents unnecessary resource consumption and potential errors. Here are ways to cancel coroutines:

1. **Cancel the Scope:** Canceling the CoroutineScope that a coroutine was launched in will automatically cancel all its child coroutines. In Jetpack Compose, the rememberCoroutineScope function provides a scope that is automatically canceled when the composable leaves the composition.

```
@Composable
fun MyComposable() {
    val scope = rememberCoroutineScope()

    LaunchedEffect(Unit) { // Launches a coroutine tied to MyComposable's
lifecycle
        while(isActive) { // Check if coroutine is still active
            // ... (do some work)
            delay(1000)
        }
    }
```

```
    // ... rest of your composable code ...
}
```

In this example, the LaunchedEffect coroutine will be automatically canceled when MyComposable is removed from the composition tree.

2. **Job.cancel():** You can explicitly cancel a coroutine by calling the cancel() function on its Job object.

```
val job = scope.launch { /* ... */ }
job.cancel()
```

Examples in Jetpack Compose:

Error Handling in LaunchedEffect:

```
@Composable
fun MyComposable(viewModel: MyViewModel) {
    val state by viewModel.state.collectAsState()

    LaunchedEffect(key1 = state) {
        try {
            viewModel.fetchData()
        } catch (e: Exception) {
            // Show error message in the UI
        }
    }

    // ... rest of your composable code ...
}
```

In this example, if viewModel.fetchData() throws an exception, the catch block will handle the error, potentially by displaying an error message to the user.

Cancellation in LazyColumn:

When an item is scrolled off the screen in a LazyColumn, its corresponding composable is removed from the composition. Any LaunchedEffect coroutines associated with that composable will be automatically canceled, preventing unnecessary work and potential resource leaks.

Key Points:

- Error handling is crucial for robust coroutine code. Use try-catch blocks or CoroutineExceptionHandler.
- Cancel coroutines when they're no longer needed to prevent resource wastage and errors.
- Leverage the rememberCoroutineScope function and LaunchedEffect composable for automatic cancellation.

By incorporating these error handling and cancellation techniques, you can ensure that your Jetpack Compose applications remain responsive and reliable even when dealing with asynchronous operations that might fail or become unnecessary.

Practical Use Cases

Coroutines shine in Jetpack Compose when handling real-world scenarios that involve asynchronicity. Let's explore some practical examples to illustrate their versatility.

Fetching Data from a Network API using Retrofit:

In a typical app, you often need to fetch data from a remote server using a library like Retrofit. Coroutines make this process much smoother:

```
@Composable
fun NewsScreen(viewModel: NewsViewModel = viewModel()) {
    val news by viewModel.news.collectAsState()

    LaunchedEffect(Unit) {
        viewModel.fetchNews()
    }

    LazyColumn {
        items(news) { article ->
            NewsItem(article)
        }
    }
}

class NewsViewModel(private val newsRepository: NewsRepository) : ViewModel()
{
    private val _news = MutableStateFlow<List<Article>>(emptyList())
    val news: StateFlow<List<Article>> = _news.asStateFlow()

    fun fetchNews() = viewModelScope.launch {
        _news.value = newsRepository.getNews()
    }
}
```

(The code is a Jetpack Compose screen that displays a list of news articles fetched from a network API using Retrofit and Coroutines. The NewsScreen composable displays the news articles, the NewsViewModel class handles the fetching of news articles, and the NewsRepository class handles the network request to the API using Retrofit.)

In this example, the NewsViewModel uses a coroutine to fetch news from a repository (which internally uses Retrofit), and the NewsScreen composable observes the news state to display the fetched articles.

Performing Database Operations with Room:

Room provides suspend functions that work seamlessly with coroutines, simplifying database interactions:

```
@Composable
fun UserListScreen(viewModel: UserListViewModel = viewModel()) {
    // ... similar to NewsScreen example ...

    class UserListViewModel(private val userDao: UserDao) : ViewModel() {
        // ...

        fun addUser(user: User) = viewModelScope.launch {
```

```
                userDao.insertUser(user)
            }
        }
}
```

(The code is to perform a database insert operation using Room and Coroutines within the context of a Jetpack Compose ViewModel.)

Running Background Tasks:

Coroutines excel at performing background tasks, such as image processing or complex calculations:

```
@Composable
fun ImageProcessorScreen(viewModel: ImageProcessorViewModel = viewModel()) {
    var imageUri by remember { mutableStateOf<Uri?>(null) }

    // ... UI for selecting an image ...

    LaunchedEffect(imageUri) {
        imageUri?.let {
            viewModel.processImage(it)
        }
    }

    // ... UI for displaying the processed image ...
}
```

Implementing Animations and Transitions:

Coroutines are perfect for creating smooth and customizable animations in Jetpack Compose. Here's a simple example of animating the size of a box:

```
@Composable
fun AnimatedBox() {
    var size by remember { mutableStateOf(50.dp) }
    val scope = rememberCoroutineScope()

    Box(
        Modifier
            .size(size)
            .background(Color.Blue)
            .clickable {
                scope.launch {
                    size = if (size == 50.dp) 100.dp else 50.dp
                }
            }
    )
}
```

(The code is a Jetpack Compose composable function that creates a box with a blue background. The box is clickable, and when clicked, it animates its size between 50.dp and 100.dp.)

These are just a few examples of the many ways you can leverage coroutines in your Jetpack Compose applications. Their ability to handle asynchronicity with ease and grace opens up a world of possibilities for building responsive, dynamic, and user-friendly UIs.

Best Practices and Considerations

Coroutines are a powerful tool, but like any tool, they're most effective when used thoughtfully and with an understanding of their strengths and limitations. Let's delve into some best practices and considerations for working with coroutines in Jetpack Compose.

Best Practices:

1. **Choose the Right Scope:**
   - Use `viewModelScope` for coroutines that are tied to the lifecycle of a ViewModel.
   - Use `rememberCoroutineScope` for coroutines that are tied to the lifecycle of a composable function.
   - Avoid launching long-running coroutines in the `GlobalScope`.
2. **Suspend, Don't Block:**
   - Always use `suspend` functions for operations that might take time (e.g., network requests, database queries).
   - Avoid blocking the main thread with long-running computations.
3. **Error Handling:**
   - Use `try-catch` blocks or `CoroutineExceptionHandler` to gracefully handle exceptions in your coroutines.
   - Consider using the `supervisorScope` builder to prevent failures in one child coroutine from canceling others.
4. **Cancellation:**
   - Make sure to cancel coroutines when they're no longer needed.
   - Utilize `LaunchedEffect` to automatically cancel coroutines when the composable is removed.
5. **Structured Concurrency:**
   - Use `coroutineScope` and `LaunchedEffect` to enforce structured concurrency. This helps prevent coroutine leaks and simplifies error handling.
6. **Testing:**
   - Write tests for your ViewModel functions that launch coroutines to ensure they behave correctly and handle errors gracefully.

Potential Pitfalls and How to Avoid Them:

- **Blocking the Main Thread:** Don't perform long-running or blocking operations directly in composables. Always use `suspend` functions and dispatchers to offload these tasks to background threads.
- **Overusing Coroutines:** While coroutines are lightweight, creating too many of them can still consume resources. Consider using alternative mechanisms like `Flow` for continuous data streams or `remember` for caching values.
- **Ignoring Cancellation:** Failure to cancel coroutines when they're no longer needed can lead to resource leaks and unexpected behavior. Always handle cancellation properly, especially in composables that can be recomposed or removed.

Optimizing Coroutine Usage:

- **Dispatchers:** Use the appropriate dispatcher for each coroutine. `Dispatchers.IO` is suitable for I/O-bound tasks, while `Dispatchers.Default` is ideal for CPU-bound tasks. Switch to `Dispatchers.Main` only when you need to update the UI.
- **withContext:** Use `withContext` to switch between dispatchers within a coroutine. This allows you to perform different parts of a coroutine on different threads as needed.

Alternative Asynchronous Options:

While coroutines are a powerful and convenient choice for asynchronous programming in Android, there are other options available, such as:

- **RxJava:** A reactive programming library for handling asynchronous data streams.
- **Executors and Threads:** The lower-level building blocks for concurrent programming in Java.

These alternatives offer different approaches and trade-offs. While RxJava provides a rich set of operators for working with data streams, coroutines offer a more concise and structured way to write asynchronous code. Executors and threads provide the most flexibility but require more manual management and can be error-prone.

By understanding the best practices, potential pitfalls, and optimization techniques for coroutines, you can harness their power to build responsive, efficient, and maintainable Jetpack Compose applications.

Chapter Summary

This chapter has illuminated the pivotal role of Kotlin coroutines in handling asynchronous operations within Jetpack Compose. You've gained a solid understanding of why asynchronicity is crucial in Android development, especially for tasks like network requests, database operations, and background processing. We explored the challenges of traditional asynchronous approaches and how Kotlin coroutines address these issues with their sequential coding style, structured concurrency, and improved error handling.

You were introduced to fundamental coroutine concepts like coroutine builders (`launch`, `async`), suspend functions, coroutine scopes, and context. The distinctions between `launch` and `async`, as well as the importance of using the right coroutine scope, were explained in detail.

We then delved into the seamless integration of coroutines with Jetpack Compose, highlighting tools like `rememberCoroutineScope` for managing coroutine lifecycles and `LaunchedEffect` for triggering asynchronous actions in response to composable state changes. Practical examples demonstrated how to use coroutines for fetching data, running background tasks, and creating animations within Compose UIs.

The chapter also emphasized the significance of structured concurrency, provided by `coroutineScope` and `LaunchedEffect`, to prevent coroutine leaks and streamline error handling. You learned best practices for using coroutines effectively, avoiding common pitfalls, and optimizing their usage for performance. We also briefly touched upon alternative asynchronous programming options in Android.

With this newfound knowledge of coroutines, you're well-equipped to tackle the challenges of asynchronous programming in your Jetpack Compose projects. In the next chapter, we'll leverage this understanding to explore how to make network requests using Retrofit, a powerful library for interacting with REST APIs.

Making Network Requests with Retrofit

Outline

- Networking in Android
- Introducing Retrofit
- Setting Up Retrofit in Your Project
- Defining API Endpoints
- Making Network Requests
- Handling Responses
- Error Handling with Retrofit
- Best Practices and Advanced Retrofit Features
- Chapter Summary

Networking in Android

Networking is the backbone of modern Android applications, enabling them to communicate with servers, retrieve data, and provide real-time updates. From social media apps that fetch your latest feed to weather apps that deliver current conditions, networking is essential for delivering rich and dynamic experiences to users.

Why Networking Matters:

- **Data Retrieval:** Most apps need to fetch data from remote servers to display content to users. This data could be anything from news articles and social media posts to product catalogs and weather forecasts.
- **Real-Time Updates:** Apps can use networking to receive real-time updates, such as push notifications, stock prices, or sports scores. This keeps users engaged and informed.
- **Cloud Services:** Many apps rely on cloud services for features like data storage, authentication, or machine learning. Networking is the conduit for communicating with these services.

Types of Network Requests:

The most common types of network requests are:

- **GET:** Retrieves data from a server.
- **POST:** Sends data to a server to create a new resource.
- **PUT:** Sends data to a server to update an existing resource.
- **DELETE:** Removes a resource from a server.

REST APIs:

REST APIs (Representational State Transfer Application Programming Interfaces) are a popular architectural style for building web services. They provide a standardized way for clients (like your Android app) to communicate with servers over HTTP. REST APIs are resource-oriented, meaning they focus on manipulating resources (e.g., users, products, articles) identified by URLs.

Common Challenges in Network Communication:

Networking in Android comes with its own set of challenges:

- **Error Handling:** Network connections can fail, servers can be down, or responses can be malformed. Robust error handling is essential to ensure your app behaves gracefully in the face of these issues.
- **Response Parsing:** Network responses are often in formats like JSON or XML. You'll need to parse these responses to extract the data you need.
- **Security:** Protecting sensitive data transmitted over the network is crucial. This might involve using HTTPS, authentication, and encryption.
- **Efficiency:** Optimizing network requests to minimize data usage and battery drain is important for mobile devices.

In this chapter, we'll focus on using Retrofit, a powerful library that simplifies network communication in Android. Retrofit provides an elegant way to define API endpoints, make requests, and handle responses, making networking in your Jetpack Compose apps a breeze.

Introducing Retrofit

Retrofit is a widely adopted library that simplifies network communication in Android apps. It's a type-safe HTTP client that provides a declarative and intuitive way to interact with REST APIs. Retrofit is built on top of OkHttp, a powerful and efficient networking library, and adds a layer of abstraction that makes it easier to define API endpoints, make requests, and handle responses.

What Makes Retrofit So Popular?

Retrofit's popularity stems from its many benefits:

- **Declarative API:** Retrofit uses interfaces and annotations to define API endpoints. This declarative approach results in concise and readable code, focusing on what you want to achieve rather than the low-level details of making the request.
- **Automatic JSON Parsing:** Retrofit seamlessly integrates with converters (e.g., Gson, Moshi) to automatically parse JSON responses into your data classes. This eliminates the need for manual parsing, saving you time and effort.
- **Integration with OkHttp:** Retrofit leverages OkHttp's robust networking capabilities, including connection pooling, caching, and request/response interception.
- **Type Safety:** Retrofit's type-safe API catches errors at compile time, preventing potential runtime issues.
- **Extensibility:** Retrofit is highly extensible, allowing you to customize its behavior with features like custom converters, call adapters, and interceptors.

Key Concepts in Retrofit:

- **Interfaces for API Endpoints:** You define interfaces that represent the endpoints of your REST API. Each method in the interface corresponds to a specific endpoint, and you use annotations to specify the HTTP method, path, parameters, and other details.
- **Annotations for Request Methods:** Retrofit provides annotations like @GET, @POST, @PUT, and @DELETE to specify the HTTP method used for each request.
- **Converters:** Converters are responsible for converting between Java objects and network representations (e.g., JSON, XML). Retrofit supports various converters, allowing you to work with different data formats.

Example: A Simple Retrofit Interface:

```
interface ApiService {
    @GET("users/{id}") // GET request to /users/{id}
    suspend fun getUser(@Path("id") id: Int): User // Returns a User object
}
```

In this example, we define an `ApiService` interface with a single method, `getUser`. This method represents a GET request to the `/users/{id}` endpoint. The `@Path` annotation indicates that the `{id}` placeholder in the path should be replaced with the value of the `id` parameter. The return type `User` indicates that Retrofit should parse the response into a `User` object using a JSON converter.

By mastering these key concepts, you'll be able to harness the power of Retrofit to effortlessly communicate with REST APIs in your Jetpack Compose applications.

Setting Up Retrofit in Your Project

Before you can start making network requests with Retrofit, you need to add the necessary dependencies and configure a Retrofit instance in your project. Let's walk through the steps:

1. Add Retrofit Dependencies:

In your module-level `build.gradle` file (usually `app/build.gradle`), add the following dependencies:

```
dependencies {
    // ... other dependencies ...

    // Retrofit
    implementation 'com.squareup.retrofit2:retrofit:2.9.0'
    // Choose one converter based on your preference:
    implementation 'com.squareup.retrofit2:converter-gson:2.9.0' // Gson
converter
    // implementation 'com.squareup.retrofit2:converter-moshi:2.9.0' // Moshi
converter

    // OkHttp Logging Interceptor
    implementation 'com.squareup.okhttp3:logging-interceptor:4.11.0'
}
```

- **retrofit:** The core Retrofit library.
- **converter-gson or converter-moshi:** Choose one converter based on your preference. Gson and Moshi are popular JSON libraries for converting between Java objects and JSON.
- **logging-interceptor:** (Optional) This interceptor allows you to log network requests and responses, helpful for debugging.

2. Create a Retrofit Instance:

Use `Retrofit.Builder` to create a Retrofit instance and configure it:

```
val retrofit = Retrofit.Builder()
    .baseUrl("https://api.example.com/")  // Set your base URL
    .addConverterFactory(GsonConverterFactory.create()) // Add Gson converter
factory
    .client(OkHttpClient.Builder().addInterceptor(HttpLoggingInterceptor().apply {
        level = HttpLoggingInterceptor.Level.BODY
    }).build()) // Add logging interceptor (optional)
    .build()
```

(The code creates and configures a `Retrofit` instance. The base URL, converter factory, and logging interceptor (optional) are set.)

- **baseUrl:** The base URL of your API (e.g., "https://api.example.com/"). Make sure it ends with a trailing slash.
- **addConverterFactory:** Add the converter factory for your chosen JSON library (Gson or Moshi).
- **client (Optional):** Add the logging interceptor to see network requests and responses in the logcat (useful for debugging).

Configuration Options:

Retrofit offers various configuration options:

- **Converters:** Retrofit supports converters for different data formats like Gson, Moshi, Jackson, Protobuf, and more.
- **Call Adapters:** Call adapters allow you to use different types for asynchronous calls, such as RxJava `Observable` or `Single`.
- **Interceptors:** Interceptors can be used to add headers, modify requests or responses, or log network traffic.

Example:

```
val okHttpClient = OkHttpClient.Builder()
    .addInterceptor(AuthInterceptor()) // Add a custom interceptor for
authentication
    .build()

val retrofit = Retrofit.Builder()
    .baseUrl("https://api.example.com/")
    .addConverterFactory(GsonConverterFactory.create())
    .client(okHttpClient)
    .build()
```

By setting up and configuring Retrofit with the necessary dependencies and options, you're now prepared to define your API endpoints and start making network requests in your Jetpack Compose applications.

Defining API Endpoints

Retrofit's elegance shines when defining API endpoints. Instead of manually constructing URLs and HTTP requests, you simply declare interfaces that represent your API's structure. Retrofit then takes care of the heavy lifting, converting your interface definitions into actual network calls.

Retrofit Interfaces and Annotations:

In Retrofit, you define interfaces to represent your API endpoints. Each method in the interface corresponds to a specific endpoint, and you use annotations to provide details about the request method, path, parameters, headers, and response type.

Here's a breakdown of some common Retrofit annotations:

- **HTTP Method Annotations:**
    - @GET: Indicates a GET request.
    - @POST: Indicates a POST request.
    - @PUT: Indicates a PUT request.
    - @DELETE: Indicates a DELETE request.
- **Path and Query Parameter Annotations:**
    - @Path: Used for path parameters in the URL (e.g., @GET("users/{id}")).

- ○ @Query: Used for query parameters in the URL (e.g., @GET("search") fun search(@Query("q") query: String)).
- **Body and Header Annotations:**
  - ○ @Body: Used to send a data object as the request body (e.g., in a POST request).
  - ○ @Header: Used to add headers to the request.

Example API Endpoint Interfaces:

```
interface ApiService {
    @GET("users/{id}")
    suspend fun getUser(@Path("id") id: Int): User

    @GET("posts")
    suspend fun getPosts(): List<Post>

    @POST("posts")
    suspend fun createPost(@Body post: Post): Post

    @PUT("posts/{id}")
    suspend fun updatePost(@Path("id") id: Int, @Body post: Post): Post

    @DELETE("posts/{id}")
    suspend fun deletePost(@Path("id") id: Int)

    @GET("search")
    suspend fun searchPosts(@Query("q") query: String): List<Post>

    @GET("posts")
    suspend fun getPostsWithHeaders(@Header("Authorization") authToken:
String): List<Post>
}
```

In this example:

- getUser fetches a single user by ID using a GET request.
- getPosts retrieves a list of posts.
- createPost creates a new post using a POST request.
- updatePost updates an existing post using a PUT request.
- deletePost deletes a post by ID.
- searchPosts performs a search for posts based on a query parameter.
- getPostsWithHeaders adds an "Authorization" header to the request.

Key Points:

- Retrofit interfaces provide a clean and declarative way to define API endpoints.
- Annotations are used to specify request methods, paths, parameters, headers, and response types.
- Each method in the interface represents a specific endpoint of your API.

By defining your API endpoints using Retrofit interfaces, you create a structured and type-safe way to interact with your backend services. This approach streamlines the process of making network requests and handling responses, leading to more maintainable and reliable code.

Making Network Requests with Retrofit

Once you've defined your API endpoints using Retrofit interfaces, you're ready to start making network requests to fetch data from your server. Retrofit handles the intricacies of constructing HTTP requests, sending them over the network, and parsing the responses.

Creating an API Service Instance:

After defining your API interface and creating your retrofit instance as explained in the previous section, you can use Retrofit to create an implementation of your API interface. This implementation will handle the actual network communication for you.

```
val apiService: ApiService = retrofit.create(ApiService::class.java)
```

Making Network Requests:

With your API service instance in hand, you can call its methods to make network requests. Each method corresponds to a specific endpoint defined in your interface.

```
val user: User = apiService.getUser(123) // Fetch user with ID 123
```

(The code is to make an api request to fetch a user with specified ID and then assign the returned user object to user variable.)

Synchronous vs. Asynchronous Requests:

- **Synchronous Requests:** In a synchronous request, your code execution blocks until the response is received from the server. This can freeze the UI if the request takes a significant amount of time. Avoid using synchronous requests on the main thread, as it can lead to an unresponsive app.
- **Asynchronous Requests:** Asynchronous requests allow your code to continue executing while the network request is in progress. Once the response is received, a callback or coroutine is triggered to handle it. Asynchronous requests are essential for maintaining a responsive UI and preventing it from freezing during network operations.

Coroutines for Asynchronous Requests:

Kotlin coroutines provide a powerful and elegant way to make asynchronous network requests in Jetpack Compose. By using suspend functions and coroutines, you can write asynchronous code in a sequential style, making it more readable and easier to maintain.

Here's how you can make an asynchronous network request using Retrofit and coroutines:

```
viewModelScope.launch { // Launch a coroutine
    val response = apiService.getPosts()
    if (response.isSuccessful) {
        val posts = response.body()
        // Update UI with the retrieved posts
    } else {
        // Handle the error
    }
}
```

(The code launches a coroutine, fetches data using apiService.getPosts(), checks if the request was successful, and updates the UI (or handles the error) accordingly.)

In this example:

1. We launch a coroutine using viewModelScope.launch. This ensures that the coroutine is tied to the lifecycle of the ViewModel and will be automatically cancelled if the ViewModel is cleared.

2. We call `apiService.getPosts()`, which is a suspend function that performs the network request asynchronously.
3. We check if the response was successful using `response.isSuccessful`.
4. If successful, we get the list of posts from `response.body()` and update the UI.
5. If not successful, we handle the error appropriately (e.g., by displaying an error message to the user).

Key Points:

- Retrofit handles the underlying details of network communication, allowing you to focus on your app's logic.
- Use asynchronous requests with coroutines to keep your UI responsive during network operations.
- Handle errors gracefully to provide a good user experience.

In the next sections, we'll delve into the details of handling responses and error management with Retrofit, ensuring that your app can robustly communicate with your backend services.

Handling Responses with Retrofit

After making a network request with Retrofit, the next crucial step is handling the response from the server. Retrofit excels at this by automatically parsing responses into your desired data structures, allowing you to focus on using the data in your Jetpack Compose UIs.

Response Types:

Retrofit can handle responses in various formats, including:

- **JSON (JavaScript Object Notation):** The most common format for web APIs, JSON is a lightweight and easily parsable data interchange format.
- **XML (eXtensible Markup Language):** While less common than JSON, some APIs still use XML for data exchange.
- **Plain Text:** If your API returns plain text, you can work with it as a string.
- **Other Formats:** Retrofit is extensible, so you can create custom converters for other formats like Protocol Buffers.

Defining Data Classes for JSON/XML Responses:

To represent the structure of JSON or XML responses, you typically define Kotlin data classes that mirror the structure of the data. This makes it easier to access and use the data in your code.

Example: User Data Class for JSON:

```
data class User(
    val id: Int,
    val name: String,
    val email: String
)
```

Example: Post Data Class for XML:

```
@XmlRootElement(name = "post")
data class Post(
    @XmlElement(name = "id") val id: Int,
    @XmlElement(name = "title") val title: String,
    @XmlElement(name = "body") val body: String
```

)

Retrofit's Automatic Parsing (Converters):

Retrofit uses **converters** to automatically parse the response data into your data classes. The converter you choose depends on the response format:

- **Gson Converter:** GsonConverterFactory is a popular choice for JSON.
- **Moshi Converter:** MoshiConverterFactory is an alternative JSON converter.
- **SimpleXml Converter:** SimpleXmlConverterFactory is used for XML.
- **Scalars Converter:** ScalarsConverterFactory is used for plain text or other simple data types.

You add the converter to your Retrofit instance during setup (as shown in the previous section). Retrofit will then use the converter to parse the response body and create an instance of your data class.

Accessing Parsed Data in Composables:

Once the response is parsed, you can easily access and use the data within your composable functions. Here's an example:

```
@Composable
fun UserScreen(userId: Int, apiService: ApiService) {
    var user by remember { mutableStateOf<User?>(null) }

    LaunchedEffect(key1 = userId) { // Fetch user when userId changes
        user = apiService.getUser(userId) // Make the API call
    }

    user?.let { // Display user data if available
        Text("Name: ${it.name}")
        Text("Email: ${it.email}")
    }
}
```

In this example, the UserScreen composable makes a network request to fetch a user's details and displays them in Text composables.

Key Points:

- Retrofit handles parsing of different response formats using converters.
- Define data classes to match the structure of your JSON or XML responses.
- Use collectAsState (with Flows) or LaunchedEffect to make network requests and update the UI with the parsed data.

By understanding how Retrofit handles responses and leverages converters, you can seamlessly integrate network data into your Jetpack Compose UIs, creating dynamic and data-driven applications.

Error Handling with Retrofit

Network requests are inherently prone to failures. Whether it's due to a lost connection, a server error, or incorrect request parameters, your Jetpack Compose app needs to be prepared to handle these errors gracefully. Retrofit provides robust error handling mechanisms to help you create a resilient and user-friendly experience.

The Importance of Graceful Error Handling:

Robust error handling is essential for several reasons:

- **User Experience:** No one likes an app that crashes or displays cryptic error messages. Proper error handling allows you to provide informative and helpful feedback to the user when something goes wrong.
- **Data Integrity:** Errors in network requests can lead to data inconsistencies or loss. Proper handling ensures that your app's data remains valid and reliable.
- **Recovery:** Some errors, like temporary network outages, can be recovered from. Implementing retry mechanisms can make your app more reliable.

Retrofit's Error Handling Mechanisms:

Retrofit provides two primary mechanisms for error handling:

1. **Exceptions:** When a network request fails, Retrofit throws an HttpException (or a subclass like IOException for connection errors). You can catch these exceptions using try-catch blocks in your coroutines and handle them accordingly.
2. **Response Codes:** Retrofit's Response object provides a isSuccessful property to check if the request was successful (status code 200-299). You can also access the response code (code()) to handle specific error scenarios (e.g., 404 Not Found, 500 Internal Server Error).

Using Response Codes:

Response codes provide valuable information about the nature of an error:

- **2xx (Success):** The request was successful.
- **4xx (Client Error):** The request was invalid (e.g., 404 Not Found, 401 Unauthorized).
- **5xx (Server Error):** The server encountered an error (e.g., 500 Internal Server Error).

You can use a when expression to handle different response codes:

```
when (response.code()) {
    in 200..299 -> { /* Success */ }
    401 -> { /* Unauthorized */ }
    404 -> { /* Not Found */ }
    500 -> { /* Internal Server Error */ }
    else -> { /* Other errors */ }
}
```

Examples:

Displaying Error Messages:

```
try {
    val response = apiService.getUser(123)
    // ... handle successful response
} catch (e: HttpException) {
    val errorMessage = when (e.code()) {
        404 -> "User not found"
        else -> "An error occurred"
    }
    // Display the errorMessage to the user
}
```

Retrying Failed Requests:

```
var retryCount = 0

suspend fun fetchData() {
    try {
        // ... make network request
    } catch (e: Exception) {
        if (retryCount < MAX_RETRY_COUNT) {
            retryCount++
            delay(RETRY_DELAY) // Wait before retrying
            fetchData()
        } else {
            // Handle the error (e.g., display an error message)
        }
    }
}
```

Key Points:

- Always handle network errors to provide a good user experience.
- Use `try-catch` blocks to catch exceptions and response codes to differentiate error types.
- Consider implementing retry mechanisms for recoverable errors.

By proactively handling network errors, you can create robust Jetpack Compose applications that gracefully handle unexpected situations and maintain data integrity.

Best Practices and Advanced Retrofit Features

While the basics of Retrofit enable you to make network requests and handle responses effectively, there's much more you can do to optimize your networking code and enhance your app's capabilities. Let's delve into some best practices and explore advanced Retrofit features.

Best Practices for Designing REST APIs and Working with Retrofit:

- **Clear API Design:** Design your API endpoints with clarity and consistency. Use meaningful resource names, HTTP verbs, and status codes.
- **Documentation:** Provide comprehensive documentation for your API, detailing endpoints, request/response formats, error codes, and authentication requirements.
- **Versioning:** Implement versioning for your API to allow for backward compatibility when you make changes.
- **Security:** Prioritize security by using HTTPS, input validation, and appropriate authentication mechanisms.
- **Rate Limiting:** Consider implementing rate limiting to protect your server from excessive requests.
- **Caching:** Utilize caching mechanisms to store responses locally and reduce network traffic.

Advanced Retrofit Features:

- **Interceptors:** Interceptors are powerful tools that allow you to modify requests or responses before they are processed. You can use interceptors to add authentication headers, log request/response details, or even retry failed requests.

```
val loggingInterceptor = HttpLoggingInterceptor().apply {
    level = HttpLoggingInterceptor.Level.BODY // Log request and response
bodies
```

```
    }

    val client = OkHttpClient.Builder()
        .addInterceptor(loggingInterceptor)
        .build()

    val retrofit = Retrofit.Builder()
        // ... other configurations ...
        .client(client)
        .build()
```

- **Custom Converters:** If you need to work with data formats that Retrofit doesn't support out of the box (e.g., Protocol Buffers), you can create custom converters to handle the serialization and deserialization of your data.
- **RxJava Integration:** Retrofit can be integrated with RxJava to create a reactive data flow. You can use RxJava's operators to transform and combine network requests and handle responses in a more declarative manner.

Integration with Jetpack Compose Components:

- **ViewModel:** ViewModels are a natural place to encapsulate your network request logic. You can inject a Retrofit ApiService instance into your ViewModel using Hilt and launch coroutines to fetch data from the network.
- **LiveData or StateFlow:** Use LiveData or StateFlow in your ViewModel to expose the network response data to your composable functions. This allows your UI to update automatically when new data is available.
- **Hilt:** Hilt makes it easy to inject dependencies like Retrofit instances and API services into your ViewModels and composables.

Example: Integrating Retrofit with ViewModel and Hilt:

```
@HiltViewModel
class MyViewModel @Inject constructor(
    private val apiService: ApiService
) : ViewModel() {

    private val _data = MutableStateFlow<MyData?>(null)
    val data: StateFlow<MyData?> = _data.asStateFlow()

    fun fetchData() = viewModelScope.launch {
        _data.value = apiService.getData()
    }
}
```

In this example, the MyViewModel injects the ApiService instance using Hilt and fetches data from the network using a coroutine. The data state variable is exposed using StateFlow to the UI, which can then observe it to update the UI when the data changes.

By following best practices, leveraging advanced features, and integrating Retrofit with other Jetpack Compose components, you can create robust, efficient, and scalable networking code for your Android applications.

Chapter Summary

This chapter has equipped you with the knowledge and tools to become proficient in making network requests with Retrofit in your Jetpack Compose applications. You learned the significance of network communication in modern apps and explored the various types of network requests and their applications.

We introduced Retrofit as a powerful and popular HTTP client, highlighting its advantages like a declarative API, automatic JSON parsing, and seamless integration with OkHttp. You were then guided through the step-by-step process of setting up Retrofit in your project, including adding dependencies, creating a Retrofit instance, and configuring it with options like base URLs and converters.

Next, we focused on defining API endpoints using Retrofit interfaces and annotations, providing clear examples for common REST API operations. You learned how to make both synchronous and asynchronous network requests using Retrofit and coroutines, emphasizing the importance of asynchronous operations for maintaining a responsive UI.

We also delved into handling responses, explaining how Retrofit parses responses into data classes using converters, and showed you how to access and utilize the parsed data within your composable functions. The chapter concluded with a discussion of error handling in Retrofit, emphasizing the importance of gracefully managing network errors and providing strategies for catching exceptions and using response codes to handle different error scenarios.

With the knowledge and skills you've acquired in this chapter, you can now confidently integrate network communication into your Jetpack Compose applications, fetching data from APIs, handling responses, and gracefully dealing with errors. In the next chapter, we will continue our journey by exploring navigation within Jetpack Compose apps.

Section G:
Navigation and App Architecture

Navigating Between Screens with Jetpack Compose Navigation

Outline

- Understanding Navigation in Mobile Apps
- Jetpack Compose Navigation Library
- Setting Up Navigation in Your Project
- Creating a Navigation Graph
- Navigating with NavController
- Passing Data Between Screens
- Navigating with Arguments
- Nested Navigation
- Advanced Navigation Scenarios
- Chapter Summary

Understanding Navigation in Mobile Apps

Navigation is the cornerstone of user experience in mobile apps. It's the mechanism that allows users to move seamlessly between different screens, access various features, and accomplish their goals within your app. A well-designed navigation system is intuitive, efficient, and enhances the overall usability of your application.

Why Navigation Matters:

- **User Flow:** Navigation defines the paths users can take through your app. It guides them from the initial screen to their desired destination, whether it's viewing a product, reading an article, or completing a purchase.
- **Information Architecture:** Navigation reflects the structure of your app's content and features. A clear navigation system helps users understand the organization of information and find what they're looking for easily.
- **Engagement:** Smooth and intuitive navigation keeps users engaged by allowing them to explore different sections of your app without friction.

Common Navigation Patterns:

There are several well-established navigation patterns in mobile app design:

- **Stacks:** A stack-based navigation model is like a stack of papers, where you can add or remove screens. This is often used for hierarchical navigation, where screens are linked in a parent-child relationship (e.g., a list of products leading to a product detail screen).

- **Tabs:** Tabs provide quick access to different sections or features of your app. They are typically displayed at the bottom of the screen and allow users to switch between different sections with a single tap.
- **Drawers (Side Navigation):** Drawers are hidden menus that slide out from the side of the screen. They are often used to provide access to less frequently used features or settings.

Challenges in Navigation:

Managing navigation can become complex as your app grows:

- **Complex Flows:** Apps with numerous screens and nested navigation can lead to intricate navigation flows that are difficult to maintain.
- **Passing Data:** Sending data between screens during navigation can be tricky, especially when dealing with different navigation patterns or complex data structures.
- **Back Navigation:** Ensuring a smooth and intuitive back navigation experience can be challenging, especially when handling nested navigation or navigating from deep links.

Navigation Libraries to the Rescue:

Navigation libraries, such as the Jetpack Compose Navigation library, simplify the implementation and management of navigation in your apps. They provide:

- **Declarative Navigation:** Define your navigation structure in a declarative way using composables and navigation graphs.
- **Type Safety:** Ensure that you're navigating to valid destinations and passing the correct types of arguments.
- **Lifecycle Management:** Automatically handle the lifecycle of destinations and manage back stack operations.
- **Data Passing:** Facilitate the passing of data between screens using arguments or shared ViewModels.

In the following sections, we'll dive deeper into the Jetpack Compose Navigation library, exploring its core components and how to implement various navigation patterns to create a seamless and user-friendly experience in your apps.

Jetpack Compose Navigation Library

The Jetpack Compose Navigation library is the official and recommended solution for handling navigation in your Jetpack Compose applications. It provides a powerful, flexible, and type-safe way to define and manage your app's navigation flows.

Why Choose Jetpack Compose Navigation?

This library offers several compelling benefits:

- **Declarative Navigation:** Like the rest of Jetpack Compose, navigation is defined in a declarative style. You describe your app's navigation structure using composables and a navigation graph, making it easy to reason about and maintain.
- **Type Safety:** The library leverages Kotlin's type system to ensure type safety when navigating between destinations. You can define arguments for your destinations, and the library will enforce that the correct types are passed during navigation.
- **Seamless Compose Integration:** Jetpack Compose Navigation is built specifically for Compose. It works seamlessly with composable functions, state management, and other Compose concepts, providing a cohesive development experience.

- **Lifecycle Awareness:** The library handles the lifecycle of your composable destinations, ensuring that they are created and destroyed at the appropriate times during navigation.
- **Flexibility:** You can implement various navigation patterns, including stacks, tabs, and drawers, with ease. The library also supports nested navigation, deep links, and more advanced scenarios.

Core Components of the Library:

- **NavHost:** The NavHost composable is the central container for your navigation graph. It holds the composable destinations and manages the navigation state.
- **NavController:** The NavController is the object you use to trigger navigation actions. It provides methods like navigate to move to a new destination and popBackStack to navigate back.
- **NavBackStackEntry:** Represents an entry in the navigation back stack. It holds information about the current destination, its arguments, and its lifecycle state. You can use NavBackStackEntry to observe changes in the current back stack entry and extract arguments.
- **NavGraphBuilder:** A DSL (Domain-Specific Language) used to define your navigation graph. You use this builder to create destinations and actions within your navigation graph.

In the following sections, we'll delve deeper into these core components and show you how to create navigation graphs, navigate between screens, pass data, and handle various navigation scenarios in your Jetpack Compose applications.

Setting Up Navigation in Your Project

Before you can start defining your navigation structure, you need to add the Jetpack Compose Navigation library to your project and set up a NavController. Let's go through the steps involved:

1. **Add the Dependency:**

   Open your module-level build.gradle file (usually app/build.gradle) and add the following dependency in the dependencies block:

   ```
   implementation("androidx.navigation:navigation-compose:2.7.5")
   ```

   (Ensure you're using the latest stable version, you can look up the latest version in the official documentation)

2. **Create a NavController:**

   In your main activity or the composable where you want to initiate navigation, create a NavController instance using the rememberNavController composable function:

   ```
   @Composable
   fun MyApp() {
       val navController = rememberNavController()
       // ... rest of your composable code
   }
   ```

   The rememberNavController function creates and remembers the NavController across recompositions, ensuring that the navigation state is preserved.

3. **Set Up the NavHost:**

The NavHost composable acts as a container for your navigation graph. You provide it with the `navController` you created and the starting destination of your navigation graph:

```
NavHost(navController = navController, startDestination = "home") {
    // Define your navigation graph here
}
```

(Replace `"home"` with the route of your actual starting destination)

The NavHost composable will manage the back stack and display the appropriate composable based on the current navigation state.

Example: Basic Setup

```
@Composable
fun MyApp() {
    val navController = rememberNavController() // Create NavController

    NavHost(navController = navController, startDestination = "home") {
        composable("home") { HomeScreen(navController) } // Define a home
screen destination
        // Add more composable destinations here
    }
}

@Composable
fun HomeScreen(navController: NavController) {
    // ... composable content for the home screen ...
}
```

(The code is a basic example of setting up navigation in Jetpack Compose using `rememberNavController` and `NavHost`.)

By setting up the `NavController` and the `NavHost`, you create the infrastructure necessary for defining your navigation graph and implementing various navigation patterns in your Jetpack Compose application.

Creating a Navigation Graph

A **navigation graph** is the blueprint for how users navigate through your app. It visually represents the screens in your app (destinations) and the paths or actions that lead from one screen to another. In Jetpack Compose, you define this graph using the `NavGraphBuilder` DSL within the `NavHost` composable.

The Concept of a Navigation Graph:

Think of a navigation graph as a flowchart. Each node in the flowchart represents a screen, and the arrows between nodes represent the actions (like button clicks or navigation calls) that trigger the transition from one screen to the next. The navigation graph encapsulates the structure of your app's navigation flow.

Creating a Navigation Graph with `NavGraphBuilder`:

Within the `NavHost` composable, you use a lambda function with a `NavGraphBuilder` receiver to define your navigation graph. This builder provides several composable functions to create destinations and actions:

- **composable:** Defines a standard composable destination (a screen in your app).
- **dialog:** Defines a dialog destination.
- **navigation:** Creates a nested navigation graph, allowing you to group destinations hierarchically.

```
NavHost(navController = navController, startDestination = "home") {
    composable("home") { HomeScreen(navController) }
    composable("profile") { ProfileScreen(navController) }
    composable("settings") { SettingsScreen(navController) }
}
```

(The code is a navigation graph with three screens - home, profile, and settings.)

Defining Destinations and Actions:

Within the `NavGraphBuilder` block, you use the `composable` function to create destinations. Each destination is associated with a unique route, which is a string identifier (e.g., "home," "profile," "settings"). You also provide a composable lambda that defines the UI content for that destination.

```
composable("profile/{userId}", arguments = listOf(navArgument("userId") { type
= NavType.IntType })) {
    // Code to fetch user details and display it.
}
```

(This creates a profile screen composable destination. It has one argument named 'userId' which is of integer type.)

To create actions (transitions between destinations), you use buttons, navigation icons, or other UI elements that trigger a navigation event using `navController.navigate("route")`. For example, you might have a button on the home screen that navigates to the profile screen:

```
Button(onClick = { navController.navigate("profile") }) {
    Text("Go to Profile")
}
```

Example Navigation Graph:

```
NavHost(navController = navController, startDestination = "home") {
    composable("home") { HomeScreen(navController) }
    composable("profile") { ProfileScreen(navController) }
    composable("settings") { SettingsScreen(navController) }

    navigation(startDestination = "profile", route = "user") { // Nested
navigation
        composable("profile") { ProfileScreen(navController) }
        composable("edit_profile") { EditProfileScreen(navController) }
    }
}
```

(The code is of a navigation graph with nested navigation. The starting screen is the "Home" screen. The user can navigate from the Home screen to the Profile screen using a button on the Home screen. The user can also navigate to the Settings screen from the Home screen. The Profile screen has a nested navigation graph that allows the user to navigate to the Edit Profile screen. The Edit Profile screen allows the user to edit their profile information.)

In this example, we have a nested navigation graph for the "user" section of the app, where you can navigate between the "profile" and "edit_profile" screens.

By designing a well-structured navigation graph, you create a clear path for your users to explore your app's content and features. This improves the overall user experience and makes your app more intuitive and enjoyable to use.

Navigating with NavController

The `NavController` is your trusty navigator in Jetpack Compose. It's the object you'll use to guide users through your app's navigation graph, seamlessly transitioning between screens. Let's dive into how to use this powerful tool.

The `NavController`: Your Navigation Command Center

The NavController is typically obtained using the `rememberNavController` function within your composable functions. It serves as the central control point for all navigation actions.

```
@Composable
fun HomeScreen(navController: NavController) {
    // ... your composable content ...
}
```

The `navigate` Function: Setting Sail

The primary way to initiate navigation is through the NavController's `navigate` function. You provide it with the route of the destination you want to navigate to:

```
navController.navigate("profile") // Navigate to the "profile" screen
```

`navigate` also supports optional arguments to customize the navigation behavior:

```
navController.navigate("profile/123") { // Navigate to the "profile" screen
with argument
    popUpTo("home") { inclusive = true } // Pop up to the "home" screen and
remove it from the back stack
    launchSingleTop = true // Ensure the destination is launched only once at
the top
}
```

(Navigates to the "profile" screen with the argument 123 as a route, and then it pops back to the "home" screen, removing it from the back stack. The navigation is performed in a way that the destination screen is only launched once at the top of the back stack, even if it was already at the top.)

The `popBackStack` Function: Charting a Return

To navigate back to the previous screen, use the `popBackStack` function:

```
navController.popBackStack() // Navigate back to the previous screen
```

You can also pop up to a specific destination in the back stack:

```
navController.popBackStack("home", inclusive = false) // Pop back to the
"home" screen, but don't remove it
```

Examples: Navigating Based on User Actions:

```
Button(onClick = { navController.navigate("settings") }) { // Navigate to
settings on button click
    Text("Go to Settings")
}

Icon(
    imageVector = Icons.Filled.ArrowBack,
    contentDescription = "Back",
    modifier = Modifier.clickable { navController.popBackStack() } // Navigate
back on icon click
)
```

Examples: Navigating Based on Application Logic:

```
val isLoggedIn = // ... some logic to determine if the user is logged in
if (isLoggedIn) {
    navController.navigate("home")
} else {
    navController.navigate("login")
}
```

By understanding the NavController's capabilities and using the navigate and popBackStack functions, you can create intuitive and flexible navigation experiences within your Jetpack Compose applications.

Passing Data Between Screens

As you build more complex apps with multiple screens, the need to pass data between composables becomes increasingly common. You might need to send data from one screen to another (e.g., when a user selects an item from a list and you want to display its details on the next screen) or share data between sibling composables.

Challenges of Passing Data:

Passing data between composables in Jetpack Compose can be tricky due to the following challenges:

- **Composable Lifecycle:** Composables are transient. They are created and destroyed as needed during recomposition. This means you can't simply store data in a composable and expect it to be available when you navigate to another screen.
- **Unidirectional Data Flow:** Jetpack Compose promotes a unidirectional data flow model, where data flows down from parent composables to child composables. This can make it challenging to pass data back up the hierarchy.
- **Navigation State:** The current state of the navigation back stack needs to be managed and accessed to retrieve passed data.

Using `rememberNavController().currentBackStackEntryAsState()`:

To overcome these challenges, Jetpack Compose provides a powerful tool: `rememberNavController().currentBackStackEntryAsState()`. This composable function allows you to:

1. **Observe Current Back Stack Entry:** Keep track of the current destination (screen) and its arguments in the navigation back stack.
2. **Extract Arguments:** Retrieve arguments passed during navigation to the current destination.

Let's see how this works in practice:

```
@Composable
fun MyComposable(navController: NavController) {
    val backStackEntry by navController.currentBackStackEntryAsState()

    // Retrieve the argument from the back stack entry
    val myArg = backStackEntry?.arguments?.getString("myArg")

    // ... use the myArg value in your composable ...
}
```

In this example:

- We use `rememberNavController()` to get an instance of `NavController`.
- `navController.currentBackStackEntryAsState()` gives a `State` object that holds the current `NavBackStackEntry`.
- We use `backStackEntry?.arguments?.getString("myArg")` to get the value of the `"myArg"` argument passed during navigation, if it exists.

Passing Data as Arguments:

To pass data between screens, you can use arguments in your navigation graph. This involves:

1. **Defining Arguments:** When creating a destination using `composable`, you can define arguments using the `arguments` parameter and `navArgument`.

   ```
   composable(
       "profile/{userId}",
       arguments = listOf(navArgument("userId") { type = NavType.StringType })
   ) { backStackEntry ->
       // Extract the userId argument from the backStackEntry
       val userId = backStackEntry.arguments?.getString("userId")
   }
   ```

2. **Passing Arguments:** When navigating to the destination, you provide the arguments as part of the route:

   ```
   navController.navigate("profile/$userId") // Pass the userId as an argument
   ```

Retrieving Arguments in the Destination Composable:

In the destination composable (the screen you're navigating to), you can retrieve the arguments from the `NavBackStackEntry` using `arguments` property, as shown in the previous example.

Key Points:

- Passing data between screens is essential for dynamic UIs.
- `rememberNavController().currentBackStackEntryAsState()` allows you to observe and extract arguments from the current back stack entry.
- Define arguments in your navigation graph and pass them as part of the route when navigating.
- Retrieve and use the passed arguments in the destination composable.

By mastering these techniques, you can effectively share information between your composables and create a seamless navigation experience for your users.

Navigating with Arguments

Navigation arguments are a powerful mechanism for passing data between composables during navigation in Jetpack Compose. They allow you to send information from one screen to another in a type-safe and structured manner. Let's delve into the details of how to use navigation arguments effectively.

The Concept of Arguments:

Think of navigation arguments as parameters that you pass to a composable destination (a screen in your app). These arguments can be of various types, such as strings, integers, booleans, or even custom data classes. When you navigate to a destination, you include the arguments as part of the route, and they are then available for the destination composable to use.

Defining Arguments in Your Navigation Graph:

You define arguments for your composable destinations within your navigation graph using the `navArgument` function. Here's how you would define an argument called `itemId` of type `Int` for a destination with the route `item_details/{itemId}`:

```
composable(
    "item_details/{itemId}",
    arguments = listOf(navArgument("itemId") {
        type = NavType.IntType
        defaultValue = -1 // Optional default value
    })
) { backStackEntry ->
    // Extract the itemId from the backStackEntry
    val itemId = backStackEntry.arguments?.getInt("itemId") ?: -1
    // ... use the itemId to fetch item details and display them ...
}
```

In this example, the `navArgument` function defines the argument's name (`itemId`), its type (`NavType.IntType`), and an optional `defaultValue`. The `type` is important for ensuring type safety and proper parsing of the argument value.

Passing Arguments During Navigation:

When navigating to a destination that expects arguments, you include the arguments as part of the route. For example, to navigate to the `item_details` screen with an `itemId` of 5, you would do this:

```
navController.navigate("item_details/5")
```

Retrieving Arguments in the Destination Composable:

In the destination composable (`item_details` in this case), you can retrieve the passed arguments from the `NavBackStackEntry`. You'll need to get a reference to the `NavBackStackEntry` of the current destination using `rememberNavController().currentBackStackEntryAsState()` as explained in the last section.

Here's how you can extract the `itemId` argument in the `item_details` composable:

```
@Composable
fun ItemDetailsScreen(navController: NavController) {
    val backStackEntry by navController.currentBackStackEntryAsState()

    // Extract the itemId from the back stack entry
    val itemId = backStackEntry?.arguments?.getInt("itemId") ?: -1

    // ... use the itemId to fetch the item details and display them ...
}
```

Example: Navigating with Arguments

In a product listing screen:

```
Button(onClick = { navController.navigate("item_details/${product.id}") }) {
    Text("View Details")
}
```

(The code is to navigate to the `ItemDetailsScreen` and pass `product.id` argument.)

In the item details screen:

```
@Composable
fun ItemDetailsScreen(navController: NavController) {
    val backStackEntry by navController.currentBackStackEntryAsState()

    // Extract the itemId argument from the back stack entry
    val itemId = backStackEntry?.arguments?.getInt("itemId") ?: -1

    // ... use the itemId to fetch the item details and display them ...
}
```

(The code is to retrieve the `itemId` from the navigation arguments.)

Key Points:

- Navigation arguments offer a type-safe and structured way to pass data during navigation.
- Define arguments in your navigation graph using `navArgument`.
- Include the arguments in the route when navigating to a destination.
- Retrieve the arguments from the `NavBackStackEntry` in the destination composable.

By mastering navigation arguments, you can streamline the flow of data between your composable screens, creating a more cohesive and user-friendly application experience.

Nested Navigation

As your Jetpack Compose application grows, you might need to create hierarchical navigation structures where certain screens are grouped together within a specific section or flow. Nested navigation provides a way to organize and manage such complex navigation scenarios.

The Concept of Nested Navigation:

Imagine a shopping app with a "Home" screen, a "Shop" section, and a "Profile" section. Within the "Shop" section, users can browse categories, view product lists, and see product details. Nested navigation allows you to create a separate navigation graph specifically for the "Shop" section, making the overall navigation structure more manageable and modular.

Creating Nested Navigation Graphs:

To create a nested navigation graph, you use the `navigation` composable function within your main navigation graph. This composable function creates a new `NavHost` that's nested within the parent `NavHost`. The nested `NavHost` manages the navigation within the specific section or flow defined by the nested graph.

Here's an example:

```
NavHost(navController = navController, startDestination = "home") {
    composable("home") { HomeScreen(navController) }

    // Nested navigation graph for the "shop" section
    navigation(startDestination = "shop_home", route = "shop") {
        composable("shop_home") { ShopHomeScreen(navController) }
        composable("category/{categoryId}") { CategoryScreen(navController) }
        composable("product_list/{categoryId}") {
ProductListScreen(navController) }
        composable("product_details/{productId}") {
ProductDetailsScreen(navController) }
    }

    composable("profile") { ProfileScreen(navController) }
}
```

(The code is of a navigation graph with a nested navigation graph for the "shop" section. The starting screen is the "Home" screen. The user can navigate from the Home screen to the Shop Home screen, and then to the Category screen, the Product List screen, and the Product Details screen. The user can also navigate to the Profile screen from the Home screen.)

In this example, we have a nested navigation graph for the "shop" section of the app. This graph has its own start destination (shop_home) and several other composable destinations.

Navigating Within Nested Graphs:

To navigate within a nested graph, you use the same `navController.navigate()` function, but you prefix the route with the nested graph's route. For example, to navigate to the "category" screen within the "shop" graph, you would do this:

```
navController.navigate("shop/category/123")
```

Benefits of Nested Navigation:

- **Modularity:** Nested navigation helps you break down complex navigation flows into smaller, more manageable units. Each nested graph can be focused on a specific section or feature of your app.
- **Reusability:** You can reuse nested graphs in different parts of your app. For example, you could have a "settings" nested graph that's used in multiple places.
- **Code Organization:** Nested navigation keeps your navigation code organized and easier to understand.

By leveraging nested navigation, you can create more structured and scalable navigation systems for your Jetpack Compose applications, enhancing the overall user experience.

Advanced Navigation Scenarios

As your Jetpack Compose app grows in complexity, you'll encounter advanced navigation scenarios that require additional techniques and considerations. This section will cover some of these scenarios, such as handling deep links, customizing the navigation bar, and integrating navigation with other Compose components.

Handling Deep Links:

Deep links are URLs that can directly open specific screens within your app. They're often used for features like sharing content or launching the app from a notification.

To handle deep links in Jetpack Compose Navigation, you can use the NavDeepLink composable within your navigation graph:

```
composable(
    route = "details/{itemId}",
    deepLinks = listOf(navDeepLink { uriPattern =
"https://www.example.com/details/{itemId}" })
) { backStackEntry ->
    // ... extract itemId and display details ...
}
```

In this example, the navDeepLink function associates a URI pattern with the composable destination. When a deep link matching this pattern is clicked, the app will launch and navigate directly to the details screen, passing the itemId as an argument.

Customizing the Navigation Bar and Back Button:

You can customize the appearance of the navigation bar and back button using the TopAppBar composable and the navigationIcon parameter:

```
@Composable
fun MyScreen(navController: NavController) {
    Scaffold(
        topBar = {
            TopAppBar(
                title = { Text("My Screen") },
                navigationIcon = {
                    IconButton(onClick = { navController.popBackStack() }) {
                        Icon(Icons.Filled.ArrowBack, "Back")
                    }
                }
            )
        }
    ) { innerPadding ->
        // ... content of the screen ...
    }
}
```

Integrating Navigation with Other Components:

Jetpack Compose Navigation integrates seamlessly with other Compose components, such as:

- **Bottom Navigation:** Use BottomNavigation and BottomNavigationItem composables to create a bottom navigation bar with tabs that trigger navigation actions.

- **Navigation Drawer:** Combine `Scaffold`, `ModalDrawer`, and `NavigationRail` to create a navigation drawer that slides out from the side and contains a navigation rail for selecting destinations.

Handling Back Button Presses:

Proper handling of back button presses is crucial for a smooth user experience. Jetpack Compose Navigation automatically manages the back stack, but you might need to customize the behavior in certain scenarios:

- **Intercepting Back Presses:** You can intercept back button presses in an `Activity` or a `NavHost` and decide whether to handle the back action manually or let the Navigation library handle it.
- **Custom Back Actions:** In some cases, you might want to perform a custom action before navigating back (e.g., showing a confirmation dialog). You can use `NavController.addOnBackPressedCallback` to register a callback that's invoked when the back button is pressed.

Key Considerations:

- **State Preservation:** Use the `rememberSaveable` function to preserve state across configuration changes (like screen rotation) during navigation.
- **Navigation Arguments:** Pass data between screens using navigation arguments to ensure type safety and data integrity.
- **Nested Navigation:** Consider using nested navigation graphs to organize complex navigation flows.

By incorporating these advanced navigation techniques into your Jetpack Compose toolkit, you can create intuitive, flexible, and user-friendly navigation experiences that cater to the specific needs of your application.

Chapter Summary

This chapter has equipped you with the knowledge and skills to master navigation in your Jetpack Compose applications. You learned about the importance of navigation in mobile apps, explored common navigation patterns, and discussed the challenges of managing complex navigation flows.

We introduced the Jetpack Compose Navigation library as the recommended solution for handling navigation in Compose-based apps. You learned how to set up navigation in your project by adding the dependency, creating a `NavController`, and defining a navigation graph using the `NavGraphBuilder` DSL.

The chapter also covered how to navigate between screens using the `NavController`, passing data between composables through arguments, and organizing hierarchical navigation structures with nested navigation graphs.

Furthermore, we delved into advanced navigation scenarios, including handling deep links, customizing the navigation bar, integrating with other Compose components, and gracefully handling back button presses.

By mastering these navigation techniques, you've taken a significant step towards building comprehensive and user-friendly Jetpack Compose applications. In the next chapter, we'll shift our focus to the broader topic of app architecture and explore strategies for modularizing your Compose projects to improve maintainability and scalability.

Modularizing Your App with Multi-Module Architecture

Outline

- The Importance of Modularity
- What is Multi-Module Architecture?
- Benefits of Multi-Module Architecture
- Structuring Your Project
- Creating Modules
- Managing Dependencies
- Communication Between Modules
- Best Practices and Considerations
- Chapter Summary

The Importance of Modularity

In the realm of software development, **modularity** is a design principle that emphasizes breaking down a complex system into smaller, self-contained, and independent modules. Each module focuses on a specific aspect of the system's functionality, encapsulating its logic and data. This approach offers a plethora of benefits, especially when dealing with large and evolving applications.

What is Modularity?

Think of modularity like building with Lego blocks. Each block represents a module, a self-contained unit with a specific purpose. You can combine these blocks in various ways to create different structures. Similarly, in software development, modularity involves creating reusable components that can be assembled to form a complete application.

Challenges of Monolithic Codebases:

When an application's code is tightly interconnected and lacks clear boundaries between different functionalities, it becomes a monolithic codebase. Maintaining such codebases can be a nightmare:

- **Increased Complexity:** Monolithic codebases are inherently complex and difficult to understand. Making changes in one area can inadvertently break functionality in another, leading to a ripple effect of bugs.
- **Slow Development:** As the codebase grows, making even small changes can require extensive refactoring and testing, slowing down development cycles.
- **Limited Reusability:** Code within a monolithic structure is often intertwined, making it challenging to reuse components in other projects or parts of the application.
- **Longer Build Times:** Building a monolithic project can take a significant amount of time, especially as it grows in size. This slows down the development feedback loop.
- **Testing Challenges:** Testing becomes increasingly difficult as it's hard to isolate individual components for testing. This can lead to brittle tests that break easily.

How Modularity Addresses These Challenges:

Modularity tackles these issues head-on:

- **Reduced Complexity:** By dividing the codebase into smaller modules, you create a clear separation of concerns. Each module has a well-defined responsibility, making the code easier to understand and manage.
- **Faster Development:** Changes are localized within modules, reducing the need for extensive refactoring and testing. This accelerates development cycles and enables faster delivery of new features.
- **Improved Reusability:** Modules can be designed to be independent and reusable, allowing you to leverage them in different parts of your app or even in other projects.
- **Faster Build Times:** With modularity, you can build only the modules that have changed, significantly reducing build times and improving developer productivity.
- **Simplified Testing:** Modules can be tested independently, making it easier to write focused and reliable tests.

Benefits in Jetpack Compose:

In the context of Jetpack Compose, modularity brings additional advantages:

- **UI Component Reusability:** You can create reusable composable components (e.g., custom buttons, cards, or lists) that can be shared across different screens or even different projects.
- **Feature Isolation:** Modules can be used to isolate features, making it easier to manage dependencies and update individual features without affecting the entire app.
- **Parallel Development:** Different teams or developers can work on separate modules independently, improving collaboration and accelerating development.

By embracing modularity in your Jetpack Compose projects, you unlock a host of benefits that empower you to build more maintainable, scalable, and efficient Android applications.

What is Multi-Module Architecture?

In the realm of Android app development, a multi-module architecture is a strategic approach to organizing your project. Instead of lumping all your code into a single, monolithic module, you divide it into smaller, more manageable units called modules. Each module serves a specific purpose and encapsulates a distinct set of functionalities, promoting better code organization, maintainability, and scalability.

Dividing Your App into Gradle Modules:

At the core of multi-module architecture lies the concept of Gradle modules. Gradle is the build system used in Android Studio, and modules are the building blocks within a Gradle project. Each module is essentially a mini-project with its own `build.gradle` file, source code directory, and resources.

By splitting your app into multiple modules, you create a clear separation of concerns. Each module can focus on a particular aspect of your app, such as:

- **App Module:** This is the main module that contains the core application code, including activities, composables, and other UI-related components.
- **Feature Modules:** Each feature module encapsulates the code for a specific feature of your app, such as login, profile, or product catalog.
- **Data Modules:** Data modules handle data access and persistence, including repositories, data sources, and database interactions.
- **Shared Modules:** Shared modules contain code that's common to multiple modules, such as utility functions, UI components, or network-related logic.

Module Dependencies:

Modules can depend on each other, creating a dependency graph that defines the relationships between them. For instance, the app module might depend on several feature modules, which in turn might depend on data modules. Gradle manages these dependencies, ensuring that the necessary code and resources are included during the build process.

Independent Development, Testing, and Maintenance:

One of the significant advantages of multi-module architecture is that each module can be developed, tested, and maintained independently. This modularity brings several benefits:

- **Parallel Development:** Multiple developers can work on different modules simultaneously without stepping on each other's toes.
- **Faster Build Times:** Gradle can incrementally build only the modules that have changed, reducing build times significantly.
- **Targeted Testing:** You can write tests specifically for each module, making your test suite more focused and easier to maintain.
- **Reusability:** Modules can be reused in other projects, promoting code sharing and reducing redundant effort.

Visual Representation:

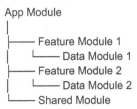

```
App Module
|
├───── Feature Module 1
|     └───── Data Module 1
├───── Feature Module 2
|     └───── Data Module 2
└───── Shared Module
```

(The figure depicts the hierarchy of modules with app module at the top and feature modules and shared module at the bottom. The data modules are sub-modules of feature modules.)

By adopting a multi-module architecture in your Jetpack Compose projects, you can create a well-structured, scalable, and maintainable codebase. It's a powerful approach that empowers you to build complex Android apps with greater efficiency and confidence.

Benefits of Multi-Module Architecture

Adopting a multi-module architecture in your Jetpack Compose projects offers a host of advantages that significantly enhance your development workflow and the overall quality of your app. Let's delve into the key benefits:

1. **Improved Code Organization and Maintainability:**
   A well-structured multi-module architecture organizes your codebase into cohesive units, each with a clear purpose and well-defined boundaries. This makes it easier for you and your team to navigate the code, understand its structure, and locate specific functionalities. Changes to one module are less likely to affect others, minimizing the risk of unintended consequences.
2. **Enhanced Scalability:**
   As your app grows, adding new features or functionalities becomes simpler with a multi-module architecture. You can introduce each new feature as a separate module, keeping your codebase well-organized and preventing it from becoming a monolithic mess. This approach also makes it easier to manage dependencies and ensures that changes to one feature don't inadvertently break others.
3. **Faster Build Times:**
   One of the most significant pain points in large Android projects is slow build times. With a

multi-module architecture, Gradle can intelligently rebuild only the modules that have changed, drastically reducing the time it takes to compile your code. This faster feedback loop allows you to iterate more quickly and efficiently.

4. **Improved Testability:**

   Modules can be tested independently, making your test suite more focused and manageable. You can write unit tests for each module, ensuring that its components work correctly in isolation. Integration tests can then verify how modules interact with each other. This approach leads to more comprehensive and reliable test coverage.

5. **Increased Reusability:**

   Modules can be designed to be self-contained and reusable. This means you can leverage them in other projects or different parts of the same app, promoting code sharing and consistency. For instance, you might have a networking module that handles API calls, a UI module with reusable composables, or a data module that provides access to your database.

By embracing a multi-module architecture in your Jetpack Compose projects, you can streamline your development process, improve code quality, and create more scalable and maintainable applications. While there might be a slight learning curve in setting up and managing modules, the long-term benefits are well worth the initial investment.

Structuring Your Project

Structuring a Jetpack Compose project into multiple modules requires careful planning and consideration of your app's architecture and features. Here's a recommended approach and some common module types to get you started.

Recommended Structure:

A typical multi-module architecture for a Jetpack Compose project might look like this:

```
:app (Application Module)
├── :core (Core Module)
│   ├── :common (Common UI Module)
│   ├── :data (Data Module)
│   └── :domain (Domain Module)
├── :feature1 (Feature Module)
├── :feature2 (Feature Module)
└── :... (More Feature Modules)
```

(The figure depicts the hierarchy of modules with app module at the top and core, feature and their sub-modules at the bottom.)

Common Module Types:

- **:app (Application Module):**
  - Contains the main entry point of your application (the `MainActivity` or its Compose equivalent).
  - Responsible for bootstrapping the app, setting up dependency injection, and connecting the different modules.
  - Typically depends on other modules to provide functionality.
- **:core (Core Module):**
  - The heart of your application, containing essential components that are shared across multiple modules.
  - Can be divided into submodules for better organization:
    - **:common:** Holds common UI components (e.g., custom buttons, layouts).

- :**data:** Handles data access (e.g., repositories, data sources, Room database).
        - :**domain:** Contains business logic (e.g., use cases, interactors, data models).
- :**feature (Feature Modules):**
    - Each feature module represents a distinct feature of your app (e.g., login, profile, search, checkout).
    - Contains composables, ViewModels, and other components specific to that feature.
    - Typically depends on the :core module and potentially other feature modules.

Organizing Components Across Modules:

- **Composables:** Place UI composables in either the :core:common module (for shared components) or within the relevant :feature module (for feature-specific components).
- **ViewModels:** Typically belong to the :feature module, as they often contain logic specific to a particular feature.
- **Data Sources/Repositories:** These usually reside in the :core:data module, as they handle data access and interaction with external sources (e.g., APIs, databases).
- **Use Cases/Interactors:** If you're using a clean architecture approach, use cases (or interactors) would typically reside in the :core:domain module, as they represent the core business logic of your app.

Example Dependencies:

- :**app:** Depends on all feature modules.
- :**feature1:** Depends on :core module.
- :**core:** Depends on nothing (except external libraries).
- :**core:common:** Depends on :core module.
- :**core:data:** Depends on :core and :core:domain modules (if using clean architecture).
- :**core:domain:** Depends on nothing (except external libraries).

This structure is just a starting point, and you can customize it to fit your project's specific needs. The key is to strive for a clear separation of concerns, keeping modules focused and independent.

Creating Modules

Creating modules in Android Studio is a straightforward process that involves a few steps. Let's dive into the details and learn how to configure these modules for your Jetpack Compose project.

Step-by-Step Guide:

1. **New Module:**
    - Right-click on your project in the "Project" view in Android Studio.
    - Navigate to "New" -> "Module."
2. **Choose Module Type:**
    - Select the type of module you want to create:
        - **Android Library:** For feature modules, data modules, and shared modules.
        - **Phone & Tablet Module:** For the main app module (if you're not using an existing one).
    - Click "Next."
3. **Configure Module Settings:**
    - **Module name:** Give your module a descriptive name (e.g., "feature_login," "data," "common_ui").
    - **Package name:** Choose a package name that follows your project's naming conventions.
    - **Minimum SDK:** Set the minimum SDK version (21 or higher for Jetpack Compose).
    - Click "Finish."

Configuring `build.gradle` **Files:**

After creating a new module, Android Studio generates a `build.gradle` file for it. This file is where you configure the module's settings, dependencies, and plugins. Here's what you need to pay attention to:

- **Plugins:**
  - For Android Library modules, apply the `com.android.library` plugin.
  - For the app module, apply the `com.android.application` plugin.
  - If you're using Kotlin in your module, apply the `org.jetbrains.kotlin.android` plugin.
- **Dependencies:**
  - Add any external dependencies your module requires (e.g., Jetpack Compose libraries, Hilt, Retrofit, etc.).
  - Specify dependencies on other modules in your project using project notation (e.g., `implementation project(":core")`).
- **Other Settings:** Configure other build settings like the `compileSdk` version, `minSdk` version, and any additional configurations specific to your module.

Example `build.gradle` **for a Feature Module:**

```
plugins {
    id 'com.android.library'
    id 'org.jetbrains.kotlin.android'
    id 'kotlin-kapt' // If using kapt for annotation processing
    id 'dagger.hilt.android.plugin' // If using Hilt
}

android {
    // ... android configurations ...
}

dependencies {
    implementation project(":core")
    // ... other dependencies ...
}
```

Module Type (`com.android.application` **vs.** `com.android.library`**):**

- `com.android.application`: Use this plugin for the main app module. It generates an APK that can be installed on a device.
- `com.android.library`: Use this plugin for all other module types (feature, data, shared). It generates an AAR (Android Archive) file that can be consumed by other modules.

Key Points:

- Creating modules in Android Studio is a straightforward process through the "New Module" dialog.
- The `build.gradle` file is where you configure module-specific settings, dependencies, and plugins.
- Use the correct plugin (`com.android.application` or `com.android.library`) based on the module type.

By carefully creating and configuring your modules, you establish a well-structured foundation for your multi-module Jetpack Compose project, enabling better code organization, maintainability, and scalability.

Managing Dependencies

In a multi-module Jetpack Compose project, dependencies are the threads that connect your modules, allowing them to access and utilize functionality from each other. Gradle, the build system in Android Studio, provides robust dependency management features to simplify this process.

Gradle Dependency Management:

Gradle handles dependency management through a declarative approach. You specify the dependencies your module needs in the `dependencies` block of your `build.gradle` file, and Gradle takes care of downloading, resolving, and including those dependencies during the build process.

`implementation` **vs.** `api` **Dependencies:**

- **implementation:** This configuration is used for dependencies that should be visible only to the module itself. Other modules that depend on this module cannot see or use the `implementation` dependencies directly. This helps reduce build times, as changes to an `implementation` dependency only require rebuilding the module that depends on it.
- **api:** This configuration is used for dependencies that should be exposed to other modules that depend on this module. This means that the `api` dependencies of a module become transitive dependencies of any module that depends on it. This can increase build times but is necessary when you want to share APIs or functionalities across multiple modules.

Example:

```
// Module: app
dependencies {
    implementation project(":core")    // :core module is not exposed to other
modules
    api project(":common-ui") // :common-ui module IS exposed to other modules
}
```

```
// Module: feature_login
dependencies {
    implementation project(":common-ui") // :common-ui module can be used in
this module
    // Cannot access :core module directly
}
```

Version Catalogs (Gradle 7.0+):

Version catalogs are a powerful new feature in Gradle that allow you to centralize the management of dependency versions. Instead of hardcoding version numbers in your `build.gradle` files, you define them in a central `libs.versions.toml` file.

```
# libs.versions.toml

[versions]
compose = "1.4.0"
retrofit = "2.9.0"

[libraries]
compose-ui = { group = "androidx.compose.ui", name = "ui", version.ref = "compose"
}
```

```
retrofit = { group = "com.squareup.retrofit2", name = "retrofit", version.ref =
"retrofit" }
```

Then, in your `build.gradle` files, you can reference the versions using:

```
dependencies {
    implementation libs.compose.ui
    implementation libs.retrofit
}
```

Benefits of Version Catalogs:

- **Centralized Management:** Makes it easier to update dependency versions in one place.
- **Improved Readability:** Reduces clutter in `build.gradle` files.
- **Version Consistency:** Ensures consistent dependency versions across your project.

Key Points:

- Gradle simplifies dependency management with declarative syntax.
- Use `implementation` for dependencies used only within a module and `api` for dependencies that need to be exposed to other modules.
- Leverage version catalogs (if using Gradle 7.0+) to centralize dependency version management.

By mastering dependency management techniques, you can create a well-structured and scalable multi-module Jetpack Compose project where modules seamlessly work together while remaining maintainable and testable.

Communication Between Modules

In a multi-module Jetpack Compose architecture, effective communication between modules is essential for a cohesive and functional app. Here are the primary techniques you can employ to facilitate this communication:

1. Interfaces and Abstract Classes: Defining Contracts

Interfaces and abstract classes act as contracts that define the expected behavior of a module or component. One module can depend on the interface or abstract class provided by another module, without needing to know the concrete implementation details.

Example:

```
// In a shared module (e.g., :core)
interface UserRepository {
    suspend fun getUser(userId: String): User
}


// In a data module (e.g., :core:data)
class UserRepositoryImpl @Inject constructor(private val apiService:
ApiService) : UserRepository {
    override suspend fun getUser(userId: String): User {
        // ...implementation using ApiService...
    }
}
```

(The code is of `UserRepository` interface and its implementation `UserRepositoryImpl` class.)

In this example, the feature module depends on the `UserRepository` interface, but the actual implementation (`UserRepositoryImpl`) is provided by the data module.

2. Dependency Injection (DI): Providing Instances

Dependency injection (DI) is a powerful technique for providing instances of classes from one module to another. By using a DI framework like Hilt, you can easily inject dependencies into your ViewModels, composables, or other classes.

```
// In a ViewModel (e.g., :feature_profile)
@HiltViewModel
class ProfileViewModel @Inject constructor(
    private val userRepository: UserRepository
) : ViewModel() {
    // ... use the userRepository instance to fetch user data ...
}
```

In this example, Hilt injects an implementation of the `UserRepository` interface into the `ProfileViewModel`.

3. Shared Data Structures or Events: Broadcasting Changes

For scenarios where you need to broadcast data changes across multiple modules, you can use shared data structures like `LiveData` or `StateFlow`. Alternatively, you can use an event bus or a custom event system to propagate events between modules.

```
// In a shared module
val userLoggedInEvent = MutableSharedFlow<User>()

// In a module that wants to trigger the event
userLoggedInEvent.emit(user)

// In a module that wants to listen for the event
viewModelScope.launch {
    userLoggedInEvent.collect { user ->
        // Handle user logged in event
    }
}
```

In this example, a `SharedFlow` named `userLoggedInEvent` is used to communicate the user logged in event between modules.

Choosing the Right Technique:

The most appropriate technique for communication between modules depends on your specific use case and the nature of the data being exchanged.

- **Interfaces/Abstract Classes:** Best for defining clear contracts between modules and promoting loose coupling.
- **Dependency Injection:** Ideal for providing complex dependencies that require their own setup or configuration.
- **Shared Data/Events:** Suitable for broadcasting data changes or events across multiple modules.

By carefully selecting and implementing the right communication mechanisms, you can create a well-structured and efficient multi-module architecture for your Jetpack Compose application.

Best Practices and Considerations

Modularizing your Jetpack Compose application requires careful planning and adherence to best practices to maximize the benefits and avoid potential pitfalls. Let's explore some key considerations and strategies to ensure a successful modularization journey.

Best Practices:

1. **Single Responsibility Principle (SRP):**
   - Each module should have a clear and focused responsibility. This helps maintain a clean separation of concerns and makes modules easier to understand, test, and maintain.
   - Avoid creating modules that handle too many unrelated tasks. Instead, break them down into smaller, more specific modules.
2. **Acyclic Dependencies:**
   - Avoid circular dependencies between modules (where module A depends on module B, and module B depends on module A). Circular dependencies make your project harder to understand and can lead to build issues.
   - If you encounter a circular dependency, consider refactoring your code to break the cycle. Often, this involves introducing interfaces or abstract classes to decouple modules.
3. **Scoped Dependencies:**
   - Use appropriate scopes for dependency injection with Hilt.
   - @Singleton should be used sparingly and only for dependencies that truly need to be shared across the entire application.
   - @ActivityScoped and @ViewModelScoped are useful for dependencies that should be bound to the lifecycle of an activity or ViewModel, respectively.
4. **Thorough Testing:**
   - Write comprehensive unit and integration tests for your modules to ensure their individual correctness and proper interaction with other modules.
   - Use Hilt's testing APIs to create test-specific components and inject mock dependencies for testing module interactions.

Considerations for Adoption:

- **Initial Setup Effort:** Setting up a multi-module architecture requires some initial effort compared to a single-module project. You'll need to create modules, define their dependencies, and adjust your project structure.
- **Learning Curve:** If your team is new to modularization, there might be a learning curve as they adapt to the new project structure and best practices.

Trade-offs:

- **Increased Complexity:** While modularity offers numerous benefits, it can increase project complexity. You need to manage multiple modules, their dependencies, and their interactions.
- **Potential Overhead:** Building and maintaining multiple modules can introduce some overhead in terms of project setup, configuration, and coordination among team members.

Additional Tips:

- **Start Small:** If you're new to modularization, start with a few key modules and gradually add more as you become comfortable with the approach.
- **Refactor Iteratively:** Don't try to modularize your entire app in one go. Refactor your codebase incrementally, starting with the most logical separations.
- **Communication is Key:** Ensure clear communication among team members about module boundaries, responsibilities, and interactions to avoid conflicts and inconsistencies.

- **Documentation:** Document your module structure and dependencies clearly to make it easier for new developers to understand and contribute to the project.
- **Continuous Integration:** Set up continuous integration (CI) to automatically build and test your modules, catching integration issues early.

By following these best practices and carefully considering the trade-offs, you can successfully adopt a multi-module architecture in your Jetpack Compose projects. This approach will lead to a more organized, maintainable, and scalable codebase, allowing you to build complex Android apps with confidence and efficiency.

Chapter Summary

This chapter has illuminated the significance of modularity in building scalable and maintainable Jetpack Compose applications. You learned about the challenges of monolithic codebases and how a multi-module architecture addresses these issues by dividing your project into smaller, more focused modules.

We explored the benefits of modularity, including improved code organization, enhanced scalability, faster build times, improved testability, and increased code reusability. We also discussed a recommended project structure for Jetpack Compose, identifying common module types such as the app module, feature modules, data modules, and shared modules.

The chapter provided a step-by-step guide on creating new modules in Android Studio and configuring their `build.gradle` files. You learned the difference between `implementation` and `api` dependencies and how to use version catalogs to manage dependency versions efficiently.

We also delved into the various techniques for enabling communication between modules, including using interfaces, dependency injection with Hilt, and shared data structures or events. Lastly, we provided best practices for modularizing Jetpack Compose applications and discussed considerations for adopting this architecture.

By applying the concepts and strategies from this chapter, you are well-equipped to embark on modularizing your Jetpack Compose projects. This approach will not only make your codebase more manageable and scalable but also improve your development workflow and the overall quality of your Android applications.

Section H:
Additional Jetpack Compose Features

Testing Your Jetpack Compose UI

Outline

- Why Test Your Compose UI?
- Testing Strategies for Jetpack Compose
- The Compose Test Environment
- Writing Basic UI Tests
- Semantics and Accessibility Testing
- Snapshot Testing
- Testing User Interactions
- Integration Testing with Hilt
- Chapter Summary

Why Test Your Compose UI?

In the fast-paced world of Android development, ensuring the quality and reliability of your app is paramount. Testing is a crucial step in this process, and specifically testing your Jetpack Compose UI offers a range of benefits that contribute to a polished and user-friendly application.

Importance of Testing:

Testing your code, including your UI, is essential for the following reasons:

- **Catching Bugs Early:** Tests act as a safety net, helping you identify and fix bugs before your app reaches your users. This saves time and effort in the long run, as fixing bugs after release is often more costly and time-consuming.
- **Ensuring Correct Behavior:** Tests verify that your UI behaves as expected under various conditions and user interactions. This helps maintain the integrity and functionality of your app as it grows and evolves.
- **Improving Confidence:** Having a comprehensive test suite gives you the confidence to make changes to your codebase without fear of breaking existing functionality. This is especially important when refactoring or adding new features.

The Role of UI Testing:

UI testing, in particular, focuses on the visual and interactive aspects of your app. It helps you catch:

- **Visual Bugs:** Issues like incorrect colors, fonts, or layout problems can be easily spotted through UI testing.
- **Layout Issues:** Testing ensures that your UI elements are displayed correctly on different screen sizes and orientations.
- **Interaction Problems:** You can verify that buttons respond to clicks, text fields accept input, and other UI elements behave as expected when interacted with.

Benefits of Automated UI Testing:

Automated UI testing involves writing code to simulate user interactions and verify UI behavior. This offers several advantages over manual testing:

- **Reduced Manual Effort:** Automated tests can be run quickly and repeatedly, saving you the time and effort of manually clicking through your app to test every scenario.
- **Consistency:** Automated tests provide consistent and repeatable results, ensuring that your UI behaves the same way across different devices and configurations.
- **Regression Prevention:** As your app grows, automated UI tests help prevent regressions by quickly identifying any issues that arise from code changes.

Types of Tests:

There are various types of tests you can write for your Jetpack Compose UI:

- **Unit Tests:** Test individual composable functions in isolation.
- **Integration Tests:** Test the interaction between multiple composables.
- **End-to-End Tests:** Simulate user interactions across multiple screens and verify the overall behavior of the app.

The specific type of test you choose depends on the level of granularity and the scope of functionality you want to verify.

By investing in UI testing, you invest in the quality and reliability of your app. It helps you create a polished and user-friendly experience, reducing the risk of bugs and ensuring that your app meets the expectations of your users.

Testing Strategies for Jetpack Compose

Testing Jetpack Compose UIs involves a blend of different strategies, each with its own strengths and tradeoffs. Let's explore these approaches and discuss when to use them to ensure your app delivers a top-notch user experience.

1. Manual Testing: The Human Touch

What is it? Manual testing Involves interacting with your app just like a user would. You navigate through screens, tap buttons, enter text, and observe how the UI responds. This approach allows you to evaluate the overall user experience, including the app's visual appeal, ease of use, and intuitiveness.

Tradeoffs:

- **Pros:** Provides a real-world perspective on how users interact with your app. Can uncover usability issues and visual bugs that automated tests might miss.
- **Cons:** Time-consuming and prone to human error. Not scalable for large apps with complex interactions.

When to Use:

- **Early Development:** Manual testing is valuable in the early stages of development when you're still iterating on the UI design and user flow.
- **Exploratory Testing:** To discover unexpected behavior or usability issues that might not be covered by automated tests.
- **Visual Verification:** To check the overall look and feel of your app and ensure it aligns with your design vision.

2. Automated Testing: The Robot Assistant

What is it? Automated testing involves writing code (using frameworks like Espresso or Compose Testing) to simulate user interactions and verify that your UI behaves as expected. These tests can be run repeatedly, ensuring consistent behavior across different devices and configurations.

Tradeoffs:

- **Pros:** Efficient, repeatable, and scalable. Can cover a wide range of scenarios and edge cases. Catches regressions quickly.
- **Cons:** Requires initial setup and ongoing maintenance. Can be brittle and might not catch all visual or usability issues.

When to Use:

- **Regression Testing:** To ensure that new changes don't break existing functionality.
- **Critical User Flows:** To test essential user interactions, such as login, registration, or checkout.
- **Large Apps:** For complex apps with many screens and interactions, automated tests are essential for comprehensive coverage.

3. Snapshot Testing: The Pixel-Perfect Inspector

What is it? Snapshot testing involves capturing a visual representation (a snapshot) of your composable UI and comparing it against a reference snapshot. This helps you detect visual regressions, ensuring that your UI hasn't changed unexpectedly.

Tradeoffs:

- **Pros:** Catches unintended visual changes quickly. Provides a visual reference for your UI.
- **Cons:** Can be sensitive to small changes (e.g., minor layout adjustments). Requires careful management of reference snapshots.

When to Use:

- **Visual Regression Testing:** To ensure that changes to your code or dependencies don't introduce visual bugs or inconsistencies.
- **UI Component Library:** To ensure the consistency of reusable UI components across your app.

Choosing the Right Strategy:

The ideal testing approach for your Jetpack Compose project often involves a combination of these strategies. You might start with manual testing to get a feel for the user experience and then gradually add automated tests to cover critical flows and ensure regression prevention. You might also incorporate snapshot testing for certain components to detect visual deviations.

The specific balance of manual, automated, and snapshot testing will depend on your project's complexity, team resources, and risk tolerance. However, a well-rounded testing strategy that incorporates all three approaches will help you deliver a high-quality, reliable, and user-friendly Jetpack Compose application.

The Compose Test Environment

To test your Jetpack Compose UIs effectively, you need a specialized environment that allows you to interact with composables and verify their behavior in a controlled setting. The Compose testing library provides the `createAndroidComposeRule` function, which sets up this environment and gives you the tools to write comprehensive UI tests.

`createAndroidComposeRule`: Setting the Stage

The `createAndroidComposeRule` function creates a test rule that launches an empty activity and sets up the necessary infrastructure for Compose testing. This rule also integrates with the Android testing framework, providing access to useful features like ActivityScenario and lifecycle management.

```
@get:Rule
val composeTestRule = createAndroidComposeRule<ComponentActivity>()
```

In this example, `createAndroidComposeRule<ComponentActivity>()` creates a test rule for a simple `ComponentActivity`. You can replace `ComponentActivity` with the specific activity you want to test if you have a more complex setup.

`setContent`: Configuring Your Composable

The `setContent` method of the test rule allows you to set the content of your composable UI. This is where you place the composable function you want to test:

```
composeTestRule.setContent {
    MyComposable()
}
```

In this example, we're setting the content of the test environment to the `MyComposable` function.

`onNode` and `onAllNodes`: Finding Composables

The `onNode` and `onAllNodes` functions are your tools for finding composable elements within the test environment.

- onNode: Finds a single composable that matches a given matcher (e.g., has specific text or a certain content description).
- onAllNodes: Finds all composables that match a given matcher.

```
val button = composeTestRule.onNodeWithText("Click Me") // Find a button
with the text "Click Me"
val images = composeTestRule.onAllNodesWithTag("product_image") // Find
all images with the "product_image" tag
```

`performClick`, `performTextInput`, and Other Interactions:

Compose Testing provides various functions to simulate user interactions with your composables:

- `performClick()`: Simulates a click on a composable.
- `performTextInput(text)`: Simulates typing text into a text field.
- `performScrollTo()`: Scrolls to a specific composable.
- `performGesture` : To perform gestures

Example: Testing a Button Click:

```
@Test
fun testButtonClick() {
    composeTestRule.setContent {
        var count by remember { mutableStateOf(0) }
        Button(onClick = { count++ }) {
            Text("Click Me")
```

```
        }
    }

    composeTestRule.onNodeWithText("Click Me").performClick() // Find the
button and click it

    composeTestRule.onNodeWithText("Count: 1").assertExists() // Assert that
the count is updated
}
```

(The code is to test if the text updates when the button is clicked.)

Key Points:

- createAndroidComposeRule: Creates a test environment for your composables.
- setContent: Configures the composable under test.
- onNode, onAllNodes: Find composables by their attributes.
- performClick, performTextInput, etc.: Simulate user interactions.
- Write assertions to verify UI behavior.

By leveraging the Compose test environment and its powerful tools, you can write comprehensive UI tests that ensure the correctness and reliability of your Jetpack Compose UIs.

Writing Basic UI Tests

Let's dive into the practical aspects of writing UI tests for your Jetpack Compose components. We'll focus on basic tests that verify the presence, visibility, and content of composables, as well as how to simulate user interactions like clicks and text input.

Example 1: Testing a Simple Composable

Let's say you have a simple composable that displays a greeting message:

```
@Composable
fun Greeting(name: String) {
    Text(text = "Hello, $name!")
}
```

Here's a basic UI test for this composable:

```
@Test
fun testGreeting() {
    composeTestRule.setContent {
        Greeting("Alice")
    }

    composeTestRule.onNodeWithText("Hello, Alice!").assertExists()
}
```

In this test:

1. We use composeTestRule.setContent to set up the Greeting composable in the test environment.
2. We use onNodeWithText("Hello, Alice!") to find the Text composable with the specific greeting message.

3. We use `assertExists()` to verify that the `Text` composable exists in the UI hierarchy.

Example 2: Testing Button Clicks and State Changes

```
@Composable
fun Counter() {
    var count by remember { mutableStateOf(0) }
    Button(onClick = { count++ }) {
        Text("Count: $count")
    }
}
```

Here's how you would test the button click and state change in this composable:

```
@Test
fun testCounter() {
    composeTestRule.setContent {
        Counter()
    }

    // Initial state
    composeTestRule.onNodeWithText("Count:
0").assertExists().assertIsDisplayed()

    // Perform click
    composeTestRule.onNodeWithText("Count: 0").performClick()

    // Verify updated state
    composeTestRule.onNodeWithText("Count:
1").assertExists().assertIsDisplayed()
}
```

Example 3: Testing Text Input

```
@Composable
fun NameInput() {
    var name by remember { mutableStateOf("") }
    TextField(value = name, onValueChange = { name = it }, label = {
Text("Name") })
}
```

Here's how to test text input in this composable:

```
@Test
fun testNameInput() {
    composeTestRule.setContent {
        NameInput()
    }

    // Find the TextField and enter text

composeTestRule.onNodeWithTag("NameInputTextField").performTextInput("Alice")

    // Verify the entered text is displayed
    composeTestRule.onNodeWithText("Alice").assertExists().assertIsDisplayed()
}
```

(Make sure you have assigned the tag "NameInputTextField" to your `TextField` composable.)

Key Assertions:

- `assertExists()`: Verifies that a composable exists in the UI hierarchy.
- `assertIsDisplayed()`: Checks if a composable is currently visible on the screen.
- `assertTextEquals(text)`: Asserts that the text content of a composable matches the expected text.

Key Interactions:

- `performClick()`: Simulates a click on a composable.
- `performTextInput(text)`: Simulates typing text into a text field.
- `performScrollTo()`: Scrolls to a specific composable.

By combining these techniques, you can create a comprehensive suite of UI tests to ensure the correctness and robustness of your Jetpack Compose applications. Remember to test different scenarios, edge cases, and configurations to guarantee a seamless user experience across a variety of devices.

Semantics and Accessibility Testing

In Jetpack Compose, **semantics** are metadata that describe the meaning and functionality of your UI elements. This metadata is not visible to the user but is crucial for accessibility features like screen readers and other assistive technologies. Testing the semantics of your composables is essential to ensure that your app is usable by everyone, including people with disabilities.

Semantics and Accessibility:

Semantics provide information about:

- **Role:** What the element is (e.g., button, image, header).
- **State:** The current state of the element (e.g., enabled, disabled, checked).
- **Description:** A textual description of the element (e.g., "Play button" for a button with a play icon).
- **Actions:** The actions that can be performed on the element (e.g., click, long press).

This information allows screen readers to announce the content and functionality of your UI elements, making your app accessible to users who are blind or have low vision.

Importance of Accessibility Testing:

Accessibility testing ensures that your app is usable by everyone, regardless of their abilities. This is not only a matter of social responsibility but also a legal requirement in many regions. By testing for accessibility, you can:

- **Reach a Wider Audience:** Make your app available to a broader range of users, including those with disabilities.
- **Comply with Regulations:** Ensure your app complies with accessibility guidelines and laws.
- **Enhance Usability:** Improve the user experience for all users, as accessibility features often benefit everyone.

Testing Semantics with `SemanticsNodeInteraction`:

The Compose testing library provides the `SemanticsNodeInteraction` class to interact with and test the semantics properties of your composables. Here's an example of how you can use it:

```
@Test
fun testButtonSemantics() {
    composeTestRule.setContent {
        Button(onClick = { /* ... */ }, modifier =
Modifier.testTag("myButton")) {
            Text("Click Me")
        }
    }

    composeTestRule
        .onNodeWithTag("myButton")
        .assert(
            SemanticsMatcher.expectValue(SemanticsProperties.Role,
Role.Button)
        )
        .assert(
            SemanticsMatcher.expectValue(SemanticsProperties.Text, "Click Me")
        )
}
```

(The code is to test if the button role is `Role.Button` and its text is `Click Me`.)

In this example:

1. We find the button using onNodeWithTag.
2. We use `SemanticsMatcher.expectValue` to assert that the button has the correct role (`Role.Button`) and text ("Click Me").

Key Points:

- Semantics are essential for accessibility.
- Accessibility testing ensures your app is inclusive.
- Use `SemanticsNodeInteraction` to test semantics properties.
- Provide meaningful descriptions and actions for all UI elements.
- Refer to accessibility guidelines (e.g., WCAG) for best practices.

By incorporating accessibility testing into your Jetpack Compose development process, you can create apps that are not only visually appealing and functional but also usable by a wider range of users.

Snapshot Testing

Snapshot testing is a valuable technique in Jetpack Compose for ensuring the visual integrity of your UI. It involves capturing an image of your composable's rendered output and comparing it against a previously saved reference snapshot. This allows you to detect unintended visual changes or regressions that might occur due to code modifications or dependency updates.

How Snapshot Testing Works:

1. **Capture Snapshot:** The first time you run a snapshot test, it captures an image of the composable's current state. This image becomes the reference snapshot.
2. **Compare on Subsequent Runs:** On subsequent test runs, a new snapshot is captured and compared pixel by pixel to the reference snapshot. If any differences are found, the test fails, alerting you to a potential visual regression.

3. **Review and Update:** You then have the opportunity to review the changes. If the changes are intentional (e.g., a deliberate design update), you can update the reference snapshot to reflect the new expected appearance.

Benefits of Snapshot Testing:

- **Catch Visual Regressions:** Snapshot testing is highly effective at detecting unintended changes in the visual appearance of your UI. This helps maintain a consistent look and feel across different versions of your app.
- **Visual Documentation:** Reference snapshots serve as visual documentation of your UI, making it easier to understand how composables should look and behave.
- **Faster Feedback Loop:** Snapshot tests run quickly and provide immediate feedback if there are any visual discrepancies, allowing you to address them promptly.

Writing Snapshot Tests with `captureToImage` and `assertAgainstGolden`:

Jetpack Compose provides functions to simplify snapshot testing:

- `captureToImage()`: This function captures an image representation of a composable.
- `assertAgainstGolden`: This function compares the captured image to a reference snapshot (a "golden" image). The golden image is typically stored as a PNG file in your project's resources.

```
@Test
fun myComposableSnapshotTest() {
    composeTestRule.setContent {
        MyComposable() // The composable you want to test
    }

    composeTestRule.onRoot() // Find the root composable
        .captureToImage()
        .assertAgainstGolden("my_composable_golden") // Compare to the
golden image
}
```

(The code is to compare the image of a composable with a golden image saved in your project's resources.)

In this example:

1. We use `composeTestRule.setContent` to set up the composable.
2. We use `onRoot()` to find the root composable of the UI hierarchy.
3. We use `captureToImage()` to capture an image of the composable.
4. We use `assertAgainstGolden("my_composable_golden")` to compare the captured image to the "my_composable_golden.png" image stored in your project's resources.

Key Points:

- Snapshot testing is a powerful tool for detecting visual regressions in Jetpack Compose UIs.
- `captureToImage` and `assertAgainstGolden` simplify the process of writing snapshot tests.
- Reference snapshots act as visual documentation and help maintain UI consistency.

By incorporating snapshot testing into your testing strategy, you can catch visual bugs early, ensure the consistency of your UI across updates, and provide a valuable visual reference for your composable designs.

Testing User Interactions

Testing user interactions in Jetpack Compose involves simulating the actions a user would perform within your app and verifying that the UI responds correctly. This can range from simple button clicks to complex sequences of actions that trigger state changes, navigation, and asynchronous operations.

Testing Complex Interactions:

Let's consider an example of a screen with a button that increments a counter when clicked, and a text field for entering a name:

```
@Composable
fun CounterScreen(viewModel: CounterViewModel = viewModel()) {
    val state by viewModel.uiState.collectAsState()

    Column {
        Text(text = "Count: ${state.count}")
        Button(onClick = { viewModel.incrementCount() }) {
            Text("Increment")
        }
        TextField(value = state.name, onValueChange = {
viewModel.updateName(it) }, label = { Text("Name") })
    }
}

class CounterViewModel: ViewModel() {
    private val _uiState = MutableStateFlow(CounterUiState())
    val uiState: StateFlow<CounterUiState> = _uiState.asStateFlow()

    fun incrementCount() {
        _uiState.value = uiState.value.copy(count = uiState.value.count + 1)
    }

    fun updateName(name: String) {
        _uiState.value = uiState.value.copy(name = name)
    }
}

data class CounterUiState(val count: Int = 0, val name: String = "")
```

To test this interaction, we can simulate button clicks, text input, and verify that the UI updates accordingly:

```
@Test
fun testCounterScreen() {
    composeTestRule.setContent {
        CounterScreen()
    }

    // Initial state
    composeTestRule.onNodeWithText("Count: 0").assertExists()
    composeTestRule.onNodeWithTag("NameInputTextField").assertTextEquals("")

    // Increment the counter
    composeTestRule.onNodeWithText("Increment").performClick()
```

```
composeTestRule.onNodeWithText("Count: 1").assertExists()

    // Enter text

composeTestRule.onNodeWithTag("NameInputTextField").performTextInput("Alice")
    composeTestRule.onNodeWithText("Alice").assertExists()
}
```

Testing Navigation:

To test navigation, you can simulate user actions that trigger navigation events (like button clicks) and then verify that the correct destination is displayed:

```
@Test
fun testNavigation() {
    composeTestRule.setContent {
        // ... set up NavHost ...
    }

    composeTestRule.onNodeWithText("Go to Profile").performClick() // Navigate

    //Check if the profile screen is opened.
    composeTestRule.onNodeWithText("Profile Screen").assertExists()
}
```

(The code is to test navigation to profile screen when "Go to Profile" button is clicked.)

Testing Asynchronous Operations:

For testing asynchronous operations like data fetching, you can use idling resources or the `runTest` function to pause the test execution until the asynchronous operation completes:

```
@Test
fun testDataFetching() = runTest {
    composeTestRule.setContent {
        MyComposable()
    }

    // ... trigger data fetching ...

    composeTestRule.waitUntil {
        composeTestRule.onNodeWithText("Data loaded").exists()
    }

    // ... assert UI elements after data is loaded ...
}
```

(The code is to test if the data fetched asynchronously from server is displayed in the UI.)

Key Strategies:

- **State Observation:** Observe state variables in your ViewModels or composables using `collectAsState` or `LiveData.observeAsState` to verify that the UI updates correctly when the state changes.
- **Mocking Dependencies:** Use mock objects to simulate responses from data sources or external systems during testing.

- **Idling Resources:** If you're using Espresso, utilize idling resources to synchronize your tests with asynchronous operations.
- **TestCoroutineDispatcher:** For testing coroutines, use `TestCoroutineDispatcher` to control the execution of coroutines and simulate delays or timeouts.
- **runTest:** Use `runTest` function when your composable uses coroutines and you want to test it with a controlled dispatcher

By employing these strategies, you can write comprehensive and effective tests for your Jetpack Compose UIs, ensuring that they are robust, user-friendly, and behave correctly in the face of complex interactions and asynchronous operations.

Integration Testing with Hilt

Hilt, as a powerful dependency injection library, seamlessly integrates with your Compose UI tests, making it easier to provide the necessary dependencies to your composables and verify their interactions with other components, such as ViewModels and repositories. Let's delve into how you can leverage Hilt for comprehensive integration testing.

Integrating Hilt with Compose UI Tests:

To enable Hilt in your Compose UI tests, follow these steps:

1. **Annotate Your Test Class:** Annotate your test class with `@HiltAndroidTest`. This tells Hilt to generate a test-specific Hilt component and provides access to Hilt testing features.
2. **Use the `HiltAndroidRule`:** Add a `HiltAndroidRule` to your test class and annotate it with `@get:Rule`. This rule will manage the Hilt component's lifecycle during your tests.
3. **Inject Dependencies:** Use `@Inject` to inject the dependencies you need into your test class.

Using the `HiltAndroidRule`:

The `HiltAndroidRule` is a JUnit rule that simplifies the setup and teardown of Hilt components for testing. It ensures that the correct Hilt component is created and destroyed for each test, preventing state leakage between tests.

```
@HiltAndroidTest
class MyComposableTest {

    @get:Rule
    val hiltRule = HiltAndroidRule(this)

    @Inject
    lateinit var repository: MyRepository // Inject a repository dependency

    // ... Your test methods ...
}
```

(The code is to inject repository into the composable test class using `HiltAndroidRule`.)

Example: Integration Test with ViewModel:

Let's consider an example where you want to test a composable that interacts with a ViewModel to fetch data and display it:

```
@HiltAndroidTest
```

```
@RunWith(AndroidJUnit4::class)
class MyComposableTest {

    @get:Rule
    val hiltRule = HiltAndroidRule(this)

    @get:Rule
    val composeTestRule = createAndroidComposeRule<ComponentActivity>()

    @Inject
    lateinit var repository: MyRepository

    @Test
    fun myComposableShowsDataFromRepository() {
        // Setup
        val expectedData = Data("test data") // Example test data
        whenever(repository.getData()).thenReturn(expectedData) // Mocking the
repository's behavior
        hiltRule.inject() // Inject dependencies into the test

        // UI Test
        composeTestRule.setContent {
            val viewModel: MyViewModel = viewModel()
            MyComposable(viewModel)
        }
        composeTestRule.onNodeWithText(expectedData.text).assertExists()
    }
}
```

(The code sets up an integration test for MyComposable using Hilt and Compose Test Rule. It mocks the repository and verifies that the correct data is displayed in the composable.)

In this example:

1. We use HiltAndroidRule to inject the repository dependency into the test.
2. We mock the repository to return expectedData when its getData() function is called.
3. We set up the composable under test (MyComposable) and inject the MyViewModel.
4. We then assert that the MyComposable displays the expected data from the repository.

Key Points:

- Hilt integration simplifies testing composables that depend on injected components.
- @HiltAndroidTest and HiltAndroidRule are essential for setting up the Hilt test environment.
- Use @Inject to inject dependencies into your test class.
- Utilize mocking libraries (e.g., Mockito) to simulate the behavior of your dependencies for testing.

By effectively integrating Hilt into your Compose UI tests, you can ensure that your composables interact correctly with their dependencies, leading to more robust and reliable tests.

Chapter Summary

This chapter has illuminated the importance of testing Jetpack Compose UIs and equipped you with the essential tools and techniques to ensure the quality and reliability of your applications. You explored different testing strategies, including manual testing, automated testing, and snapshot testing, understanding their strengths and tradeoffs.

We introduced you to the Compose test environment, demonstrating how to set it up using the `createAndroidComposeRule` function. You learned how to find composables within the test environment using `onNode` and `onAllNodes`, and how to simulate user interactions like button clicks and text input using `performClick` and `performTextInput`.

We then provided examples of writing basic UI tests to verify the presence, visibility, and content of composables using assertions like `assertExists`, `assertIsDisplayed`, and `assertTextEquals`. The concept of semantics and accessibility testing was also covered, highlighting the importance of ensuring your UIs are accessible to all users.

You delved into snapshot testing, learning how it helps detect visual regressions by comparing composable snapshots against reference images. We also explored strategies for testing complex user interactions involving multiple composables and asynchronous operations like data fetching.

Finally, we discussed the integration of Hilt with your Compose UI tests, enabling seamless dependency injection for more comprehensive testing.

Armed with this knowledge, you're well-prepared to create a robust testing framework for your Jetpack Compose applications, ensuring they function correctly, look as expected, and deliver a great user experience to everyone. The next chapter will introduce you to the world of animations and transitions in Compose, adding a dynamic touch to your UIs.

Animations and Transitions in Jetpack Compose

Outline

- The Role of Animations in Modern UI/UX Design
- Basic Animation Concepts in Jetpack Compose
- Animating with `animate*AsState`
- Creating Custom Animations
- Choreographing Animations
- Using `rememberInfiniteTransition`
- Crossfading and Other Transitions
- AnimatedVisibility
- Advanced Animation Techniques
- Chapter Summary

The Role of Animations in Modern UI/UX Design

Animations are no longer a luxury in modern user interface (UI) and user experience (UX) design; they're a necessity. Animations elevate the user experience beyond the static and mundane, injecting life, dynamism, and engagement into your Jetpack Compose applications.

Importance of Animations:

- **Enhanced User Experience:** Animations make your app feel more polished, professional, and delightful to use. They create a sense of visual interest and interactivity that keeps users engaged and coming back for more.
- **Visual Feedback:** Animations provide essential visual feedback to users, confirming that their actions have been recognized and are being processed. A simple button press animation or a loading spinner can reassure users that the app is working as expected.
- **Guiding User Attention:** Animations can subtly guide the user's attention to important elements on the screen, making the interface more intuitive and easier to navigate. A gentle highlight on a new feature or a subtle animation that reveals a hidden menu can effectively draw the user's focus.
- **Making Interactions Intuitive:** Animations can make complex interactions more understandable by visually illustrating how elements on the screen are connected and how actions affect the UI. A transition that smoothly animates a list item into a detailed view, for instance, helps users understand the relationship between the two screens.

Types of Animations:

Jetpack Compose offers a wide range of animation capabilities, allowing you to create various types of animations to suit different purposes:

- **Microinteractions:** These are small, subtle animations that provide feedback for user actions, such as a button ripple effect or a subtle color change when a checkbox is toggled. Microinteractions enhance the user experience by making the interface feel more responsive and alive.
- **State Changes:** These animations accompany changes in the state of a composable, such as the expansion or collapse of a view, the transition between different states of a button, or the loading of new content. They provide visual continuity and make transitions feel natural.
- **Screen Transitions:** These animations occur when navigating between screens in your app. They can range from simple fades or slides to more elaborate custom transitions. Screen transitions help create a sense of continuity and make the navigation flow feel more seamless.

By strategically incorporating animations into your Jetpack Compose applications, you can create interfaces that are not only visually appealing but also more intuitive, engaging, and user-friendly. In the following sections, we'll delve into the technical aspects of implementing animations in Compose, exploring various animation APIs, techniques, and best practices to bring your UI to life.

Basic Animation Concepts in Jetpack Compose

Animations in Jetpack Compose are built upon a few core concepts that empower you to create dynamic and visually engaging user interfaces. Let's explore these fundamental building blocks.

State-Driven Animations:

In Compose, animations are intrinsically linked to the state of your composables. When the state of a composable changes (e.g., a button being clicked, a value being updated), Compose automatically triggers an animation to smoothly transition the UI from the old state to the new state. This declarative approach to animation simplifies your code and makes it more predictable.

Easing Curves and Durations:

- **Easing Curves:** Easing curves define the rate of change over time for an animation. They control the acceleration and deceleration of the animation, influencing how natural and smooth it feels. Compose provides various easing curves, such as `LinearEasing`, `FastOutSlowInEasing`, and `CubicBezierEasing`, each with its own characteristic motion.
- **Durations:** The duration of an animation determines how long it takes to complete. You can specify durations in milliseconds or using the `Duration` class. Shorter durations create snappy animations, while longer durations are suitable for more gradual transitions.

Implicitly Animated Values:

Jetpack Compose introduces the concept of **implicitly animated values**. These are special types of state variables that, when changed, automatically trigger an animation to smoothly transition to the new value. The animation uses the default easing curve and duration provided by the Compose framework.

Here are some examples of implicitly animated values:

- `animateFloatAsState`: For anImating `Float` values (e.g., size, opacity).
- `animateColorAsState`: For animating `Color` values.
- `animateDpAsState`: For animating Dp (density-independent pixel) values (e.g., padding, offset).

Example: Animating the Size of a Box:

```
@Composable
fun MyAnimatedBox() {
    var size by remember { mutableStateOf(50.dp) }

    Box(
        Modifier
            .size(animateDpAsState(targetValue = size).value) // Implicit
animation
            .background(Color.Blue)
            .clickable { size = if (size == 50.dp) 100.dp else 50.dp }
    )
}
```

(The code is to animate the size of a box in Jetpack Compose using `animateDpAsState`. The initial size of the box is 50.dp. When the box is clicked, the size changes to 100.dp if the current size is 50.dp, and vice versa.)

In this example, `animateDpAsState` creates an animated value that transitions smoothly between 50.dp and 100.dp whenever the `size` state variable changes.

Key Points:

- Animations in Compose are driven by state changes.
- Easing curves and durations control the timing and feel of animations.
- Implicitly animated values provide a convenient way to create smooth transitions.
- Compose handles most of the animation complexity for you.

By understanding these basic animation concepts, you're well on your way to creating engaging and visually appealing animations in your Jetpack Compose UIs. The following sections will dive deeper into creating custom animations, choreographing multiple animations, and exploring various animation techniques in Compose.

Animating with `animate*AsState`

The `animate*AsState` family of functions in Jetpack Compose are your go-to tools for creating simple yet powerful animations. They offer a convenient way to animate various types of values, such as floats, colors, sizes, and offsets, making it incredibly easy to add smooth transitions to your UI elements.

Introducing `animate*AsState` Functions:

Jetpack Compose provides several `animate*AsState` functions, each tailored for a specific data type:

- `animateFloatAsState`: For animating `Float` values (e.g., opacity, rotation).
- `animateColorAsState`: For animating `Color` values.
- `animateDpAsState`: For animating Dp (density-independent pixels) values (e.g., size, padding).
- `animateIntAsState`: For animating `Int` values (e.g., counters).
- `animateOffsetAsState`: For animating `Offset` values (e.g., position).
- `animateRectAsState`: For animating Rect values.

How `animate*AsState` Works:

These functions work by creating an animated value that smoothly transitions between the current state and the target state whenever the target state changes. They handle the animation logic for you, taking care of calculating intermediate values and applying easing curves to create a natural and pleasing animation.

The basic pattern for using `animate*AsState` is:

1. **Define Target State:** Store the target value in a state variable (e.g., `targetValue by remember { mutableStateOf(initialValue) }`).
2. **Use animate*AsState:** Call the appropriate `animate*AsState` function, passing the `targetValue` as a parameter.
3. **Apply the Animated Value:** Use the returned `value` property of the `animate*AsState` result as the input for your composable's attribute or modifier.

Examples:

Animating Size:

```
@Composable
fun MyAnimatedBox() {
    var size by remember { mutableStateOf(50.dp) }

    Box(
        Modifier
            .size(animateDpAsState(targetValue = size).value)
            .background(Color.Blue)
            .clickable { size = if (size == 50.dp) 100.dp else 50.dp }
    )
}
```

(The code is to animate the size of a box in Jetpack Compose.)

Animating Opacity:

```
@Composable
fun MyAnimatedText() {
    var showText by remember { mutableStateOf(true) }
    val alpha by animateFloatAsState(targetValue = if (showText) 1f else 0f)

    Column {
        Button(onClick = { showText = !showText }) {
            Text(if (showText) "Hide Text" else "Show Text")
        }
        Text(
            text = "Hello, world!",
            modifier = Modifier.alpha(alpha) // Animate alpha value
        )
    }
}
```

(The code is to animate the visibility of text using alpha (opacity) in Jetpack Compose.)

Animating Color:

```
@Composable
fun MyAnimatedBackground() {
    var isRed by remember { mutableStateOf(false) }
    val color by animateColorAsState(if (isRed) Color.Red else Color.Blue)

    Box(Modifier.fillMaxSize().background(color))
}
```

(This code defines a composable function `MyAnimatedBackground` that animates the background color of a box. It uses `animateColorAsState` to smoothly transition between red and blue when the boolean state `isRed` is toggled.)

By leveraging the `animate*AsState` functions and understanding the principles of state-driven animations, you can easily add smooth and engaging transitions to your Jetpack Compose UIs. These functions abstract away the complexity of animation logic, making it simple for you to create visually appealing and interactive user experiences.

Creating Custom Animations

While the `animate*AsState` functions are convenient for simple animations, Jetpack Compose offers more advanced tools that give you fine-grained control over how your UI elements move and change. Let's explore how you can create custom animations using `AnimationSpec`, `rememberInfiniteTransition`, and `Animatable`.

`AnimationSpec`: Defining the Animation's Behavior

An `AnimationSpec` defines the timing and easing of an animation. It determines how the animation progresses over time, including its duration, easing curve, and other parameters. Compose provides several built-in `AnimationSpec` implementations:

- **tween:** A simple animation that transitions between two values over a specified duration with an optional easing curve.
- **spring:** A physics-based animation that simulates a spring-like motion.
- **keyframes:** Allows you to define custom keyframes for more complex animation sequences.

```
val animationSpec = tween<Float>(
    durationMillis = 1000, // 1 second duration
    easing = LinearEasing // Linear easing curve
)
```

`rememberInfiniteTransition`: Creating Infinite Animations

The `rememberInfiniteTransition` function creates an `InfiniteTransition` object that allows you to define animations that repeat indefinitely.

```
@Composable
fun MyInfiniteAnimation() {
    val infiniteTransition = rememberInfiniteTransition()
    val color by infiniteTransition.animateColor(
        initialValue = Color.Red,
        targetValue = Color.Blue,
        animationSpec = infiniteRepeatable(
            animation = tween(durationMillis = 1000), // Each cycle takes 1
second
            repeatMode = RepeatMode.Reverse       // Reverse the animation at
the end
        )
    )

    Box(
        Modifier
            .size(100.dp)
            .background(color)
    )
}
```

In this example, the `color` value continuously animates between red and blue, creating a pulsating effect.

`Animatable`: Low-Level Animation Control

The Animatable class provides a lower-level API for creating animations. You can create an Animatable object for a specific type and then directly control its value using the animateTo function.

```
val animatedFloat = remember { Animatable(0f) }
LaunchedEffect(Unit) {
    animatedFloat.animateTo(
        targetValue = 1f,
        animationSpec = tween(durationMillis = 1000)
    )
}

// Use animatedFloat.value in your composables
```

This example animates a float value from 0 to 1 over one second.

Key Points:

- AnimationSpec: Defines the timing and easing of your animations.
- rememberInfiniteTransition: Creates infinite repeating animations.
- Animatable: Provides low-level control for creating and manipulating animated values.

By understanding and utilizing these tools, you can unlock the full potential of animations in Jetpack Compose, creating captivating and expressive user interfaces that delight your users. Remember, animation is an art, and experimenting with these techniques will help you craft unique and engaging experiences.

Choreographing Animations

While simple animations add a touch of polish to your UI, choreographing multiple animations together can create truly captivating and dynamic visual effects. In Jetpack Compose, the updateTransition and AnimatedContent composables empower you to orchestrate complex animation sequences effortlessly.

Concept of Choreographing Animations:

Choreographing animations involves coordinating the timing and behavior of multiple animations to achieve a cohesive and visually pleasing effect. Think of it like a dance performance, where different dancers move in harmony to create a beautiful spectacle. In your UI, this could involve elements fading in and out, sliding into position, or changing size and color, all in perfect synchronization.

updateTransition and AnimatedContent: Your Choreography Tools

- **updateTransition:** This composable function helps you manage the state transitions of a composable and create animations that are linked to those transitions. It provides a way to define different target states and smoothly animate between them.
- **AnimatedContent:** This composable simplifies the process of animating content changes. It automatically animates the appearance and disappearance of content based on the current state and the provided transition.

Example: Expanding and Collapsing a View:

Let's see how to choreograph animations for a view that expands or collapses when clicked:

```
@Composable
```

```
fun ExpandableCard() {
    var expanded by remember { mutableStateOf(false) }
    val transition = updateTransition(targetState = expanded, label =
"cardTransition")

    Card(modifier = Modifier.fillMaxWidth().clickable { expanded = !expanded
}) {
        Column(modifier = Modifier.padding(16.dp)) {
            Text(text = "My Expandable Card")

            // Animated Visibility
            AnimatedVisibility(visible = expanded) {
                Text(
                    text = "This is the expanded content. It shows up when the
card is expanded.",
                    modifier = Modifier.padding(top = 8.dp)
                )
            }
        }
    }
}
```

In this example:

1. We use a boolean state variable expanded to track whether the card is expanded or collapsed.
2. updateTransition creates a Transition object that manages the animation between the expanded and !expanded states.
3. The AnimatedVisibility composable animates the appearance or disappearance of the additional content based on the expanded state.

Additional Considerations:

- **Animation Timing:** You can control the duration and easing of each individual animation within the choreography to fine-tune the visual effect.
- **State Management:** Ensure that your state variables are updated correctly to trigger the appropriate transitions and animations.
- **Performance:** Avoid overusing complex animations, as they can impact performance. Keep your animations simple and optimized for your target devices.

By mastering the art of choreographing animations with updateTransition and AnimatedContent, you can create visually stunning and interactive UIs that enhance the user experience and set your Jetpack Compose applications apart.

Using rememberInfiniteTransition

The rememberInfiniteTransition function is a specialized tool in Jetpack Compose designed for creating animations that loop continuously. These infinite animations are perfect for scenarios where you want to add a touch of dynamism or visual interest to your UI, such as loading indicators, pulsating buttons, or subtle background effects.

How rememberInfiniteTransition Works:

Similar to the updateTransition function, rememberInfiniteTransition provides a Transition object. However, instead of being tied to a specific state change, this transition continues indefinitely, cycling through its animations repeatedly.

To define the animations within an infinite transition, you use the .animate* functions (e.g., animateFloat, animateColor) and specify the initial and target values for each property you want to animate. You also provide an InfiniteRepeatableSpec to define the animation's duration, easing curve, and repeat mode.

Example: Creating a Pulsating Button:

```
@Composable
fun PulsatingButton(onClick: () -> Unit) {
    val infiniteTransition = rememberInfiniteTransition()
    val scale by infiniteTransition.animateFloat(
        initialValue = 1f,
        targetValue = 1.1f, // Slightly larger scale
        animationSpec = infiniteRepeatable(
            animation = tween(durationMillis = 1000), // Each pulse takes 1
second
            repeatMode = RepeatMode.Reverse // Reverse the animation to create
a pulse
        )
    )

    Button(
        onClick = onClick,
        modifier = Modifier.scale(scale) // Apply the animated scale to the
button
    ) {
        Text("Pulse!")
    }
}
```

In this example, the button's scale property is animated to create a subtle pulsing effect. The animation continuously loops, transitioning between the initial scale of 1.0 and a slightly larger scale of 1.1.

Example: Creating a Loading Indicator:

```
@Composable
fun LoadingIndicator() {
    val infiniteTransition = rememberInfiniteTransition()
    val rotation by infiniteTransition.animateFloat(
        initialValue = 0f,
        targetValue = 360f, // Rotate a full circle
        animationSpec = infiniteRepeatable(
            animation = tween(durationMillis = 1500), // One rotation takes
1.5 seconds
            easing = LinearEasing
        )
    )

    Icon(
        imageVector = Icons.Default.Refresh,
        contentDescription = "Loading",
        modifier = Modifier.rotate(rotation) // Apply the animated rotation
```

```
    )
}
```

(The code is to create a loading indicator that continuously rotates an icon.)

In this example, the icon's `rotation` property is animated to make it spin continuously. The animation is linear and takes 1.5 seconds to complete a full rotation.

Key Points:

- `rememberInfiniteTransition` is ideal for creating animations that repeat indefinitely.
- Use the `.animate*` functions to define the properties you want to animate.
- Customize the animation behavior using `InfiniteRepeatableSpec`.

By leveraging `rememberInfiniteTransition` and experimenting with different animation specifications, you can craft captivating looping animations that add flair and interactivity to your Jetpack Compose UIs.

Crossfading and Other Transitions

Transitions in Jetpack Compose provide a way to create smooth and visually appealing changes in your UI. They can be used to animate the appearance or disappearance of elements, switch between different content states, or create seamless transitions between screens. Compose offers several built-in transitions, with `Crossfade` being a versatile and popular option.

`Crossfade`: A Smooth Transition Between Elements

The `Crossfade` composable is designed to smoothly fade between two pieces of content based on a state change. It automatically handles the fading in and out of the content, creating a seamless visual effect.

```
@Composable
fun MyCrossfade() {
    var currentPage by remember { mutableStateOf("A") }

    Column {
        Button(onClick = { currentPage = if (currentPage == "A") "B" else "A"
}) {
            Text("Switch Page")
        }

        Crossfade(targetState = currentPage) { screen ->
            when (screen) {
                "A" -> Text("Page A")
                "B" -> Text("Page B")
            }
        }
    }
}
```

In this example, the `Crossfade` composable takes the `currentPage` state as its `targetState`. When the button is clicked, the state changes, triggering a smooth fade transition between the two text composables.

Other Built-in Transitions:

Jetpack Compose offers a variety of other built-in transitions, each with its unique style:

- **Slide:** Slides content in or out from a specific direction (e.g., `Slide.InHorizontally`, `Slide.OutVertically`).
- **Fade:** Fades content in or out. You can control the duration and initial/target alpha values.
- **Scale:** Scales content up or down.
- **Rotate:** Rotates content.
- **animateContentSize Modifier:** Animates the size change of a composable based on the change in its content.

Using Transitions for Different Scenarios:

- **Animating Visibility Changes:** You can use transitions to animate the appearance and disappearance of composables when their visibility state changes:

```
AnimatedVisibility(visible = showContent, enter = fadeIn(), exit = fadeOut())
{
    MyContent()
}
```

(The code is to smoothly show `MyContent` composable on screen with `fadeIn` effect and hide it from the screen with `fadeOut` effect.)

- **Animating State Changes:** Transitions are ideal for animating the visual changes that accompany state transitions within a composable.
- **Screen Transitions:** In conjunction with the Jetpack Compose Navigation library, you can use transitions to create custom animations between screens.

Key Points:

- Transitions provide a way to animate changes in your Jetpack Compose UI.
- `Crossfade` is a versatile transition for smoothly fading between content.
- Compose offers various built-in transitions like `Slide` and `Fade`.
- You can use transitions to animate visibility changes, state changes, and screen transitions.

By incorporating transitions into your app, you can enhance the visual appeal, improve user experience, and create a more engaging and polished feel.

AnimatedVisibility

The `AnimatedVisibility` composable is a specialized tool within Jetpack Compose for elegantly animating the appearance and disappearance of UI elements. It provides a convenient way to create smooth transitions whenever a composable's visibility state changes.

How `AnimatedVisibility` Works:

`AnimatedVisibility` takes a `visible` parameter that determines whether the wrapped content should be visible or not. When the `visible` state changes, `AnimatedVisibility` automatically applies an enter transition when the content becomes visible and an exit transition when it becomes invisible.

Enter and Exit Transitions:

You have several options for the enter and exit transitions:

- **fadeIn/fadeOut:** Gradually fade in or out the content.
- **slideIn/slideOut:** Slide the content in or out from a specific direction (e.g., slideInVertically, slideOutHorizontally).
- **expandIn/shrinkOut:** Expand or shrink the content from or to a specific direction (e.g., expandVertically, shrinkHorizontally).
- **Custom Transitions:** You can create your own custom transitions using the EnterTransition and ExitTransition types.

Examples:

Fading In and Out:

```
@Composable
fun MyFadingContent() {
    var visible by remember { mutableStateOf(false) }

    Column {
        Button(onClick = { visible = !visible }) {
            Text("Toggle Visibility")
        }
        AnimatedVisibility(
            visible = visible,
            enter = fadeIn(animationSpec = tween(200)), // Fade in
            exit = fadeOut(animationSpec = tween(200))   // Fade out
        ) {
            Text("This text fades in and out")
        }
    }
}
```

(The code is to create a simple text toggle button in Jetpack Compose.)

Sliding In and Out:

```
@Composable
fun MySlidingContent() {
    // ... (similar structure as MyFadingContent)

    AnimatedVisibility(
        visible = visible,
        enter = slideInVertically(),  // Slide in from top
        exit = slideOutVertically()    // Slide out to top
    ) {
        // ... your content ...
    }
}
```

Expanding and Shrinking:

```
@Composable
fun MyExpandableContent() {
    // ... (similar structure as MyFadingContent)
```

```
    AnimatedVisibility(
        visible = visible,
        enter = expandVertically(), // Expand from top
        exit = shrinkVertically()    // Shrink to top
    ) {
        // ... your content ...
    }
}
```

(The code is to expand and shrink UI content vertically.)

Custom Transitions:

```
@Composable
fun MyCustomTransitionContent() {
    // ... (similar structure as MyFadingContent)

    AnimatedVisibility(
        visible = visible,
        enter = fadeIn() + expandVertically(), // Combine fade and expand
        exit = fadeOut() + shrinkVertically()  // Combine fade and shrink
    ) {
        // ... your content ...
    }
}
```

(The code defines a custom transition that fades in and expands the content vertically on enter, and fades out and shrinks the content vertically on exit.)

By utilizing `AnimatedVisibility`, you can effortlessly add elegant animations to the appearance and disappearance of your composable elements, enhancing the visual appeal and user experience of your Jetpack Compose applications.

Advanced Animation Techniques: Taking Your Animations Further

While Jetpack Compose provides a solid foundation for animations, you can dive deeper into more advanced techniques to create truly unique and captivating visual experiences. Let's explore some of these techniques and where you can find resources to further your animation skills.

1. `AnimatedContent`: Dynamic Content Transitions

The `AnimatedContent` composable is designed specifically for animating changes in your content. It works seamlessly with the `updateTransition` function to create smooth transitions between different UI states. You can customize the animation behavior using `ContentTransform` and `slideIntoContainer`, `slideOutOfContainer`, `fadeIn`, and `fadeOut`.

```
@Composable
fun MyAnimatedContent(currentScreen: Screen) {
    AnimatedContent(targetState = currentScreen, transitionSpec = {
        // Example: Slide transition between screens
        if (targetState.ordinal > initialState.ordinal) {
            slideInHorizontally { width -> width } + fadeIn() with
                    slideOutHorizontally { width -> -width } + fadeOut()
        } else {
            slideInHorizontally { width -> -width } + fadeIn() with
```

```
                      slideOutHorizontally { width -> width } + fadeOut()
        }.using(
            SizeTransform(clip = false) // Avoid clipping during animation
        )
    }) { screen ->
        when (screen) {
            Screen.Screen1 -> Screen1Content()
            Screen.Screen2 -> Screen2Content()
        }
    }
}
```

(The code is to create a smooth transition between screens in Jetpack Compose using
AnimatedContent.)

2. Custom Keyframes: Precision Control

The keyframes animation spec allows you to define a sequence of keyframes, each representing a
specific point in the animation with its own values and durations. This gives you precise control over the
animation's progression.

```
val animationSpec = keyframes {
    durationMillis = 2000 // Total duration
    0 to 100 with LinearEasing // From 0 to 100 over 500ms (25% of total duration)
    100 to 200 with FastOutSlowInEasing // From 100 to 200 over 1000ms (50%)
    200 to 0 with LinearEasing // From 200 to 0 over 500ms (25%)
}
```

(The code is to animate some value between 0-100-200-0 with different easings.)

3. Physics-Based Animations: Natural Motion

Physics-based animations mimic real-world physics, creating more natural and dynamic movements.
Compose's spring animation spec is a great starting point. It simulates a spring with properties like
stiffness and damping.

```
val animationSpec = spring<Float>(
    stiffness = Spring.StiffnessLow, // Less stiffness for a looser spring
    dampingRatio = Spring.DampingRatioMediumBouncy // Medium bouncy damping
)
```

Resources for Further Learning:

- **Official Documentation:** The Jetpack Compose documentation provides comprehensive guides
  and examples on animations: https://developer.android.com/jetpack/compose/animation
- **Codelabs and Tutorials:** Google offers interactive codelabs and tutorials to help you learn
  animation concepts and practice building animations in Compose.

By exploring these advanced animation techniques and diving into the available resources, you'll be well
on your way to becoming a master of animation in Jetpack Compose, creating captivating and memorable
user experiences for your Android applications.

Chapter Summary

This chapter has opened the door to the captivating world of animations and transitions in Jetpack
Compose. You've learned how animations play a pivotal role in enhancing user experience, providing
visual feedback, guiding user attention, and making interactions more intuitive. We explored the different

types of animations commonly used in modern UI/UX design, ranging from subtle microinteractions to impactful screen transitions.

You gained an understanding of the core animation concepts in Compose, such as state-driven animations, easing curves, and durations. You were introduced to the convenient `animate*AsState` functions for effortlessly creating smooth animations for various data types, including size, opacity, and color.

We delved into more advanced animation techniques, including using `AnimationSpec` for precise control over timing and easing, `rememberInfiniteTransition` for crafting looping animations, and `Animatable` for low-level animation manipulation. You learned how to choreograph multiple animations together using `updateTransition` and `AnimatedContent`, creating complex and visually engaging sequences.

The chapter also covered the `AnimatedVisibility` composable, a powerful tool for animating the appearance and disappearance of UI elements, and briefly touched upon even more advanced techniques like custom keyframes and physics-based animations.

By mastering these animation techniques, you'll be well-equipped to elevate the visual appeal and interactivity of your Jetpack Compose applications. Remember, animation is a powerful tool for communication and storytelling within your UI, so embrace its potential and experiment with different approaches to create truly delightful user experiences.

Section I:
Advanced Topics and Integrations

Integrating Camera and Image Handling in Jetpack Compose

Outline

- The Importance of Camera and Image Features in Mobile Apps
- CameraX: The Modern Camera Library
- Setting Up CameraX in Your Project
- Capturing Images with CameraX
- Displaying Captured Images
- Image Manipulation and Transformation (Optional)
- Best Practices and Considerations for Camera and Image Handling
- Chapter Summary

The Importance of Camera and Image Features in Mobile Apps

In the era of visual communication, camera and image handling features have become indispensable in a wide array of Android applications. They empower users to capture and share moments, express their creativity, and interact with the world around them in new and engaging ways.

Ubiquity Across Applications:

Camera and image features are no longer limited to photography apps. They've become essential components of:

- **Social Media Apps:** Users share photos and videos to connect with friends and family, express themselves, and document their lives.
- **E-commerce Apps:** Product images are critical for showcasing items, and camera features enable users to upload pictures of products for reviews or returns.
- **Messaging Apps:** Sending images and videos has become a primary mode of communication, allowing for richer and more expressive conversations.
- **Productivity Apps:** Camera features are used for document scanning, note-taking, and even augmented reality experiences.
- **Healthcare Apps:** Patients can capture images of their symptoms for remote consultations, and healthcare providers can use images for diagnosis and treatment planning.

Diverse Use Cases:

The use cases for camera and image handling are vast and varied:

- **Capturing Photos and Videos:** This is the most fundamental use case, allowing users to take pictures and record videos directly within your app.
- **Scanning Barcodes and QR Codes:** Image analysis can be used to decode barcodes and QR codes, enabling features like product scanning, inventory management, and contactless payments.

- **Augmented Reality (AR):** Camera input can be used to overlay digital information onto the real world, creating immersive AR experiences.
- **Image Editing and Filtering:** Applying filters, cropping, and adjusting image parameters are common features in many apps.
- **Object Detection and Recognition:** Advanced image analysis techniques can be used to identify objects, faces, or text within images, unlocking a wide range of possibilities.

Challenges:

Working with camera and image data presents unique challenges:

- **Permissions:** You need to request and handle camera permissions to access the device's camera.
- **Image Processing:** Processing images can be computationally intensive, requiring careful optimization to avoid performance issues.
- **Memory Management:** Images can consume a significant amount of memory, especially when dealing with high-resolution photos or videos. Efficient memory management is crucial to prevent your app from crashing.
- **Compatibility:** Different devices have varying camera capabilities. Ensuring your app works across a wide range of devices can be challenging.

In the next sections, we'll explore how to overcome these challenges by using CameraX, a modern and versatile library for camera development, and Jetpack Compose to build your app's UI. By the end of this chapter, you'll be well-equipped to integrate powerful camera and image features into your Android applications.

CameraX: The Modern Camera Library

In the realm of Android camera development, **CameraX** emerges as a game-changer. Introduced by Google, CameraX is a Jetpack support library that simplifies the process of building camera-powered features into your apps. It's designed to be more intuitive, efficient, and reliable than the older Camera API, making it the preferred choice for modern Android development.

Advantages Over the Older Camera API:

CameraX addresses several pain points that developers faced with the older Camera API:

- **Ease of Use:** CameraX provides a higher-level, use-case-driven API that abstracts away the complexities of camera hardware interactions. This means you can focus on implementing features rather than dealing with intricate camera configurations.
- **Lifecycle Management:** CameraX seamlessly integrates with Android's lifecycle components (Activities and Fragments), automatically handling camera initialization, resource allocation, and release. This reduces the risk of memory leaks and crashes, leading to more stable apps.
- **Feature Support:** CameraX supports a wide range of camera features, including image capture, video recording, image analysis, and more. It also offers extensions for features like HDR (High Dynamic Range) and night mode.
- **Device Compatibility:** CameraX aims to provide consistent behavior across different Android devices, minimizing compatibility issues and ensuring your app works well on a variety of hardware.

Core Components of CameraX:

CameraX is built around several core components that work together to provide a comprehensive camera experience:

- **Preview:** The `Preview` use case allows you to display a live camera feed on the screen. This is essential for providing a viewfinder experience and letting users see what they're capturing.

- **Image Analysis:** The ImageAnalysis use case enables you to process individual camera frames in real-time. This is ideal for tasks like barcode scanning, object detection, or image processing.
- **Image Capture:** The ImageCapture use case simplifies the process of capturing high-quality images from the camera. It handles image compression, format selection, and other details for you.
- **Video Capture (Optional):** If your app needs to record videos, the VideoCapture use case provides a convenient way to do so.
- **Extensions:** CameraX offers extensions that add extra functionalities to your camera app. Examples include HDR (High Dynamic Range) imaging, night mode, and portrait effects.

Choosing the Right Use Cases:

The choice of which CameraX use cases to include in your app depends on the specific features you want to provide. For example, if your app only needs to capture photos, you can focus on Preview and ImageCapture. If you also need video recording, you'll include VideoCapture.

In the following sections, we'll delve into the practical aspects of setting up CameraX in your Jetpack Compose project and using its various components to capture and display images. You'll learn how to create a camera preview, capture high-quality photos, and integrate these features seamlessly into your Compose UIs.

Setting Up CameraX in Your Project

Before you can harness the power of CameraX in your Jetpack Compose app, you need to add the necessary dependencies and request the required permissions. Let's walk through the steps involved:

1. Add CameraX Dependencies:

Open your module-level build.gradle file (usually located at app/build.gradle) and add the following dependencies to the dependencies section:

```
dependencies {
    // ... other dependencies ...

    // CameraX core library using the camera2 implementation
    implementation "androidx.camera:camera-camera2:1.4.0-alpha02" // Update to
the latest stable version

    // If you want to additionally use the CameraX Lifecycle library
    implementation "androidx.camera:camera-lifecycle:1.4.0-alpha02" // Update
to the latest stable version

    // If you want to additionally use the CameraX View class
    implementation "androidx.camera:camera-view:1.4.0-alpha02" // Update to
the latest stable version
}
```

(Remember to replace the version numbers with the latest stable version. You can check for the latest version in the official documentation.)

- **camera-camera2:** The core CameraX library using the Camera2 implementation (recommended for most cases).
- **camera-lifecycle:** (Optional) This library provides lifecycle-aware components to simplify CameraX integration with Activities and Fragments.

- **camera-view:** (Optional) This library provides the `PreviewView` class, which is a view for displaying the camera preview within traditional Android layouts. We will use this view in the `AndroidView` composable later to integrate the preview within Jetpack Compose UI.

2. Request Camera Permissions:

Starting from Android 6.0 (API level 23), apps need to request permissions at runtime before accessing certain features, including the camera. To request camera permissions in your Jetpack Compose app:

- **Add permission to the manifest:**

```
<manifest ...>
    <uses-permission android:name="android.permission.CAMERA" />

    <application ...>
    </application>
</manifest>
```

- **Check and request permission in your activity:**

```
class MainActivity : ComponentActivity() {

    override fun onCreate(savedInstanceState: Bundle?) {
        super.onCreate(savedInstanceState)
        // Check camera permissions
        if (ContextCompat.checkSelfPermission(
                this, Manifest.permission.CAMERA) !=
PackageManager.PERMISSION_GRANTED) {
            // Request camera permissions
            ActivityCompat.requestPermissions(
                this,
                arrayOf(Manifest.permission.CAMERA),
                REQUEST_CODE_PERMISSIONS
            )
        } else {
            // Permission has already been granted
            startCamera()
        }
    }
}
```

(The code is a snippet from an Android Activity that checks and requests camera permissions at runtime. `startCamera()` function will be called when the permission is granted to start using camera.)

In this example:

1. We first check if the CAMERA permission has already been granted using `ContextCompat.checkSelfPermission`.
2. If not granted, we request the permission using `ActivityCompat.requestPermissions`.
3. When the user responds to the permission request, the onRequestPermissionsResult method in your activity will be called, where you can handle the user's decision (whether they granted or denied the permission).
4. If the permission is granted, we proceed to initialize and start the CameraX preview.

With the CameraX dependencies added and permissions requested, you are now ready to dive into using CameraX's core components to build camera features into your Jetpack Compose app.

Capturing Images with CameraX

Now that CameraX is set up, let's capture photos using its core components: Preview and ImageCapture. We'll integrate this seamlessly into your Jetpack Compose UI.

Creating a Preview Composable:

The Preview component provides a live viewfinder experience, displaying the camera feed directly in your composable UI. Here's how you can create a basic Preview composable:

```
@Composable
fun CameraPreview(
    modifier: Modifier = Modifier,
    scaleType: PreviewView.ScaleType = PreviewView.ScaleType.FILL_CENTER,
    cameraSelector: CameraSelector = CameraSelector.DEFAULT_BACK_CAMERA,
) {
    val lifecycleOwner = LocalLifecycleOwner.current // Get the lifecycle
owner
    val context = LocalContext.current
    val cameraProviderFuture = remember { // Create a future to get a camera
provider asynchronously
        ProcessCameraProvider.getInstance(context)
    }

    AndroidView(
        modifier = modifier,
        factory = { context ->
            val previewView = PreviewView(context).apply {
                this.scaleType = scaleType
            }

            // Request a ProcessCameraProvider asynchronously.
            cameraProviderFuture.addListener({
                val cameraProvider: ProcessCameraProvider =
cameraProviderFuture.get()
                val preview = Preview.Builder().build().also {
                    it.setSurfaceProvider(previewView.surfaceProvider)
                }

                // Bind the use case(s) to the camera.
                try {
                    cameraProvider.unbindAll()
                    cameraProvider.bindToLifecycle(
                        lifecycleOwner,
                        cameraSelector,
                        preview
                    )
                } catch (e: Exception) {
                    // Handle any errors
                }
            }, ContextCompat.getMainExecutor(context))
```

```
            previewView
        }
    )
}
```

(The code is a Jetpack Compose composable function for rendering the preview from a `CameraX` `Preview` object. It takes in the modifier, scaleType and the cameraSelector as parameters to customize the preview according to the user.)

In this composable:

- We obtain the lifecycle owner for binding to lifecycle as CameraX is lifecycle aware.
- We fetch the camera provider using `ProcessCameraProvider.getInstance(context)`. The camera provider is used to bind lifecycle and use cases to a camera.
- We create a `PreviewView` using the `AndroidView` composable so that it can be rendered within Jetpack Compose UI. The `PreviewView` is a view to display the camera preview using CameraX.
- We set the preview use case to display the camera output using `Preview.Builder`.
- We use `cameraProvider.bindToLifecycle` to bind the lifecycle of the composable with the lifecycle of camera. This is done so that camera is opened when the composable is added to the UI and closed when it is removed from the UI.
- We use `cameraProvider.unbindAll()` to unbind all the previously bound use cases from the camera to prevent conflict between the use cases.

Using ImageCapture to Take Pictures:

The `ImageCapture` component allows you to capture and save images from the camera. Here's how you can use it:

```
val imageCapture: ImageCapture = remember { ImageCapture.Builder().build() }

// In the callback when the user wants to take a picture
imageCapture.takePicture(
    ContextCompat.getMainExecutor(context), // Provide an executor
    object : ImageCapture.OnImageSavedCallback {
        override fun onImageSaved(outputFileResults:
ImageCapture.OutputFileResults) {
            val savedUri = outputFileResults.savedUri // Access the captured image
URI
            // ... process the image (e.g., display in your UI, upload to server)
...
        }

        override fun onError(exception: ImageCaptureException) {
            // ... handle error ...
        }
    }
)
```

In this code:

- The image capture object is created and remembered.
- `takePicture` is called to capture a picture.
- A callback is created where in we can access the captured image and do whatever we want to do with it.

Saving Captured Images:

You can save captured images to different locations:

- **Device Storage:** Use the `MediaStore` API to save the image to the device's gallery.

```
val contentValues = ContentValues().apply {
    put(MediaStore.MediaColumns.DISPLAY_NAME,
"my_image_${System.currentTimeMillis()}.jpg")
    put(MediaStore.MediaColumns.MIME_TYPE, "image/jpeg")
}
imageCapture.takePicture(
    ImageCapture.OutputFileOptions.Builder(
        context.contentResolver,
        MediaStore.Images.Media.EXTERNAL_CONTENT_URI,
        contentValues
    ).build(), // Output file options
    // ... rest of the takePicture code ...
)
```

- **Temporary File:** Save the image to a temporary file within your app's cache directory.

```
val file = File(context.cacheDir, "my_image.jpg")
imageCapture.takePicture(
    ImageCapture.OutputFileOptions.Builder(file).build(), // Output file
options
    // ... rest of the takePicture code ...
)
```

With these techniques, you can empower your Jetpack Compose applications to capture stunning images and seamlessly integrate them into your UI, opening up a world of possibilities for your users' creativity and engagement.

Displaying Captured Images

Once you've successfully captured an image using CameraX, the next step is to display it within your Jetpack Compose UI. The `Image` composable, combined with the `rememberImagePainter` function, makes it a breeze to load and present images from various sources, including the files or URIs where you saved your captured photos.

Using `rememberImagePainter` for Loading:

The `rememberImagePainter` function from the `coil-compose` library is a convenient way to load images asynchronously and efficiently. It automatically handles tasks like image decoding, caching, and error handling, freeing you from these low-level details.

Example: Loading an Image from a URI:

```
@Composable
fun DisplayCapturedImage(imageUri: Uri?) { // Assuming you have the captured
image URI
    val painter = rememberImagePainter(data = imageUri)

    Image(
        painter = painter,
```

```
        contentDescription = "Captured image",
        modifier = Modifier
            .fillMaxWidth()
            .height(200.dp), // Adjust size as needed
        contentScale = ContentScale.Crop
    )
}
```

In this example:

- `rememberImagePainter(data = imageUri)`: Creates an `ImagePainter` object that loads the image from the `imageUri`. The `remember` block ensures that the painter is cached across recompositions to avoid reloading the image unnecessarily.
- `Image(painter = painter, ...)`: The Image composable uses the `painter` to display the loaded image. We also provide a `contentDescription` for accessibility and modify the image size and scale as needed.

Displaying Images with the `Image` Composable:

The `Image` composable is the fundamental element for displaying images in Compose. You provide it with an `ImageBitmap` (for images loaded in memory) or a `Painter` (like the one created by `rememberImagePainter`). You can also customize the appearance of the image using modifiers.

Example: Displaying an Image from a File:

```
@Composable
fun DisplayImageFromFile(filePath: String) { // Assuming you have the image
file path
    val painter = rememberImagePainter(data = File(filePath))

    Image(
        painter = painter,
        contentDescription = "Image from file",
        // ... other modifiers ...
    )
}
```

Handling Loading and Error States:

The `rememberImagePainter` function provides a `state` property that you can use to track the loading progress of the image and handle potential errors.

```
val painterState = painter.state
if (painterState is ImagePainter.State.Loading) {
    CircularProgressIndicator() // Show a loading indicator
} else if (painterState is ImagePainter.State.Error) {
    // Handle the error (e.g., display an error message)
}
```

Key Points:

- `rememberImagePainter` simplifies image loading in Jetpack Compose.
- `Image` composable displays images loaded from various sources.
- Handle loading and error states for a smooth user experience.

By combining CameraX for image capture and Jetpack Compose for UI rendering, you can seamlessly integrate camera features into your Android apps. With the `rememberImagePainter` function, loading and displaying images becomes a straightforward task, enabling you to create visually rich and engaging user experiences.

Image Manipulation and Transformation (Optional)

While Jetpack Compose provides basic image loading and display capabilities, you might need to perform additional manipulations or transformations on your captured images. Libraries like **Coil** and **Glide** offer powerful tools for resizing, cropping, rotating, and applying various effects to your images.

Coil: A Modern Image Loading Library

Coil is a fast, lightweight, and Kotlin-first image loading library that integrates seamlessly with Jetpack Compose. It provides a simple and intuitive API for loading images from various sources (including files, URLs, and resources), caching them efficiently, and applying transformations.

Example: Resizing and Cropping an Image with Coil:

```
@Composable
fun MyImageComposable(imageUrl: String) {
    Image(
        painter = rememberImagePainter(
            data = imageUrl,
            builder = {
                transformations(
                    CircleCropTransformation(), // Apply circle crop
                    ResizeTransformation(200, 200) // Resize to 200x200
                )
            }
        ),
        contentDescription = "My Image",
        modifier = Modifier.fillMaxWidth()
    )
}
```

(The code is a Jetpack Compose composable function for displaying an image. The `rememberImagePainter` function from the `coil-compose` library is used to load the image from a URL and apply two transformations: `CircleCropTransformation` to crop the image into a circle and `ResizeTransformation` to resize the image to 200x200.)

Glide: A Popular and Feature-Rich Image Library

Glide is another widely used image loading library that offers a rich set of features for loading, caching, and manipulating images. Like Coil, it integrates well with Jetpack Compose and provides a simple API for image transformations.

Example: Rotating an Image with Glide:

```
@Composable
fun MyImageComposable(imageUri: Uri) {
    Image(
        painter = rememberGlidePainter(
            request = imageUri,
            requestBuilder = {
```

```
            it.transform(CenterCrop(), Rotate(90)) // Apply center crop
and 90-degree rotation
        }
    ),
    contentDescription = "My Image",
    // ... other modifiers ...
    )
}
```

In this example, we use `rememberGlidePainter` to load an image and apply a `CenterCrop` and `Rotate` transformation using Glide's request builder.

Additional Image Transformations:

Both Coil and Glide offer a wide range of image transformations:

- **Blur:** Apply a blur effect to images.
- **Rounded Corners:** Create images with rounded corners.
- **Grayscale:** Convert images to grayscale.
- **Color Filters:** Apply color filters to change the look of images.
- **And Many More:** Explore the documentation of Coil and Glide to discover the full range of available transformations.

Key Considerations:

- **Performance:** Be mindful of the computational cost of image transformations. Avoid applying complex transformations to large images, as it can impact performance. Consider using background threads or optimizing your transformations for efficiency.
- **Memory Usage:** Keep track of memory usage when loading and manipulating images. Use appropriate image sizes and compression techniques to avoid out-of-memory errors.

By leveraging image loading and manipulation libraries like Coil or Glide, you can add a touch of visual sophistication to your Jetpack Compose applications. Remember to use these libraries judiciously, keeping performance and memory usage in mind, to create a smooth and enjoyable user experience.

Best Practices and Considerations for Camera and Image Handling

Working with the camera and image data in your Jetpack Compose apps requires careful attention to detail. Here's a collection of best practices and considerations to help you create a seamless and user-friendly experience while ensuring performance and security.

Best Practices:

1. **Managing Camera Lifecycle:**
   - **Bind and Unbind:** Always bind the `Preview`, `ImageCapture`, and `ImageAnalysis` use cases to the camera when your composable is active, and unbind them when it's no longer needed. You can use the `remember` function to create and remember these use cases.
   - **Lifecycle Awareness:** If you are using the `camera-lifecycle` library, use the `LifecycleCameraController` to manage the camera lifecycle in sync with your composable's lifecycle. This ensures that the camera is opened and closed at the appropriate times, preventing resource leaks and potential crashes.
2. **Image Size and Quality:**

- **Resolution:** Choose the appropriate resolution for your use case. High-resolution images consume more memory. Consider using lower resolutions for previews or when memory is constrained.
- **Compression:** Compress images before saving or transmitting them to reduce file sizes and bandwidth usage. You can use libraries like `Compressor` or built-in Android APIs for image compression.
- **Aspect Ratio:** Maintain the correct aspect ratio of images to avoid distortion when displaying them.

3. **Permissions:**
   - **Request Permissions:** Always request the `CAMERA` permission at runtime before accessing the camera.
   - **Handle Denial:** Gracefully handle cases where the user denies the camera permission. Provide clear instructions on how to enable it.

4. **Error Handling:**
   - **Camera Errors:** Be prepared to handle camera errors, such as the camera being unavailable or disconnected. Provide informative error messages to the user.
   - **Image Capture Errors:** Handle errors that might occur during image capture, such as file saving failures or capture exceptions.
   - **Use `ImageCapture.OnImageSavedCallback`:** Use `ImageCapture.OnImageSavedCallback` to get callbacks on a background thread when the image is saved.

5. **Memory Management:**
   - **Avoid Large Bitmaps:** Be cautious when loading and displaying large bitmaps, as they can quickly consume a lot of memory. Consider downsampling or loading them in a background thread.
   - **Release Resources:** Release camera resources (e.g., `ImageProxy` objects) promptly when you're done with them to avoid memory leaks.

Common Challenges and Solutions:

- **Camera Initialization Issues:** If you encounter issues initializing the camera, double-check your permissions, dependencies, and CameraX configuration.
- **Image Orientation:** Captured images might be rotated incorrectly due to device orientation. You can use Exif data or libraries like `ExifInterface` to correct the orientation.
- **Large Image Handling:** To efficiently handle large images, consider loading them in smaller chunks or using a library like Glide or Coil, which offer features like downsampling and placeholders.

Privacy and Security:

- **Transparency:** Be transparent with users about how you're using the camera and image data. Explain why you need the permissions and how the data will be used and stored.
- **Data Minimization:** Collect only the necessary image data and avoid storing sensitive information (like faces) without the user's explicit consent.
- **Secure Storage:** If you need to store images, use secure storage mechanisms like encrypted files or databases.

By following these best practices and carefully considering the potential challenges, you can create Jetpack Compose applications that leverage camera and image features responsibly, efficiently, and securely.

Chapter Summary

This chapter has empowered you with the knowledge and tools to seamlessly integrate camera and image handling into your Jetpack Compose applications. You learned about the importance of these features in modern apps and their wide range of use cases, from capturing photos and videos to scanning barcodes and applying image filters.

We introduced CameraX as the go-to library for camera development on Android, highlighting its advantages over the older Camera API. You gained a solid understanding of the core CameraX components, including `Preview`, `ImageAnalysis`, and `ImageCapture`, and how they work together to provide a comprehensive camera experience.

A step-by-step guide walked you through the process of setting up CameraX in your project, adding the necessary dependencies, and requesting camera permissions at runtime. You learned how to create a `Preview` composable to display the camera feed and capture images using the `ImageCapture` component. We also explored different options for saving captured images, either to device storage or temporary files.

To showcase your captured masterpieces, you learned how to display images in your Compose UI using the `Image` composable and the `rememberImagePainter` function. We even touched upon advanced image manipulation techniques with libraries like Coil and Glide, allowing you to resize, crop, rotate, and apply various effects to your images.

Finally, we discussed best practices for working with CameraX and handling images in Jetpack Compose. You gained insights into managing the camera lifecycle, optimizing image sizes for performance, compressing images for efficient storage, handling permissions, and addressing common challenges like camera errors. We also emphasized the importance of user privacy and security when dealing with camera and image data.

With this newfound knowledge and practical guidance, you are now equipped to create compelling Android apps that leverage the full potential of camera and image capabilities. In the next chapter, we'll venture into the world of maps and location services, exploring how to integrate location-based features into your Jetpack Compose applications.

Working with Maps and Location Services in Jetpack Compose

Outline

- Location and Maps in Modern Apps
- Introducing the Maps Compose Library
- Obtaining Location Permissions
- Getting the User's Current Location
- Displaying a Map
- Customizing the Map (Markers, Styles, etc.)
- Handling Map Interactions (Clicks, Gestures, etc.)
- Best Practices and Considerations for Maps and Location
- Chapter Summary

Location and Maps in Modern Apps

Location-based features have revolutionized the way we interact with mobile apps. By leveraging the user's location, apps can provide personalized experiences, offer relevant recommendations, and enable a wide range of location-aware functionalities. Let's delve into the significance of location and maps in modern apps and explore the challenges they present.

The Importance of Location-Based Features:

- **Navigation:** Turn-by-turn directions, traffic updates, and estimated arrival times have become indispensable for many users. Apps like Google Maps and Waze have transformed the way we navigate the world.
- **Local Search:** Finding nearby restaurants, stores, or services based on the user's location has become a common feature in many apps. This helps users discover local businesses and make informed decisions.
- **Location Sharing:** Apps like Find My Friends and Glympse allow users to share their location with friends and family, enhancing safety and coordination.
- **Personalized Experiences:** Apps can use location data to tailor their content and recommendations to the user's interests and location. For example, a food delivery app might suggest nearby restaurants based on the user's current location.
- **Geo-fencing:** Apps can trigger actions or notifications when a user enters or exits a specific geographical area. This can be used for features like location-based reminders or personalized advertising.

Maps vs. Location Services:

It's important to distinguish between maps and location services:

- **Maps:** Maps are visual representations of the Earth's surface. They allow users to visualize their location, explore different areas, and plan routes. In Android, Google Maps is the most popular mapping platform, offering a rich set of features and customization options.
- **Location Services:** Location services, on the other hand, provide the underlying technology for determining the user's location. This can be done using GPS, Wi-Fi, or cellular networks. The Fused Location Provider API in Android simplifies the process of accessing location data from various sources.

Challenges in Working with Location Data:

While location-based features offer immense value, they also come with challenges:

- **Privacy Concerns:** Users are increasingly sensitive about how their location data is used and shared. It's crucial to be transparent about your app's location practices and obtain user consent before collecting or using their location data.
- **Accuracy Variations:** Location accuracy can vary depending on the available technology (GPS, Wi-Fi, cellular) and environmental factors. Your app needs to handle these variations gracefully and provide accurate information to the user.
- **Battery Usage:** Continuous location updates can drain the device's battery. It's important to optimize your app's location usage and minimize battery consumption.

In the next sections, we'll explore how to integrate Google Maps and location services into your Jetpack Compose applications using the Maps Compose library and the Fused Location Provider API. You'll learn how to handle permissions, fetch location data, display maps, and create interactive location-based experiences for your users.

Introducing the Maps Compose Library

The **Maps Compose library** is Google's official solution for seamlessly integrating Google Maps into your Jetpack Compose applications. It provides a declarative and intuitive way to display maps, add markers, customize the map's appearance, and handle user interactions.

Advantages of Using Maps Compose:

- **Declarative API:** Like the rest of Jetpack Compose, the Maps Compose library embraces a declarative approach. You describe your map UI using composable functions, making it easier to reason about and maintain.
- **Easy Customization:** The library offers a wide range of customization options, allowing you to tailor the map's appearance and behavior to fit your app's design and requirements. You can add markers, change the map type, adjust the camera position, and more, all within your composable functions.
- **Seamless Compose Integration:** Maps Compose is designed to work harmoniously with other Jetpack Compose components. You can easily embed maps within your existing UI layouts and interact with them using familiar Compose concepts.

Core Components of the Library:

- `GoogleMap`: This is the main composable for displaying the map. It provides the canvas on which you can render map tiles, markers, and other elements.
- `Marker`: Markers are used to pinpoint specific locations on the map. You can customize their appearance with icons, labels, and info windows.
- `CameraPositionState`: This object represents the current position and zoom level of the map's camera. You can use it to programmatically control the camera, for example, to move to a specific location or zoom in/out.

By using Maps Compose, you can easily add interactive and visually appealing maps to your Android applications. The declarative nature of Compose, combined with the library's customization options, empowers you to create maps that perfectly match your app's design and functionality.

In the following sections, we'll guide you through the process of setting up the Maps Compose library, requesting location permissions, and building your first map in Jetpack Compose. You'll also learn how to customize the map and handle user interactions to create a truly immersive map experience for your users.

Obtaining Location Permissions

Before your Jetpack Compose app can access the user's location, you must first obtain the necessary permissions. Android requires you to explicitly request these permissions at runtime to protect user privacy. Let's walk through the steps involved in requesting and handling location permissions.

1. Add Permissions to Your Manifest:

Open your app's AndroidManifest.xml file and add the following permissions within the <manifest> tag:

```
<uses-permission android:name="android.permission.ACCESS_FINE_LOCATION" />
<uses-permission android:name="android.permission.ACCESS_COARSE_LOCATION" />
```

- **ACCESS_FINE_LOCATION:** This permission allows your app to access the device's precise location (e.g., using GPS).
- **ACCESS_COARSE_LOCATION:** This permission allows your app to access the device's approximate location (e.g., using Wi-Fi or cell towers).

It's recommended to request only the permission you need. If your app doesn't require precise location, you might only need ACCESS_COARSE_LOCATION.

2. Request Permissions at Runtime:

Use the Accompanist Permissions library to request the necessary permissions at runtime within your composable functions.

Add the dependency: Open your module-level build.gradle file and add the following dependency in the dependencies section:

```
implementation "com.google.accompanist:accompanist-permissions:0.32.0"
```

(Remember to replace the version number with the latest stable version. You can check for the latest version in the official documentation.)

Request permissions:

```
@Composable
fun LocationPermissionRequest(onPermissionGranted: () -> Unit) {
    val locationPermissionsState = rememberPermissionState(
        android.Manifest.permission.ACCESS_FINE_LOCATION // or
ACCESS_COARSE_LOCATION
    )

    if (locationPermissionsState.hasPermission) {
        // Permission is granted, proceed with location-related tasks
        onPermissionGranted()
    } else {
        Column {
            val textToShow = if (locationPermissionsState.shouldShowRationale)
{
```

```
                // If the user has denied the permission previously, explain
why you need it.
                "The location is important for this app. Please grant the
permission."
            } else {
                // First time requesting permission or user has asked not to
be asked again.
                "Location permission required for this feature to be
available."
            }
            Text(textToShow)
            Button(onClick = {
locationPermissionsState.launchPermissionRequest() }) {
                Text("Request permission")
            }
        }
    }
}
```

(The composable function LocationPermissionRequest will show rationale text and a button for requesting the permission based on the permission state.)

In this composable:

- rememberPermissionState is used to obtain the permission state. It will trigger recomposition when the state changes.
- If permission is already granted, we execute the onPermissionGranted callback function, which is a lambda function that takes no parameters and returns no value. The purpose of the callback is to be called when the permission is granted and the user can proceed with location-related tasks.
- If the permission has not been granted, we show the relevant message to the user and provide the option for the user to request the permission.

By following these steps, you ensure that your app adheres to Android's permission model and respects user privacy while accessing location data.

Getting the User's Current Location

To provide location-based features, your app needs to know the user's current location. Android's Fused Location Provider API, combined with the power of Kotlin coroutines, offers a streamlined way to retrieve location data.

Using FusedLocationProviderClient:

The FusedLocationProviderClient is your primary tool for accessing location data in Android. It intelligently combines various location providers (GPS, Wi-Fi, cellular) to provide the most accurate and efficient location information.

```
val fusedLocationClient: FusedLocationProviderClient =
LocationServices.getFusedLocationProviderClient(context)
```

(The code snippet uses the LocationServices class to get a FusedLocationProviderClient instance, which is the main entry point for interacting with the fused location provider.)

Checking for Location Permissions:

Before accessing the user's location, always check that you have the necessary permissions (either ACCESS_FINE_LOCATION or ACCESS_COARSE_LOCATION). You can use the rememberPermissionState as shown in previous section or the traditional method using ContextCompat.checkSelfPermission.

Requesting Location Updates:

Once you have the permissions, you can request location updates from the FusedLocationProviderClient:

```kotlin
val locationRequest = LocationRequest.Builder(Priority.PRIORITY_HIGH_ACCURACY,
10000).build()
val locationCallback = object : LocationCallback() {
    override fun onLocationResult(locationResult: LocationResult) {
        for (location in locationResult.locations) {
            // Update UI or perform other actions with the new location
        }
    }
}
fusedLocationClient.requestLocationUpdates(locationRequest, locationCallback,
Looper.getMainLooper())
```

In this example:

- We create a LocationRequest to specify the desired location update frequency.
- We define a LocationCallback to handle the location results.
- We call requestLocationUpdates on the fusedLocationClient, passing the location request and callback.

Handling Location Results in Jetpack Compose:

You can use state variables in your composable functions to store and display the current location:

```kotlin
@Composable
fun MyLocationComposable(fusedLocationClient: FusedLocationProviderClient) {
    var currentLocation by remember { mutableStateOf<Location?>(null) }

    LaunchedEffect(Unit) {
        // ... (check permissions and request location updates here) ...

        // Update the currentLocation state with the new location
        currentLocation = location
    }

    Column {
        Text("Current Latitude: ${currentLocation?.latitude}")
        Text("Current Longitude: ${currentLocation?.longitude}")
    }
}
```

(The code is a Jetpack Compose composable function that displays the user's current location. It uses LaunchedEffect to request location updates in a coroutine scope, and mutableStateOf to store the current location.)

Key Points:

- `FusedLocationProviderClient`: The main API for accessing location data.
- Permissions: Always check for and request permissions before accessing location.
- `LocationRequest`: Configure location update frequency and priority.
- `LocationCallback`: Handle location updates in the background.
- `collectAsState`: (with Flows) or `LaunchedEffect`: Use these to update UI with new location data.

By integrating location services into your Jetpack Compose app, you can unlock a new dimension of functionality, from personalized content to real-time location-based interactions. Always remember to respect user privacy and handle location data responsibly.

Displaying a Map

With the Maps Compose library, embedding a Google Map into your Jetpack Compose UI is a breeze. This library provides the `GoogleMap` composable, a powerful tool that lets you display maps, customize their appearance, and handle user interactions with ease.

Displaying the Map:

To display a map, follow these steps:

1. **Add the Dependency:** Make sure you've added the Maps Compose library dependency to your project's `build.gradle` file:

   ```
   implementation 'com.google.maps.android:maps-compose:2.11.4' // Update to
   the latest version
   ```

   (Always refer to the official documentation for the latest version)

2. **Get Your API Key:** Obtain a valid Google Maps API key from the Google Cloud Console. This key is required to access the maps service.

3. **Use the GoogleMap Composable:**

   ```
   @Composable
   fun MyMapComposable() {
       GoogleMap(
           modifier = Modifier.fillMaxSize(),
           properties = MapProperties(isMyLocationEnabled = true), // Enable
   current location
           uiSettings = MapUiSettings(zoomControlsEnabled = true) // Add
   zoom control buttons
       )
   }
   ```

   In this basic example:

   - `modifier = Modifier.fillMaxSize()`: Makes the map fill the available space.
   - `properties = MapProperties(isMyLocationEnabled = true)`: Enables the "My Location" button on the map (ensure you have location permissions).
   - `uiSettings = MapUiSettings(zoomControlsEnabled = true)`: Enables the zoom control buttons on the map.

Setting the Initial Camera Position and Zoom Level:

To control the initial view of the map (where it's centered and how zoomed in it is), you can use the `cameraPositionState` parameter of the `GoogleMap` composable. This state object represents the current position and zoom level of the map's camera.

```
val cameraPositionState = rememberCameraPositionState {
    position = CameraPosition.fromLatLngZoom(LatLng(30.9010, 75.8573), 10f) //
Centered on Ludhiana, Punjab with zoom level 10
}

GoogleMap(
    modifier = Modifier.fillMaxSize(),
    cameraPositionState = cameraPositionState,
    // ... other properties
)
```

In this example, the map will initially be centered on Ludhiana, Punjab with a zoom level of 10. You can adjust the latitude, longitude, and zoom level to fit your requirements.

The Importance of the Google Maps API Key:

A valid Google Maps API key is essential for using the Maps Compose library. Without it, your map will not display correctly. Here's how to obtain and provide your API key:

1. **Obtain API Key:** Get your API key from the Google Cloud Console. Follow the instructions provided by Google.
2. **Add the API Key to Your Manifest:** Add the API key to your app's `AndroidManifest.xml` file:

   ```
   <application>
       <meta-data
           android:name="com.google.android.geo.API_KEY"
           android:value="YOUR_API_KEY" />
   </application>
   ```

With these steps, you'll be able to display a fully functional Google Map in your Jetpack Compose UI. In the upcoming sections, we'll explore how to customize the map's appearance, add markers, and handle user interactions to create rich and engaging location-based experiences in your Android apps.

Customizing the Map

The Maps Compose library offers a plethora of customization options to help you tailor the map's appearance and behavior to align with your app's design and functionality. Let's explore some of the most common and powerful ways to customize your maps.

1. Adding Markers: Pinpointing Locations

Markers are essential for highlighting specific locations on your map. You can use the `Marker` composable to add markers with custom icons, titles, and snippets.

```
GoogleMap(
    modifier = Modifier.fillMaxSize(),
    cameraPositionState = cameraPositionState,
    // ... other properties
) {
```

```
    Marker(
        state = MarkerState(position = LatLng(30.9010, 75.8573)), // Ludhiana,
Punjab
        title = "Ludhiana",
        snippet = "The Manchester of India"
    )
}
```

(The code is a marker to pin Ludhiana city on the map.)

2. Changing Map Type: Choosing the Right Perspective

Maps Compose supports various map types to suit different scenarios:

- MapType.NORMAL: The standard road map view.
- MapType.SATELLITE: Satellite imagery.
- MapType.TERRAIN: Topographical map with elevation details.
- MapType.HYBRID: A combination of normal and satellite views.

```
GoogleMap(
    modifier = Modifier.fillMaxSize(),
    properties = MapProperties(mapType = MapType.SATELLITE),
    // ... other properties
)
```

3. Styling with Custom Colors and Themes:

You can apply custom styles to your map using the MapProperties and MapUiSettings objects.

```
val mapProperties = MapProperties(
    mapStyleOptions = MapStyleOptions.loadRawResourceStyle(context,
R.raw.map_style_json)
)
val mapUiSettings = MapUiSettings(
    zoomControlsEnabled = false, // Disable default zoom controls
    myLocationButtonEnabled = true // Show the "My Location" button
)
GoogleMap(
    modifier = Modifier.fillMaxSize(),
    properties = mapProperties,
    uiSettings = mapUiSettings,
)
```

In this example, we load a custom map style from a JSON file in the raw resources folder. We also disable the default zoom controls and enable the "My Location" button.

4. Enabling/Disabling Gestures:

You can control which gestures are enabled on the map using MapUiSettings:

```
val mapUiSettings = MapUiSettings(
    zoomGesturesEnabled = true,
    scrollGesturesEnabled = true,
    rotateGesturesEnabled = false,
    tiltGesturesEnabled = false
)
```

In this example, we enable zoom and scroll gestures but disable rotation and tilt gestures.

Key Points:

- `Marker`: Used to add markers to the map.
- `MapProperties`: Customizes the appearance of the map (e.g., map type, style).
- `MapUiSettings`: Controls map gestures and UI elements.
- `CameraPositionState`: Programmatically control the camera position and zoom.

With these customization options, you can create a map that seamlessly integrates with your app's design and provides a rich and interactive experience for your users.

Handling Map Interactions

Jetpack Compose's `GoogleMap` composable offers a rich set of callbacks to handle various user interactions with the map. This enables you to create dynamic and responsive map experiences that react to user input.

Map Clicks and Long Clicks:

You can use the `onMapClick` and `onMapLongClick` lambdas in the `GoogleMap` composable to detect when the user taps or long-presses on the map:

```
GoogleMap(
    modifier = Modifier.fillMaxSize(),
    // ... other properties
    onMapClick = { latLng ->
        // Handle map click (e.g., add a marker)
    },
    onMapLongClick = { latLng ->
        // Handle map long click (e.g., show a context menu)
    }
)
```

Marker Clicks:

When using the `Marker` composable, you can provide an `onClick` lambda to handle clicks on the marker:

```
Marker(
    state = MarkerState(position = myLatLng),
    title = "Marker Title",
    snippet = "Marker Description",
    onClick = {
        // Handle marker click (e.g., show details in a dialog)
    }
)
```

Camera Movements:

You can observe changes in the camera position using the `cameraPositionState` object and react to those changes within your composable:

```
val cameraPositionState = rememberCameraPositionState()
```

```
var currentLocation by remember {
mutableStateOf(cameraPositionState.position.target) }
var currentZoom by remember {
mutableStateOf(cameraPositionState.position.zoom) }

LaunchedEffect(cameraPositionState.isMoving) { // Trigger when camera is
moving
    if (!cameraPositionState.isMoving) {
        currentLocation = cameraPositionState.position.target
        currentZoom = cameraPositionState.position.zoom
        // Perform actions based on new camera position and zoom
    }
}


GoogleMap(
    modifier = Modifier.fillMaxSize(),
    cameraPositionState = cameraPositionState,
    // ... other properties
)
```

In this example, LaunchedEffect is used to observe changes in the cameraPositionState. Whenever the camera stops moving, we update the currentLocation and currentZoom state variables and can then perform actions based on the new camera position.

Examples of Handling Interactions:

```
// Add a marker on map click:
var markerPosition by remember { mutableStateOf<LatLng?>(null) }

GoogleMap(
    // ...other properties
    onMapClick = { latLng -> markerPosition = latLng }
) {
    markerPosition?.let {
        Marker(
            state = MarkerState(position = it),
            title = "Marker",
            snippet = "Added on click"
        )
    }
}

// Show a dialog on marker click:
Marker(
    // ... other properties
    onClick = {
        showDialog = true
    }
)

if (showDialog) {
    AlertDialog(
        onDismissRequest = { showDialog = false },
        title = { Text("Marker Details") },
        text = { Text(marker.snippet ?: "") },
        confirmButton = {
            Button(onClick = { showDialog = false }) {
                Text("OK")
```

```
                }
            }
        )
}
```

```
// Show current latitude and longitude on map
Text("Latitude: ${currentLocation.latitude}, Longitude:
${currentLocation.longitude}")
```

By utilizing these event handlers and state variables, you can create dynamic and responsive maps in Jetpack Compose that seamlessly react to user interactions.

Best Practices and Considerations for Maps and Location

Integrating maps and location services into your Jetpack Compose applications opens up a world of possibilities, but it's important to do so responsibly and efficiently. Here are some best practices and considerations to keep in mind:

Best Practices:

1. **Efficient Location Updates:**
   - **Interval and Priority:** Request location updates only as frequently as your app requires. Use the LocationRequest to specify the desired interval and priority (e.g., PRIORITY_HIGH_ACCURACY for navigation, PRIORITY_BALANCED_POWER_ACCURACY for less frequent updates).
   - **Fused Location Provider:** Utilize the FusedLocationProviderClient, as it intelligently manages the underlying location providers to balance accuracy and battery usage.
   - **Remove Updates:** Stop requesting location updates when your app is in the background or when they're no longer needed. You can use the removeLocationUpdates() method to do this.
2. **Graceful Handling of Unavailable Services:**
   - **Check Availability:** Before requesting location updates or displaying a map, check if location services are enabled on the device.
   - **Alternative UI:** If location services are unavailable, provide alternative UI elements or information to the user. For example, you could display a message suggesting they enable location services or offer a way to manually enter their location.
3. **Privacy and Security:**
   - **Request Permissions:** Always request the necessary permissions (e.g., ACCESS_FINE_LOCATION, ACCESS_COARSE_LOCATION) at runtime, explaining why your app needs them.
   - **Transparent Data Usage:** Be transparent with users about how you collect, store, and use location data.
   - **Minimize Data Collection:** Only collect and store the location data that is absolutely necessary for your app's functionality.
   - **Secure Storage:** If you store location data, use secure storage mechanisms (e.g., encryption) to protect it from unauthorized access.

Common Challenges and Solutions:

- **Location Accuracy Issues:** GPS signals can be unreliable indoors or in areas with poor reception. Consider using Wi-Fi or cellular network positioning as a fallback.
- **Map Interaction Errors:** Be prepared to handle errors that might occur during map interactions, such as when a user tries to zoom in beyond the maximum level or clicks on an invalid area of the map. Provide appropriate error messages or feedback to the user.

- **Map Performance:** If your map is slow or unresponsive, optimize the number of markers you display, simplify the map style, or consider using clustering for large numbers of markers.

Further Learning:

- **Official Documentation:** The Android Developers website provides comprehensive documentation on location services and the Maps SDK for Android:
  - **Location Services:** https://developer.android.com/training/location
  - **Maps SDK for Android:** https://developers.google.com/maps/documentation/android-sdk/intro
  - **Maps Compose Library:** https://developers.google.com/maps/documentation/android-sdk/maps-compose

By adhering to these best practices and addressing common challenges, you can create location-aware Jetpack Compose applications that are both functional and user-friendly while respecting user privacy and ensuring optimal performance.

Chapter Summary

This chapter has opened the door to the world of location-based features in your Jetpack Compose applications. You learned how to harness the power of maps and location services to enhance your app's functionality and provide personalized experiences to users.

We discussed the importance of location and maps in modern apps, highlighting their role in navigation, local search, location sharing, and more. You gained an understanding of the distinction between maps (visual representations) and location services (the technology for determining location).

The chapter introduced the Maps Compose library, a powerful tool for integrating Google Maps into your Jetpack Compose UIs. We explored its core components: GoogleMap for displaying the map, Marker for adding location markers, and CameraPositionState for controlling the map's view. You also learned how to obtain the necessary location permissions at runtime and fetch the user's current location using the FusedLocationProviderClient.

With practical examples, you discovered how to display a map in your Compose UI, set its initial camera position and zoom level, and customize its appearance and behavior. You also learned how to handle user interactions with the map, such as clicks, long clicks, marker clicks, and camera movements.

Finally, we discussed best practices and considerations for working with maps and location services, emphasizing the importance of efficient location updates, graceful error handling, and responsible data privacy practices. We also addressed common challenges and provided solutions for dealing with issues like location accuracy and map performance.

With the knowledge and techniques presented in this chapter, you're now equipped to create compelling location-aware applications using Jetpack Compose. Feel free to explore the vast possibilities of maps and location services to enrich your Android apps and deliver exceptional user experiences.

Publishing Your App to the Google Play Store

Outline

- Preparing Your App for Release
- Creating a Google Play Developer Account
- Setting Up Your App in Play Console
- Uploading Your App Bundle
- Creating Store Listing and Promotional Materials
- Managing Releases and Updates
- Post-Launch Considerations
- Chapter Summary

Preparing Your App for Release

Before you unleash your Jetpack Compose creation on the Google Play Store, it's crucial to meticulously prepare your app for release. This final phase involves thorough testing, optimization, and configuration to ensure that your app delivers a polished and seamless user experience.

The Importance of Testing:

Thorough testing is non-negotiable. Your app needs to work flawlessly across a wide range of devices and Android versions. Here's what you should focus on:

- **Functional Testing:** Verify that all features and user flows work as intended. Test edge cases, error scenarios, and unexpected user inputs.
- **Device Compatibility Testing:** Test your app on various devices with different screen sizes, resolutions, and hardware configurations to ensure a consistent experience.
- **Android Version Compatibility Testing:** Ensure your app functions correctly on different Android versions, including older ones that your target audience might be using.
- **Performance Testing:** Identify and address performance bottlenecks to ensure smooth animations, fast loading times, and minimal battery drain.
- **Security Testing:** Conduct security tests to protect user data and prevent vulnerabilities.

Optimization:

Optimization is key to delivering a high-quality user experience:

- **Performance Optimization:**
    - Analyze your app's performance using profiling tools.
    - Optimize your composable functions to minimize recompositions and improve rendering efficiency.
    - Consider using lazy loading for images and data to reduce memory usage.
- **Size Optimization:**
    - Shrink your app's size by compressing images, removing unused resources, and enabling code shrinking (ProGuard or R8).
    - Consider using Android App Bundles to deliver optimized APKs for different device configurations.

Creating a Release Build:

1. **Generate a Signed APK or App Bundle:** In Android Studio, go to "Build" -> "Generate Signed Bundle / APK."
2. **Choose Build Variant:** Select "release" as the build variant.
3. **Create or Select a Keystore:** If you don't have a keystore, create a new one. If you have an existing one, select it and enter the correct password.
4. **Sign Your App:** Provide the necessary details for your keystore and key alias, and click "Finish." Android Studio will generate a signed release build of your app.

Code Obfuscation and Optimization:

- **Enable ProGuard or R8:** Code shrinking (ProGuard or R8) removes unused code and resources, reducing your app's size. It also obfuscates your code to make it more difficult to reverse engineer.
- **Configure ProGuard Rules:** If you're using ProGuard, create and maintain ProGuard rules to ensure that your code isn't removed or obfuscated incorrectly.

Removing Debugging and Testing Code:

Before releasing your app, make sure to:

- **Remove Log Statements:** Excessive logging can impact performance. Remove unnecessary log statements using ProGuard or manually.
- **Disable Debugging Features:** Disable any debugging tools or features that should not be accessible in the release version.
- **Clean Up Test Resources:** Remove any test-specific code, data, or resources that are not needed in the final build.

By meticulously preparing your Jetpack Compose app for release, you ensure that your users will have a smooth, polished, and enjoyable experience with your app.

Creating a Google Play Developer Account

Before you can publish your app on the Google Play Store, you'll need a Google Play Developer account. This account gives you access to the Play Console, where you manage your app listings, releases, and financial details.

Step-by-Step Guide:

1. **Go to the Google Play Console:** Visit the Google Play Console website: https://play.google.com/console
2. **Sign In or Create an Account:** If you have a Google account, sign in. If not, you'll need to create one.
3. **Accept the Developer Agreement:** Read and accept the Google Play Developer Distribution Agreement. This agreement outlines the terms and conditions for publishing apps on the Play Store.
4. **Pay the Registration Fee:** There is a one-time registration fee of $25 (USD) to create a Google Play Developer account. You can pay using a credit or debit card.
5. **Provide Account Details:** Fill in your developer account details, including your name or the name of your organization, contact information, and physical address.
6. **Verify Your Account:** Google will typically require you to verify your account via email or phone. Follow the instructions provided to complete the verification process.

Associated Fees:

- **Registration Fee:** The one-time registration fee of $25 is required to create a Google Play Developer account.

- **Transaction Fees:** Google takes a percentage of your app's revenue as a transaction fee. This fee varies depending on your location and the type of transaction (e.g., app purchase, in-app purchase, subscription).

Required Information:

When creating your developer account, you'll need to provide the following information:

- **Account Type:** Individual or organization.
- **Developer Name:** Your name or the name of your organization.
- **Contact Email:** An email address where you can be reached.
- **Physical Address:** Your physical address (this is required for tax purposes).
- **Payment Method:** A valid credit or debit card to pay the registration fee.

Additional Tips:

- **Use a Professional Email:** Consider using a professional email address that is associated with your developer name or organization.
- **Choose a Memorable Developer Name:** Your developer name will be displayed on the Play Store, so choose a name that represents your brand or identity.

By creating a Google Play Developer account, you unlock the door to publishing your Jetpack Compose app on the world's largest Android app marketplace. In the following sections, we'll guide you through setting up your app listing in the Play Console and preparing your app for submission.

Setting Up Your App in Play Console

Once you have a Google Play Developer account, it's time to create your app's listing in the Play Console. This listing is your app's storefront on the Google Play Store, showcasing its features, functionality, and visual appeal to potential users.

Step-by-Step Guide:

1. **Access the Play Console:** Log in to your Google Play Console account.
2. **Create a New App:**
   - Click the "Create App" button.
   - Choose the default language for your app (you can add more languages later).
   - Enter your app's title and click "Create."
3. **Complete the Store Listing:**
   Your app listing consists of several sections, each playing a crucial role in attracting and informing users:
   - **App Title:** Choose a catchy and informative title that reflects your app's purpose and stands out in search results.
   - **Short Description:** Write a brief description (up to 80 characters) that quickly summarizes your app's key features and benefits.
   - **Full Description:** Provide a more detailed description of your app (up to 4000 characters), highlighting its functionality, unique selling points, and how it solves users' problems.
   - **Screenshots and Videos:** Upload high-quality screenshots and videos that showcase your app's UI and demonstrate its features in action.
   - **Promotional Graphics:** Create eye-catching promotional graphics (e.g., feature graphic, icon) that visually represent your app's brand.
4. **Categorize Your App:**
   - Choose the category (e.g., Education, Entertainment, Health & Fitness) and a subcategory that best describes your app.
5. **Set Content Rating:**

- Complete the content rating questionnaire to determine the appropriate rating for your app. This rating indicates the age group for which your app is suitable.
6. **Provide Contact Details:**
   - Include your contact email and website so users can easily reach you for support or feedback.
   - You can also provide a privacy policy URL if your app collects user data.
7. **Set Up In-App Products and Subscriptions (Optional):**
   - If your app offers in-app purchases or subscriptions, you can configure them in the Play Console. This involves creating products, setting prices, and managing your payment system integration.

Tips for an Effective Store Listing:

- **Compelling Title and Descriptions:** Use keywords that users are likely to search for, highlight your app's unique features, and clearly communicate its value proposition.
- **High-Quality Visuals:** Invest in visually appealing screenshots and promotional graphics to make your app stand out.
- **Localization:** If you're targeting a global audience, localize your store listing and promotional materials into different languages.
- **A/B Testing:** Experiment with different versions of your store listing to see which one performs best.
- **Monitor Analytics:** Track your app's downloads, ratings, reviews, and other metrics in the Play Console to gain insights into user behavior and optimize your listing over time.

By meticulously crafting your app's presence in the Play Console, you lay the groundwork for a successful launch and increased visibility on the Google Play Store.

Uploading Your App Bundle

Once your Jetpack Compose app is ready for release, the next step is to generate a signed app bundle and upload it to the Google Play Console. Android App Bundles are the modern way to distribute Android apps, offering several advantages over traditional APKs (Android Package Kits).

Step-by-Step Instructions:

1. **Generate a Signed App Bundle:**
   - In Android Studio, go to "Build" -> "Generate Signed Bundle / APK."
   - Select "Android App Bundle" and click "Next."
   - **Choose or Create a Keystore:**
     - If you have an existing keystore, select it and enter your password.
     - If not, create a new one by providing the required details (keystore path, password, alias, etc.).
   - **Build and Sign:**
     - Select the "release" build variant.
     - Click "Finish" to generate the signed app bundle.
2. **Upload to Google Play Console:**
   - Go to your app's listing in the Play Console.
   - Navigate to the "Production" -> "Releases" section (or the appropriate release track).
   - Click "Create new release."
   - Under "App bundles," click "Browse files" and select your signed app bundle.
   - Fill in release notes and other details, then click "Save."

Release Tracks:

Google Play offers several release tracks for your app:

- **Internal:** For quick internal testing and quality assurance.
- **Alpha:** For a small group of trusted testers to get early feedback.
- **Beta:** For a wider group of testers to gather more feedback.
- **Production:** The final release available to all users on the Play Store.

By using different release tracks, you can gradually roll out your app to a larger audience and gather feedback at each stage before making it available to everyone.

Managing App Versions and Version Codes:

- **Version Name:** A user-friendly string that represents the app's version (e.g., "1.0.0").
- **Version Code:** An integer that uniquely identifies a specific version of your app. It must be incremented with each release.

You can specify the version name and code in your module-level `build.gradle` file:

```
android {
    defaultConfig {
        versionCode 1
        versionName "1.0"
    }
}
```

Key Points:

- App bundles are the preferred way to distribute Android apps.
- Generate a signed app bundle using Android Studio's built-in tools.
- Upload your bundle to the Play Console and choose the appropriate release track.
- Carefully manage version names and codes to keep track of your app's releases.

By following these steps, you can successfully publish your Jetpack Compose app on the Google Play Store, making it accessible to millions of Android users worldwide.

Creating Store Listing and Promotional Materials

Your app's store listing is its first impression on potential users. It's your chance to grab their attention, showcase your app's unique features, and convince them to download it. Let's explore how to create a compelling store listing and promotional materials that maximize your app's visibility and appeal.

Crafting an Effective Store Listing:

1. **App Title:** Your app's title should be concise, memorable, and relevant to its core functionality. Consider using keywords that users are likely to search for.
2. **Short Description:** This brief description (up to 80 characters) is your elevator pitch. Highlight your app's most compelling features and benefits in a way that grabs attention.
3. **Full Description:** The full description allows you to elaborate on your app's features, functionality, and benefits. Use persuasive language, focus on user needs, and explain how your app solves their problems.
4. **Icon:** Your app icon is a visual representation of your brand and should be eye-catching and memorable. Design a high-quality icon that aligns with your app's theme and resonates with your target audience.

5. **Feature Graphic:** The feature graphic is the first visual element users see in your store listing. Create a visually striking graphic that captures the essence of your app and makes users want to learn more.
6. **Screenshots and Videos:** Show, don't just tell. Use high-quality screenshots and videos to demonstrate your app's UI, key features, and user flow. Ensure your visuals are clear, visually appealing, and relevant to the text descriptions.
7. **Promotional Video (Optional):** A short promotional video can be a powerful way to showcase your app in action and create excitement.

Tips for Compelling App Descriptions:

- **Focus on Benefits:** Explain how your app solves users' problems or improves their lives.
- **Use Clear and Concise Language:** Avoid jargon and technical terms. Make your description easy to understand for a broad audience.
- **Highlight Unique Features:** Emphasize what sets your app apart from competitors.
- **Call to Action:** Encourage users to download your app by including a clear call to action (e.g., "Download now" or "Try it for free").

Selecting Appropriate Keywords:

Keywords play a crucial role in app store optimization (ASO). Research relevant keywords that users are likely to search for when looking for apps like yours. Include these keywords strategically in your app title, short description, and full description.

Localization: Reaching a Global Audience:

If your app targets a global audience, localization is essential. Translate your store listing and promotional materials into multiple languages to cater to users in different regions. This can significantly increase your app's discoverability and appeal.

Example:

App Title: "FitTrack: Your Personal Fitness Companion"

Short Description: "Track your workouts, monitor your progress, and achieve your fitness goals with FitTrack."

Full Description: "FitTrack is your all-in-one fitness app, designed to help you stay motivated and reach your health and fitness goals. Track your workouts, log your meals, monitor your progress, and get personalized recommendations. With FitTrack, you can easily create workout routines, set goals, and track your calories burned. The app also provides a library of healthy recipes and nutrition tips. Download FitTrack now and start your journey to a healthier you!"

By investing time and effort in creating an effective store listing and promotional materials, you'll increase your app's visibility, attract more users, and ultimately achieve greater success on the Google Play Store.

Managing Releases and Updates

After publishing your initial release, your work as a developer doesn't end. Managing releases and updates is an ongoing process that involves rolling out new features, fixing bugs, and responding to user feedback. The Google Play Console provides tools to streamline this process and gain valuable insights into your app's performance.

Rolling Out Your App:

When you create a new release in the Play Console, you have several options for how to roll it out:

- **Phased Rollout:** This allows you to gradually release your update to a percentage of your users over time. This helps you monitor for issues and gather feedback before making the update available to everyone. You can start with a small percentage (e.g., 5%) and gradually increase it if no major problems are found.
- **Staged Rollout:** Similar to a phased rollout, but you can define specific stages and manually control when each stage is released. This gives you more fine-grained control over the rollout process.
- **Full Rollout:** This releases the update to all users at once. This is typically used after you've tested the update thoroughly in internal, alpha, or beta tracks.

Monitoring App Performance and User Feedback:

The Play Console provides a wealth of data and tools to help you monitor your app's performance:

- **Statistics:** View metrics like downloads, active users, crashes, and ANRs (Application Not Responding).
- **Ratings and Reviews:** Read user reviews and respond to feedback to improve your app and address any issues.
- **Android vitals:** Monitor your app's performance metrics like battery usage, rendering time, and startup time to identify areas for optimization.
- **Crashes and ANRs:** Analyze crash reports and ANRs to pinpoint and fix bugs.
- **Pre-launch reports:** See potential issues and errors before they occur for the user

Submitting App Updates:

To submit an update:

1. **Increment Version Code:** Increase the versionCode in your module's build.gradle file.
2. **Update Version Name (Optional):** You can also update the versionName to reflect the new version.
3. **Generate a New Signed App Bundle:** Repeat the steps for generating a signed app bundle.
4. **Upload to Play Console:** Upload the new bundle to the desired release track.
5. **Review and Rollout:** Review the release details, set the rollout percentage (if using a phased rollout), and click "Start rollout to production."

Handling Versioning and Compatibility:

- **Backward Compatibility:** Ensure that your updates are backward compatible with older versions of Android that you still support.
- **Deprecation:** If you remove features or APIs, provide deprecation warnings in previous versions and clearly communicate changes to users.
- **Gradual Rollouts:** Use phased or staged rollouts to test your updates on a smaller audience before releasing them to everyone.

By effectively managing releases and updates, you can continuously improve your Jetpack Compose app, deliver new features, fix bugs, and provide a better experience for your users.

Post-Launch Considerations

Publishing your app on the Google Play Store is just the beginning. The post-launch phase is critical for your app's success. This involves actively promoting your app, engaging with users, and continuously improving your product based on data and feedback.

Strategies for Promoting Your App:

- **App Store Optimization (ASO):** Optimize your app's store listing with relevant keywords, compelling descriptions, and high-quality visuals.
- **Social Media Marketing:** Promote your app on social media platforms like Twitter, Facebook, and Instagram.
- **Content Marketing:** Create blog posts, videos, or other content that highlights your app's features and benefits.
- **Paid Advertising:** Consider running targeted ad campaigns on Google Ads or social media platforms.
- **Public Relations:** Reach out to tech bloggers, journalists, and influencers to get your app featured in articles and reviews.
- **Community Engagement:** Participate in online forums, social media groups, and developer communities to connect with potential users.

Responding to User Reviews and Feedback:

- **Be Responsive:** Respond to user reviews, both positive and negative, in a timely and professional manner. Thank users for their feedback and address any issues they raise.
- **Show Empathy:** When responding to negative reviews, acknowledge the user's concerns and offer solutions or explanations.
- **Learn and Improve:** Use user feedback to identify areas where your app can be improved. Consider implementing feature requests or fixing bugs based on user feedback.
- **Don't Engage in Arguments:** Avoid getting into arguments with users, even if they are being unreasonable. Keep your responses professional and respectful.

Analyzing App Metrics and Usage Data:

The Play Console provides a wealth of data about your app's performance. Utilize this data to:

- **Track Downloads and Installs:** See how many users are downloading and installing your app.
- **Monitor Engagement:** Track metrics like daily active users, session duration, and retention rate to understand how users are interacting with your app.
- **Analyze User Acquisition:** Understand where your users are coming from (e.g., organic search, referral links, ads) to optimize your marketing efforts.
- **Identify Crashes and Errors:** Analyze crash reports and ANRs to pinpoint and fix bugs.

By analyzing this data, you can gain valuable insights into your app's strengths and weaknesses, identify areas for improvement, and make informed decisions about future updates and features.

Additional Resources and Guidelines:

- **Google Play Academy:** Google offers a comprehensive training program to help you learn about publishing and promoting apps on Google Play: https://playacademy.exceedlms.com/student/catalog
- **Google Play Console Help Center:** Find answers to common questions and troubleshooting guides: https://support.google.com/googleplay/android-developer

By actively promoting your app, engaging with users, and analyzing data, you can ensure that your Jetpack Compose app thrives in the competitive landscape of the Google Play Store.

Chapter Summary

This chapter has guided you through the essential steps of publishing your Jetpack Compose app on the Google Play Store. You learned about the importance of thoroughly preparing your app for release by conducting comprehensive testing and optimization. We discussed the process of creating a Google Play Developer account, setting up your app listing in the Play Console, and uploading your signed app bundle.

We also provided valuable tips for creating an effective store listing, including writing compelling descriptions, choosing the right keywords, and creating eye-catching visuals. You learned about the different release tracks available on Google Play and how to manage your app's releases and updates.

Furthermore, we emphasized the importance of post-launch activities like app promotion, responding to user feedback, and analyzing app metrics. We provided resources and guidelines to help you navigate the post-launch phase and ensure the continued success of your app on the Google Play Store.

By following the steps and best practices outlined in this chapter, you can confidently launch your Jetpack Compose app and reach a global audience of Android users. Remember that publishing your app is not the end of the journey, but rather the beginning of a new phase of growth and improvement. Continuously monitor user feedback, analyze app performance, and iterate on your app to deliver the best possible experience to your users.

Appendices

Appendix A: Jetpack Compose Cheat Sheet

This cheat sheet provides a quick reference for essential Jetpack Compose concepts, composables, modifiers, and other helpful tips. Use it as a handy guide while building your Compose UIs.

Core Concepts:

- **Declarative UI:** UI as a function of state. UI automatically updates when state changes.
- **Composables:** Functions annotated with @Composable, the building blocks of your UI.
- **Modifiers:** Chainable functions to customize composables' appearance and behavior.
- **State:** Data that drives your UI. Use `remember` and `mutableStateOf` to manage state.
- **Recomposition:** The process of re-executing composables when their dependencies change.

Basic Composables:

- `Text`: Displays text content.
- `Image`: Displays images (bitmaps, vectors, etc.).
- `Button`: Creates interactive buttons.
- `TextField`: Captures text input.
- `Column`: Arranges composables vertically.
- `Row`: Arranges composables horizontally.
- `Box`: Allows for overlapping composables.

Layout Modifiers:

- `padding`: Adds space around a composable.
- `size`: Sets the width and height.
- `fillMaxWidth`, `fillMaxHeight`: Fills available width or height.
- `weight`: Distributes space proportionally (for `Row` and `Column`).
- `offset`: Offsets a composable's position.
- `align`: Aligns a composable within its parent.

State and Input Modifiers:

- `clickable`: Makes a composable clickable.
- `toggleable`: Creates a toggleable element (checkbox, switch).
- `scrollable`: Makes content scrollable.
- `selectable`: Makes text selectable.

Commonly Used Composables:

- `LazyColumn`, `LazyRow`: Efficiently display lists.
- `Scaffold`: Basic structure for screens (AppBar, content, FAB).

- **Card:** Material Design card container.
- **AlertDialog:** Creates alert dialogs.
- **Divider:** Creates dividers between elements.

Styling and Theming:

- **MaterialTheme:** Provides a default Material Design theme.
- **Surface:** A base composable for styling (background, shape, elevation).
- **TextStyle, Colors, Shapes:** Customize typography, colors, and shapes.

Navigation:

- **NavHost:** Holds your navigation graph.
- **NavController:** Triggers navigation actions.
- **composable:** Defines a screen destination.
- **navigate(route):** Navigates to a destination.
- **popBackStack():** Navigates back.

Advanced Concepts:

- **ConstraintLayout:** Powerful layout for complex arrangements.
- **remember:** Caches a value across recompositions.
- **mutableStateOf:** Creates observable state.
- **LaunchedEffect:** Launches coroutines tied to a composable's lifecycle.
- **animate*AsState:** Creates animated values.

Additional Tips:

- **Preview:** Use @Preview to preview composables in Android Studio.
- **Testing:** Use Compose Test Rules and assertions to write UI tests.
- **Explore:** Check out the official documentation and community resources for more advanced features and use cases.

Appendix B: Resources for Further Learning

Your journey with Jetpack Compose doesn't have to end with this book! The world of Android development is constantly evolving, and there's always more to explore and master. This appendix provides a curated list of resources to help you deepen your knowledge, stay updated with the latest advancements, and connect with the vibrant Jetpack Compose community.

Official Documentation:

- **Jetpack Compose:** The official documentation is your primary source of truth. It covers all aspects of Jetpack Compose, from the basics to advanced topics, with detailed explanations, code examples, and best practices: https://developer.android.com/jetpack/compose
- **Android Developers Website:** The broader Android Developers website offers a wealth of information on Android development in general, including guides, tutorials, and API references: https://developer.android.com
- **Kotlin Documentation:** Jetpack Compose is built on Kotlin, so a solid understanding of Kotlin is essential. Refer to the Kotlin documentation for language features and best practices: https://kotlinlang.org/docs

Online Courses and Tutorials:

- **Jetpack Compose Pathway:** Google's learning pathway on their developer website provides a structured learning experience to learn about and master different aspects of Compose. https://developer.android.com/courses/pathways/compose
- **Other Platforms:** Explore other platforms like Udemy, Udacity, or Pluralsight for courses specifically on Jetpack Compose.

Blogs and Articles:

- **Android Developers Blog:** The official Android Developers Blog often features articles and updates about Jetpack Compose: https://android-developers.googleblog.com/
- **Medium:** Many Android developers share their knowledge and insights on Medium. Search for "Jetpack Compose" to find relevant articles.

Community and Forums:

- **r/androiddev (Reddit):** The Android developer community on Reddit is a great place to ask questions, share ideas, and find solutions to problems: https://www.reddit.com/r/androiddev/
- **Stack Overflow:** Stack Overflow is a valuable resource for finding answers to technical questions and getting help from the community: https://stackoverflow.com/

Additional Resources:

- **Jetpack Compose Samples:** Google provides a collection of sample projects that demonstrate various Jetpack Compose features and use cases: https://github.com/android/compose-samples
- **Awesome Jetpack Compose:** A curated list of Jetpack Compose resources, including libraries, tutorials, and articles.

By actively engaging with these resources, you can continue your learning journey and stay at the forefront of Jetpack Compose development.

Conclusion

Congratulations! You've completed your journey through "Jetpack Compose: A Complete Guide for Kotlin Android Developers." By now, you've gained a comprehensive understanding of Jetpack Compose, from its fundamental concepts to advanced techniques for building stunning, responsive, and efficient Android user interfaces.

You've learned how to leverage the declarative power of Compose to create UIs that are easy to reason about and maintain. You've mastered core composables, advanced layout techniques, and the art of styling and theming to craft visually appealing interfaces. You've also delved into working with data and lists, integrating with data sources like Room, and building robust app architectures with MVVM and dependency injection.

Furthermore, you've explored asynchronous programming with Kotlin coroutines, making network requests with Retrofit, implementing navigation between screens, and modularizing your app for better organization and scalability. You even ventured into advanced topics like testing, animations, camera integration, and maps, unlocking a wide array of possibilities for your Android projects.

Embracing the Future of Android UI Development:

Jetpack Compose represents a paradigm shift in Android UI development. Its declarative nature, Kotlin-first approach, and focus on modern UI patterns make it a powerful tool for building the next generation of Android apps. By mastering Jetpack Compose, you're not only improving your current development skills but also future-proofing your career as an Android developer.

Your Journey Continues:

This book has provided a solid foundation, but your learning journey doesn't end here. The Android ecosystem is constantly evolving, with new Jetpack Compose features and libraries emerging regularly. Stay curious, explore new possibilities, and continue experimenting with different techniques to push the boundaries of what you can create.

Remember:

- **Practice Makes Perfect:** The best way to solidify your knowledge is to build real-world projects with Jetpack Compose. Start small, experiment with different features, and gradually tackle more complex challenges.
- **Stay Informed:** Keep up with the latest developments in Jetpack Compose by following official blogs, attending conferences, and participating in online communities.
- **Share Your Knowledge:** Help others learn and grow by sharing your experiences and insights with the Android community.

As you continue your exploration of Jetpack Compose, I hope this book has served as a valuable guide, inspiring you to create exceptional Android experiences. The possibilities are limitless, so embrace the power of Compose and unleash your creativity to build the apps of tomorrow.